Basque Explorers

Occasional Papers Series
No. 25

Basque Explorers
in the Pacific Ocean

William A. Douglass

Center for Basque Studies
University of Nevada, Reno

This book was published with the generous financial assistance of the Basque Government

Occasional Papers Series, No. 25
Series Editors: Joseba Zulaika and Cameron J. Watson
Center for Basque Studies
University of Nevada, Reno
Reno, Nevada 89557
http://basque.unr.edu

Book and cover layout: Jose Luis Agote

Library of Congress Cataloging-in-Publication
information forthcoming.

Contents

Introduction

Australian historian O. H. K. Spate's magnificent work on European voyages of discovery in the Pacific is entitled *The Spanish Lake*.[1] The reference is to Spain's near monopoly of the European probing of that vast region throughout the two and a half centuries after Magellan's voyage of circumnavigation (1519–1522) until that of Captain Cook's *Endeavour* (1768–1770). It is the purpose of this book to consider Basque involvement in the Spanish exploration and colonization of "the Spanish Lake." The Basque presence in Pacific waters was episodic and inextricably intertwined with that of other Spanish nationals. At no time was there an exclusively Basque expedition or colonial undertaking, although, as we will see, individual Basques were key figures in Pacific exploration, and there is evidence of Basque ethnic networking within particular expeditions. But why single out Basques at all?[2]

---

1. O. H. K. Spate, *The Spanish Lake*. (Canberra: Australian National University Press, 1979).

2. A methodological note is in order. Given that Basque surnames are quite distinctive, when one appears in a document, it is likely that the person is Basque. The caveat regards the fact that the exercise is far from precise. On one hand, throughout southern and central Spain, there are many Basque-surnamed individuals who are centuries removed from their cultural roots. This was a function of Christian resettlement of the Muslim-occupied parts of Iberia as the Reconquest advanced. During the apogee of Muslim control of the peninsula, much of the Basque Country remained a part of unconquered Christian Spain and subsequently provided settlers (from both modest and prominent social backgrounds) to the shifting borderland between the two civilizations. Furthermore, as preeminent mariners and merchants, Basques settled in Sevilla and Cádiz in order to be able to engage in New World commerce, given the two cities' monopoly on it at various periods. Basque mariners also gravitated to the seaports of Galicia, Asturias, and Santander. Conversely, some persons born in the Basque Country do not bear etymologically distinctive Basque surnames. Their Basque "credentials" might in every respect be impeccable, but they must be verified from other sources in order for them to be ascribed Basque identity in the present account.

A further qualification of the use of surnames regards the orthographic challenges posed by late medieval and early modern documents. The same surname may be recorded differently, according to the whims and literacy level of the inscriber. Furthermore, it was common for individuals to employ more than a single identity. Consequently, full siblings might

There is a marked tendency among historians to treat "Spaniards" monolithically, that is, counterpoised to other "nationalities" such as the French, English, Dutch, Portuguese, and so on. While valid at one level, at another, this violates the marked internal regional differences among Las Españas of the epoch.[3] It disregards the fact that Colum-

---

use different surnames. While the above is true of all Spaniards, the problem with respect to Basque naming practices is more egregious and even persists down to the present. For example, there is the case of contemporary Basque historian José Ignacio Telletxea Idigoras. Under the dictatorship of Francisco Franco, Basque personal names and surnames were prohibited and therefore Hispanicized. Since Franco's death (1975), many writers and artists have modified the orthography of their personal identity. Tellechea Idígoras was a prolific scholar before the transition. I cite some of his work that appeared in volumes 2 (1988) and 4 (1992) of the multi-volume maritime history entitled *Itsasoa*. He signs his 1988 essay "Tellechea" and his 1992 one with the Basque "Telletxea." In both instances, however, he retains the Spanish José Ignacio instead of the Basque Josu Iñaki.

Finally, I would note the Tellechea [Telletxea] Idígoras [Idigoras] caveats regarding Basque maritime history (and Spanish maritime history, as well). He comments that in most cases, the mariners failed to document their activities and that even when they did so, the majority of the extant texts still languish largely unexamined in both Spanish and Basque archives. José Ignacio Tellechea Idígoras, "Historias de la mar," in *Itsasoa: El mar de Euskalerria*, ed. Enrique Ayerbe, vol. 2, *La naturaleza, el hombre y su historia* (Donostia/San Sebastián: Eusko Kultur Eragintza Etor, 1988), 249. Rather, to date, Spanish and Basque maritime history is known largely from the few diaries and official reports of the principals and the published chronicles of their contemporaries. Most of the events of relevance to this chapter transpired half a millennium ago, and their historiography is largely of the "oft-repeated tale" variety. That is, over the centuries, the tendency has been to recount periodically the same narrative, rather than elaborating upon it with new evidence or paradigms.

The same criticism is applicable to the present treatment, since it rests entirely upon published secondary sources. Regarding Basque maritime history, the two primary figures are Segundo de Ispizúa, *Historia de los vascos en América*, vol. 1 (Bilbao: Impr. J. A. de Lerchundi, 1914), vol. 2 (Bilbao: Impr. J. A. de Lerchundi, 1915), and vol. 3 (Bilbao: Impr. J. A. de Lerchundi, 1917); and José de Arteche, *Urdaneta, el dominador de los espacios del Océano Pacífico* (Madrid: Espasa Calpe, 1943). Relying heavily upon the latter, Mairin Mitchell provides book-length treatments in English of two key Basques in the Pacific voyages of discovery: *Elcano: The First Circumnavigator of the World* (London: Herder Publications, 1958), and *Friar Andrés de Urdaneta, O. S. A.* (London: Macdonald and Evans, 1964). Stephen Clissold performs a similar service with his work *Conquistador: The Life of Don Pedro de Sarmiento* (London: Derek Verschoyle, 1954). In the present work, all translations from the Spanish are my own, except when they are quoted in English in the works of others.

3. As we will see, "Spain" was ultimately cobbled together out of a plethora of northern kingdoms, duchies, counties, and the recently reconquered central and southern reaches of the peninsula. The confederation embraced at least four major language groups (Portuguese-Galician, Basque, Castilian, and Catalonian), each with a bewildering array of subdialectal variations. Within Spanish national discourse, there emerged the twin notions of the individual's *patria grande* ("great native land," that is, Spain) and the equally potent *patria chica* ("little native land," that is, one's region). The two little lands of Catalunya and Euskal Herria bridged both sides of the subsequent French-Spanish border, while there is great cultural and linguistic similarity between Galicia and northern Portugal.

bus argued his case before a Castilian queen who, along with her consort, had yet to complete the political consolidation of what would eventually become today's Spain. It fails to consider that despite the centralizing successes of Emperor Charles V (as reflected in the defeat of the Comuneros in 1521), under the Hapsburgs, throughout the sixteenth and seventeenth centuries, Spain was as much a decentralized federation as a single integrated state.

While barely more than a hundred miles across on an east-west tangent, Euskal Herria (the entire Basque homeland) is strategically located where the western Pyrenees meet the Cantabrian Sea. It is currently divided into Hegoalde—the three Spanish Basque provinces of Bizkaia, Gipuzkoa, and Araba, as well as Navarra—on the one hand, and Iparralde, which contains the three traditional French Basque territories of Lapurdi, Benafarroa, and Xiberoa, on the other. In terms of territory, Hegoalde is about six times larger than Iparralde. Today, the population of the former is about 2.8 million and that of the latter two hundred thousand.

The coastline of Euskal Herria is blessed with many natural harbors, and as a consequence, Basques have long numbered among Europe's quintessential mariners. During the Middle Ages, they were particularly active in the fishing and maritime commerce in European Atlantic waters. Basques were possibly Europe's earliest (and certainly its most accomplished) whalers. By the fourteenth century, Bizkaians maintained their own legation, or "House of Bizkaia," in Bruges to facilitate Bilbao's extensive trade with Northern Europe, and they were concluding commercial treaties with England. Mention might also be made of the curious Navarrese intervention in the eastern Mediterranean, where, from about 1370 to 1419, they held sway over much of the Peloponnesian Peninsula.[4]

---

4. Luis, brother of Navarrese King Carlos II, was to have received Albania as the dowry of his wife, Juana of Sicily and Durazzo. When it was not forthcoming, Carlos arranged for an expeditionary force (commanded by Luis) that descended the Ebro River from Navarra, crossed the Mediterranean, and conquered Albania. According to Rachel Bard, "Lacking resources to go home, the Navarrese constituted an 'autonomous military republic.' Under a succession of leaders, they stayed on, fighting Catalan mercenary forces and French and all comers for possession of much of Greece. They took Athens in 1380. They were still in Greece in 1390, with Venetians as allies. . . . Their last recorded battle was in 1419." Rachel Bard, *Navarra: The Endurable Kingdom* (Reno: University of Nevada Press, 1982), 73–74.

Basques also participated in the initiatives of both Castilla and Portugal directed at North Africa and the Canary Islands, as well as in Mediterranean commercial and military ventures. Near the beginning of the fifteenth century, in Cádiz, they founded the Colegio de Pilotos Vizcaínos (College of Bizkaian Pilots), with its set of ordinances regulating the activities of Basque ships' captains in African and Mediterranean waters. It provided memorial services in its own chapel for those who lost their lives at sea.[5] There is also evidence, by 1484, of a monastery in the Basque Country dedicated to the training of Franciscan missionaries for evangelization of the Canary Islanders.[6]

Antonio de Nebrija, a contemporary of Christopher Columbus, commented, "Those who resided in the County of Bizkaia and the province of Gipuzkoa are people wise in the art of navigation and forceful in naval battles, and they have ships and appurtenances for them, and in these three regards they are better informed than any other nation of the world."[7] Indeed, regarding the defining vessel of the epoch's transoceanic exploration, the caravel, French historian Pierre Chaunu noted, "The oldest caravels appeared in the Gulf of Biscay: from 40 to 50 tons and with two square sails. There is evidence [of them] as early as the thirteenth century. This ship, transformed progressively, was used by Henry the Navigator."[8]

The Portuguese are commonly regarded to be the fifteenth century's master shipbuilders and navigators. While there is much evidence for this, particularly in the second half of the century, it is clear that the Portuguese were well aware of earlier Basque naval technology.[9] Referring to the mid-1400s, the eve of the explorations, Spate notes,

> Shipbuilding underwent a virtual revolution in the fifteenth century. . . . Iberian builders, particularly those of Biscay, played an important role in this development, without which the Discoveries would not have been possible. . . . Thus, from about 1430 a bewildering variety of hybrids [ships]

---

5. Tellechea Idígoras, "Historias de la mar," 268.

6. Ibid., 248.

7. Carlos Clavería Arza, *Los vascos en el mar* (Pamplona: Editorial Aramburu, 1966), 120.

8. Antonio de Nebrija, cited in Miguel Laburu, "Jalones en la historia de la arquitectura naval vasca," in Ayerbe, *Itsasoa*, vol. 2, *El mar de Euskalerria: La naturaleza, el hombre y su historia*, 222.

9. In 1412, Gipuzkoan and Bizkaian ships sailed in the service of Portugal in its expeditionary force directed at Ceuta and the Canary Islands. Ibid., 260.

were developed, initially it seems largely by the Basques. . . . The end result, the standard big ship for most of the sixteenth century, was the carrack: three masts with a lateen mizzen, high castles (especially aft), and a large central cargo hatch. This was the *nao* of the Spanish *Carrera* and the *nau* of the Portuguese *Carreira* to the West and East Indies respectively.[10]

It should therefore come as no surprise that Basques played a significant (and at times key) role in the unfolding drama of Spain's maritime explorations.

There is considerable imprecision regarding Basque maritime history, perhaps best illustrated by the speculation surrounding Columbus's first voyage. Some have hypothesized that the Genoese explorer learned about the New World while in the Cape Verde Islands, where he met a Basque ship's captain who had returned from Brazil after having been blown off course. Others have suggested that Basque cod fishermen may have been visiting the coast of Terranova prior to Columbus's first expedition and may have inspired it.[11]

Then, too, while biding his time in Córdoba awaiting his first opportunity to present his project to Queen Isabella, Columbus had frequented a pharmacy owned by a fellow Genoese, and it was there that he made the acquaintance of a young Basque named Diego de Arana.[12] Diego introduced Columbus to his cousin, Beatriz Enríquez de Arana,[13] and she became his lover. Although they never married, she bore him a son, Hernando. It is possible that Beatriz's family invested money in the venture, and she would eventually become his heiress upon the admiral's death.

And there is also the considerable ink expended on whether or not the *Santa María* was constructed in a Basque shipyard, not to

---

10. Spate, *The Spanish Lake*, 16.

11. William A. Douglass and Jon Bilbao, *Amerikanuak: Basques in the New World* (Reno: University of Nevada Press, 1975), 53–55. Mark Kurlansky has further popularized this viewpoint in his two books *Cod: A Biography of a Fish That Changed the World* (New York: Penguin Books, 1998), 17–29 and *The Basque History of the World* (London: Jonathan Cape, 1999), 56–60. This is surprising since Kurlansky was aware of the compelling evidence to the effect that the earliest Basque whalers in Terranova likely arrived in the 1520s, as discussed by Mariano Ciriquiain-Gaiztarro, *Los vascos en la pesca de la ballena* (Donostia-San Sebastián: Biblioteca Vascongada de los Amigos del País, 1961), 204–207.

12. The family was from the Valley of Arana in Araba.

13. She may have had Converso roots on her father's side.

mention on the ethnic makeup of its captain and crew. We have at least the surnames, and in a few instances, more information regarding a partial list of some eighty-five members of Columbus's first expedition. There are thirteen Basques on it. Nine were on the *Santa María*, including Columbus's bailiff and "cousin," Diego de Arana.[14] However, subsequent testimonials, including that of Columbus's son Hernando, state that the majority of the *Santa María*'s crew was Basque.[15]

This foundational voyage established at the outset two nearly irreconcilable characteristics of future Basque participation in Spanish exploratory and imperial ventures. On the one hand, Basques were the empire's quintessential mariners and consequently likely to be overrepresented in the ranks of the explorers. In this regard, they were handmaidens of imperial policy. Conversely, Basques were equally capable of becoming obstreperous critics of authority and, at times, subverters of it.[16] Indeed, if there were many Basques in the crew of the *Santa María*, as a bloc, they were the disgruntled contingent that bordered upon mutiny (even threatening to throw their admiral into the sea) when the promised landfall proved elusive.[17] Furthermore, upon losing his flagship, Columbus was forced to leave behind thirty-nine men on Hispaniola under the command of Diego de Arana. After separating into two factions, due either to discord among the Bizkaians or between them and the non-Basques, the colony was annihilated by the natives.[18]

---

14. José Manuel Azcona Pastor, *Possible Paradises: Basque Emigration in Latin America* (Reno: University of Nevada Press, 2004), 12–13.

15. After considering all of the evidence, Tellechea Idígoras concludes conservatively that there may have been a dozen Basques in all in the famed voyage of discovery. Tellechea Idígoras, "Historias de la mar," 264.

16. Within Spanish circles, the Vizcaínos or Bizkaians (at the time, the generic term for all Basques) became notorious for pursuing their own agendas, including, according to at least some of their critics, formulation of cabals whereby well-placed Basques accorded preferential treatment to their fellow ethnics. See Douglass and Bilbao, *Amerikanuak*, 80–83, 87–94.

17. Azcona Pastor, *Possible Paradises*, 14.

18. Bartolomé de las Casas, *Historia de las Indias*, 3 vols. (Mexico City: Fondo de Cultura Económica, 1951), 1:357–58; Antonio de Herrera y Tordesillas, *Historia general de los hechos de los castellanos en las islas y tierras firmes de el Mar Océano*, 10 vols. (Asunción del Paraguay: Guarania, 1944–47), 1:277; Jon Bilbao, *Vascos en Cuba (1492–1511)* (Buenos Aires: Editorial Ekin, 1958), 92–97.

Configuring Spain and Portugal

There has never been a more transformational period in the history of this particular planet than the near century from 1492, demarcated by Columbus's first voyage, until the destruction of the Spanish Armada in 1588—or what might be called "The Iberian Age on the World Stage." In 1492, there were four Iberian Christian kingdoms (Castilla, Aragón, Navarra, and Portugal), and a small part of the peninsula (Granada) remained under Islamic control. By 1512, two Christian kingdoms (Spain and Portugal) controlled all of Iberia, and in 1580, these were merged into a unified realm under King Philip II. In 1492, there was but a single Christian church; by 1524, that unity had been shattered, and Occidental Europe entered upon more than a century of internecine warfare (until the Treaty of Westphalia, in 1648) among elements of a Catholic Holy Roman Empire and several Protestant states. In 1492, the inhabitants of Europe and parts of Africa and Asia knew of each other and were tied together, at least loosely, by trade links, while an "Old World" and a "New World" (the Americas) were essentially unaware of one another's existence. While, in 1492, in the Occidental world, an inward-looking medieval order still obtained in which church, crown, and the aristocracy contested political power, by 1588, the continent was embroiled in an early modern age that would come to be characterized by mercantilism and secularism. While, in 1492, Islam, and particularly Ottoman Turks, posed a major military and political challenge to Europe, and even Barbary pirates were capable of disrupting Mediterranean commerce, by 1571, the victory of Christians at the Battle of Lepanto removed Islam permanently as a serious threat to European expansionism, including ultimately into the Islamic heartland itself.

By 1522, the overseas empires of the two Iberian powers literally spanned the globe, prompting both the concern and the envy of other aspiring European maritime powers—notably, England, Holland, and France. Consequently, by this time, the seeds had been sown of a global competition among European powers that would ultimately number the days of Indian rajahs and Chinese emperors, not to mention Inca god-kings and Cherokee chiefs. In 1492, Australian Aborigines, Amazonian Indians, and South Sea Islanders might still be blissfully ignorant of the fate that awaited their descendants, but the imperialist aliens were on their way, bearing superior weaponry, irresistible trade goods, an obsession with a strange god intolerant of any other, and the political demands of monarchs who were half a world away, but nevertheless insistent upon loyalty and subservience—a rapacious phalanx of explorers obsessed with finding and appropriating "treasure," followed by waves of colonists who would lay claim to the "vacant" land itself while enslaving or indenturing the locals to work it, when not importing slaves or indentured workers from elsewhere.

In sum, the Reconquest of the Iberian Peninsula and the imperial expansion in northern Africa of both Spain and Portugal melded the cross with the sword—a blending of celestial zeal with terrestrial greed. And who were these Iberians? How had they come to launch their hegemonic planetary initiatives?

The Iberians

At the dawn of the second millennium, Iberia was divided geopolitically by a nearly even line running from the Atlantic to the Mediterranean that separated a Christian northern quarter of the peninsula from the Muslim three-quarters constituted by the Caliphate of Córdoba (with holdings in adjacent North Africa, as well). Rachel Bard refers to the reign of Navarrese monarch Sancho the Great (1004–1035) as "pivotal"[1] in this context—a claim that could be made for both the Basque homeland and the future Spain.

When Sancho ascended the throne of the tiny kingdom of Navarra (Pamplona), Christian Iberia was fragmented into several monarchies and counties, the major entities being the kingdoms of Gali-

---

1. Rachel Bard, *Navarra: The Durable Kingdom* (Reno: University of Nevada Press, 1982), 29–40.

cia (including a part of northern Portugal) and that of León (with its southeastern county of Castilla) and the Pyrenean counties of Aragón, Ribagorza, and Sobrarbe. During his three-decade rule, with the exception of Galicia, the capable Sancho was able to bring them all (as well as southwestern France) under his direct rule or influence through military conquest, political maneuvering, and by virtue of earlier marital alliances that allowed him to become regent for under-age heirs to power in Castilla, León, and Gascony.[2]

The expanded kingdom of Navarra served as Western Europe's Christian borderland and bulwark against any further expansion of Islam, becoming (if but briefly) one of the continent's most important states. Navarra's triumph was far from accidental, in that it possessed strategic advantages over all of the other Christian monarchies and counties. Almost immediately after the initial incursion of the Moors into the Iberian Peninsula in the early eighth century, the rulers of present-day southern Navarra, the Banu Qasi family, converted to Islam. Over the next two centuries (and with but brief interludes of strife), there would be several marriages between that lineage and the monarchs of the kingdom of Pamplona to the north.

In the first half of the tenth century, the ruler of the emirate (kingdom) of Córdoba, Adb-al-Rahman III (891–961) conquered the several other Iberian Islamic emirates and incorporated them into a unified caliphate, or empire. His mother was Navarrese.[3] When his grandson assumed the throne of the caliphate at the tender age of twelve, real authority devolved upon a powerful hajib, or chamberlain, Al-Mansur (976–1002), who came to be known for good reason as "The Victorious." A ruthless military dictator, Al-Mansur became the scourge of the Christian north—save Navarra. Indeed, he had married his son and successor to another Navarrese princess. Consequently, when Sancho the Great assumed power, his was the sole Christian kingdom to have been spared the wrath of Al-Mansur. The opportunity that this presented for Navarrese expansion was only

2. Ibid., 30–34.

3. Stanley Payne notes, "The son of a Navarrese princess, this greatest of Cordoban rulers was a short, blue-eyed Muslim who dyed his red hair black to match that of most of his subjects." Stanley Payne, *A History of Spain and Portugal*, 2 vols. (Madison: University of Wisconsin Press, 1973), 1:23.

enhanced when, in the first decade of the new millennium, internal challenges to the Cordoban dictatorship weakened the caliphate.

The first time that the components of entire present-day Euskal Herria (as well as all of the areas contiguous to it) were united within a single polity transpired during Sancho's reign. Upon his accession, Araba, Gipuzkoa, Bizkaia, and the Rioja, as well, were all within the Castilian political orbit. Sancho's queen was herself Castilian. However, the initial expansion of his realm would be at the expense of his father-in-law, Count Sancho García (995–1017). In 1016, Sancho the Great annexed the Rioja. By 1022, Araba had recognized him as its king. In 1025, he named Gipuzkoa a seigneury within his kingdom, and in 1030, the designation was also extended to Bizkaia.[4]

However, even during Sancho's lifetime, the "empire" began to unravel when he carved out separate jurisdictions for his sons. The presumptive preeminence of the monarchy of Navarra was secured when Sancho's eldest legitimate son, García, became its ruler. The county of Castilla went to Sancho's second-born son, Fernando, and that of Aragón to the bastard Ramiro. The youngest son, Gonzalo, received the combined counties of Sobrarbe and Ribagorza. Sancho's dream that his successors would all act in consort and harmony was put paid almost immediately after his death, when his progeny became implacable competitors and even battlefield adversaries. Both Fernando and Ramiro declared themselves kings of their respective counties. During subsequent centuries, the histories of Navarra, Castilla, and Aragón would be both convoluted and intertwined—with the foundational Navarrese kingdom initially ascendant, yet subsequently subservient to the other two.

The seigneury of Bizkaia emerged under its first lord, Iñigo López Ezquerra, a nobleman at the court in Pamplona first mentioned in a document dating from 1033, during the waning years of the reign of Sancho the Great. At the time, all of present-day Bizkaia, Araba, Gipuzkoa, and the entire Rioja constituted the western reaches of the kingdom of Navarra. By 1076, Iñigo and his son Lope Iñiguez had traduced Pamplona by throwing in their lot with Castilian King Alfonso VI, who had invaded and occupied the Rioja. During the 1070s, Alfonso extended his rule to Galicia and Portugal, and in 1086, he tri-

---

4. Bard, *Navarra*, 30.

umphed over the Muslims at Toledo, proclaiming himself emperor of Spain—albeit without having wrested parts of the Iberian Peninsula from the Muslims as yet.

Alfonso VI consigned jurisdiction over the Rioja to Lope Iñiguez's son Diego, third lord of Bizkaia. The key concessions in the area included the town of Haro, located strategically on the south bank of the Ebro River at the point where Araba, Navarra, and the Castilian Rioja meet. Henceforth, the lineage of the lords of Bizkaia would bear the surname López de Haro.[5]

Subsequently, Navarra's King Sancho the Wise (1150–1194), assailed by pressure from both Castilla and Aragón, sought alliance with England by betrothing his daughter Berenguela to King Richard the Lionheart. Richard was also Duke of Aquitaine (which included by this time present-day Hegoalde). He had acquired the title at birth, derived from his mother Eleanor's dowry upon her marriage to Henry II. Richard's union with Berenguela proved childless, but it did establish strong ties between Navarra and England that would perdure for three hundred years. Indeed, Richard conferred Gascony upon his father-in-law, including the region of Behe Nafarroa.

Unfortunately for the Navarrese, Castilla also had ties with the English. In 1170, its king, Alfonso VIII, had married Eleanor, daughter of Henry II and Eleanor of Aquitaine. Alfonso believed that this gave him claim to Gascony. In 1199, he invaded it easily while the Navarrese king, Sancho the Strong (1194–1234) was absent on a visit to Andalusia. Alfonso's route passed through Araba and Gipuzkoa, and they were annexed by Castilla.[6] Henceforth, Navarra would be a landlocked and greatly weakened kingdom.[7]

Sancho the Strong's reign was pivotal in other fashions, as well. In 1212, he led his forces at the battle of Navas de Tolosa in a Christian army that included Castilian, Leonese, and Aragonese contingents. Their victory was a key turning point in Iberian history that

---

5. The main boulevard, or "Gran Via," of the major Bizkaian city of Bilbao is named for Diego López de Haro.

6. Bard, *Navarra*, 38–39.

7. It also signaled the last time that the entire Basque Country would be under a single ruler, if we exempt the brief sway of Napoleon Bonaparte over both France and Spain during the early nineteenth century.

would signal the beginning of the end of Muslim Spain and the serious expansion of the territorial holdings of both Castilla and Aragón. Instead of joining the ensuing scramble, Sancho demurred and retreated to his castle in Tudela, where he withdrew from affairs of state. The Navarrese nobility exercised de facto rule of the kingdom. They became so obsessed with local issues that Navarra would miss out on the opportunity to expand its southern frontier.

In 1234, Sancho died without legitimate heirs. At one point, he had considered making his cousin, King Jaime I of Aragón, his successor, but the plan was thwarted by the Navarrese nobility. They insisted upon naming Sancho's nephew, Count Thibaut of Champagne, as their monarch—King Teobaldo I. Thus began what might be termed dynastic drift, during which, until the kingdom's final demise in 1512, Navarra would be ruled by a series of dynasties with French ties.[8]

When the Aragonese king, Fernando II, conquered Navarra in 1512, it was the culmination of nearly a century of machinations (frequently expressed in interdynastic marriages) involving Castilla, Aragón, and Navarra. A central figure in it all was Fernando's father, Juan II, who married a Navarrese princess (but subject to his father-in-law's safeguards ensuring that Navarra would not be subsumed into Aragón) and then, upon the death of his queen, usurped the kingship from the legitimate heir, Carlos, the Prince of Viana. Eventually, Juan became king of Aragón, to be succeeded by his son Fernando, while the crown of Navarra went to Juan's daughter Leonora and then to her grandson, scion of the French Foix dynasty.

Like his father, Fernando was obsessed with Navarra. In 1512, he allied with Henry VIII of England in a campaign against the French. Supported by a contingent of English troops, he would invade Guyenne (lost by England during the Hundred Years' War) and return it to Henry. Fernando demanded that the Navarrese allow him to enter their kingdom to thwart a supposed imminent French counterattack. When this was refused, he invaded anyway, consolidating his hold upon Pamplona while abandoning any thoughts of attacking

---

8. Bard, *Navarra*, 39–40, 59–73.

France.[9] Henceforth, all of Hegoalde would be under Spanish central authority.[10]

We are at another pivotal point, one that would change the direction of Spanish, European, and world history. It was under the so-called "Catholic Monarchs," Isabella I of Castilla and Fernando II of Aragón, that we can first speak with authority of modern Spain—the outcome of the marriage between Castilla (which had long since absorbed Galicia and León) and Aragón (which included Catalunya), the conquest in 1492 of the last Moorish enclave in Iberia (Granada), and the military defeat of the Navarrese in 1512. The Catholic Monarchs were both distant descendants of Sancho the Great and, more recently, of Juan I of Castilla (1379–1390) and Leonor of Aragón and were therefore cousins. They required a papal dispensation in order to marry. Neither was a monarch when they were wedded, in 1469. Isabella then weathered a five-year power struggle to become queen of Castilla (1474–1504), and Fernando ascended the throne to rule Aragón (1479–1516) upon his father's death.

The reign of the Catholic Monarchs was more a diarchy than a unified monarchy. Yet the two rulers seemed to agree on most matters and were given to signing orders jointly. Castilla was by far the more potent power within the partnership in terms of both population and territory. The weightiness of Castilian affairs meant that Fernando spent most of his time there, visiting, rather than residing in Aragón.[11]

There was a third king of Spain in the person of the Cardinal Pedro González de Mendoza,[12] archbishop of Sevilla and later of

---

9. Ibid., 76–83.

10. It might be noted that Fernando's successors, first King Carlos I of Spain and then his son, Felipe II, were ambivalent about the conquest and entertained thoughts of restoring the Kingdom of Navarra. However, by century's end the "Navarrese question" was losing traction and was finally dismissed altogether by a commission charged by Felipe III (1598–1621) with studying the matter. (Ibid., 100–101, 103, 126).

11. Payne, *A History*, 1:172–78.

12. Here we have a prime example of a powerful Castilian family of remote Basque origin. The surname derives from the Basque terms *mendi* ("mountain") and *otza* ("cold"). Historian Helen Nader notes:

> The Mendoza came originally from the province of Alava and many incorporated themselves into Castilian society during the reign of Alfonso XI (1312–1350). . . . By 1332, the Mendoza had been feuding with the Guevara clan for at least a century, and other Alavese

Toledo, the most prestigious seat in Castilla. He presided over the Church's Council of the Realm and rode beside the queen into battle. According to Hugh Thomas,

> he was the enlightened son of Iñigo Hurtado de Mendoza, Marquis of Santillana, a poet and humane aristocrat, a man cultivated enough to rival any prince in Italy. Las Casas, in his history, wrote of the Cardinal's "great virtue, prudence, and fidelity to the monarchs," as well as his "generosity of spirit and lineage." Few would dwell on his private virtues but his other qualities were difficult to contest. The Mendoza family was the most powerful in Castile, with members of it in influential positions everywhere. The brothers, sisters, nephews and nieces of the Cardinal were the masters of church and state.[13]

Castilian hegemony over the Canary Islands and Aragonese rule in Sardinia, Sicily, and Naples meant that the new Spain had an Old World empire. In the Portuguese, it also had a prime competitor.

Portugal emerged in the twelfth century as a separate Iberian kingdom, having distanced itself from Galicia during the period when the latter was being pulled into the orbit of Castilla-León. The first Portuguese king, Afonso I (1128–1185), was descended from Castilla's King Alfonso VI through his illegitimate daughter Teresa. She was her father's favorite child, and when she married a Burgundian aristocrat and crusader, Alfonso bestowed upon them rule over Coimbra and Portugal, or approximately the northern half of the present-day country. While not necessarily a hereditary grant, their son Afonso I invoked his lineage to declare himself king. To reinforce his claim, he aligned his new realm with the papacy while paying tribute to it. In 1179, the archdiocese of Braga was created, thereby recognizing

---

clans that moved to Castile in the fourteenth century—including the Ayala, the Velasco, and the Orozco—had all shed their blood in these feuds. . . . Once the Alavese moved to Castile, they ended their feuds, incorporated themselves into the Castilian fighting force, and climbed the ladder of rewards available to those who gave military service to the king.

By virtue of being caballeros, the Alavese who moved to Castile in the fourteenth century were hidalgos (gentry). All members of the hidalgo class—caballero or letrado—shared a common responsibility for the res publica: they were the administrators of Castile.

Helen Nader, *The Mendoza Family in the Spanish Renaissance, 1350–1550* (New Brunswick, N.J.: Rutgers University Press, 1979), 36.

13. Hugh Thomas, *Rivers of Gold: The Rise of the Spanish Empire, from Columbus to Magellan* (New York: Random House, 2003), 22.

Afonso's kingship and underscoring the separation of Portugal from Galicia. The crown of Castilla-León,[14] riven as it was by internal strife and under severe external pressure from Al-Mansur, was incapable of mounting an effective challenge against such upstart Portuguese independence.

Over the next century, the Portuguese monarchs conquered all of the Muslim territory to their south, albeit by welcoming the extensive involvement of English, French, and Flemish crusaders, as well as several orders such as the Knights Templar. By the end of the reign of Afonso III (1246–1279), Portugal had matured to its present geopolitical configuration. According to Stanley Payne, "The small kingdom contained no ethnic subgroup of any importance save for a very slight Jewish population, and by the middle of the thirteenth century had become the first nation-state in Europe."[15]

The destinies of Castilla and Portugal would remain inextricably intertwined through interdynastic marriages, subsequent contested rival claims to the respective thrones, economic competition, and considerable warfare. Despite disputes and conflicts with his Castilian neighbors, in 1340, Afonso IV (1325–1357) sent a large contingent of troops to fight alongside them at the battle of Salado, in which their combined force defeated the last Muslim invaders of Iberia.[16] Nevertheless, but a few decades later, Portuguese King Fernando (1367–1383) sided with the English and the Aragonese against Castilla and its French ally in one of the phases of the Hundred Years' War. The Portuguese suffered three serious defeats in the conflict and were forced to sign unfavorable peace treaties. They lost much of their fleet and suffered such severe economic reversals that the very viability of the country was called into question.

When Fernando died without leaving a male heir, the danger of Portugal being subsumed into Castilla was heightened by a marital provision (supported by much of the Portuguese aristocracy) that the male heir of King Juan I of Castilla, husband of Fernando's daughter Beatriz, would eventually inherit the Portuguese throne. Fernando's widowed queen, Teles, was an extremely unpopular interim ruler,

---

14. Payne, *A History*, 1:116–17.

15. Ibid., 1:120–21.

16. Ibid., 1:127.

and she was overthrown by a revolt led by João, the grand master of the knightly Order of Aviz, the Portuguese section of the Knights of Calatrava. He was the bastard son of King Fernando's brother, Pedro I (1357–1367). He was acclaimed King João I (1384–1433) of Portugal by the archbishop of Braga and the Parliament of Coimbra, prompting an immediate invasion by a Castilian army. The ostensible international conflict was also a civil war within Portugal, since the country was quickly divided along regional and social-class lines.[17]

King João's forces prevailed at the battle of Aljubarrota (north of Lisbon), aided by English crossbowmen. During the conflict, much of Portugal's nobility fought on the Castilian side and were killed by the hundreds. The archbishop of Braga then planned a military campaign designed to remove the Trastamaras[18] from the Castilian throne while annexing a part of northern Castilla for Portugal. He concluded a pact with John of Gaunt (brother of the Black Prince, uncle of Richard II, and called "time honored Lancaster" by Shakespeare).[19] John arguably had his own claim to the Castilian throne, having married the daughter of Castilla's king, Pedro the Cruel (1350–1369).

John of Gaunt sailed from England with twenty thousand, occupied La Coruña, and acclaimed himself king of Castilla. The initiative proved abortive, and the English accepted a payment from the Trastamaras to depart. However, they left behind an important legacy in the form of John's daughter—Philippa. Part of the pact with the archbishop of Braga called for her marriage to João de Aviz. When he proved reluctant, John of Gaunt threatened to withhold a critical loan to Portugal and even to invade the country. So the diffident João and Philippa were married by the archbishop of Braga. According to Charles McKew Parr, "Like her grandniece, Queen Isabella the Catholic, and like her red-haired, great-great-grandniece, Queen Elizabeth

---

17. Ibid., 1:128–29.

18. When King Pedro the Cruel had his father's mistress murdered to remove a possible rival, her bastard son Enrique, backed by much of the Castilian aristocracy, led a successful rebellion against the monarchy and established his own Trastamara royal lineage. Enrique personally executed his deposed half-brother Pedro. In 1386, Enrique's son Juan I (1379–1390) was king of Castilla.

19. Charles McKew Parr, *Ferdinand Magellan, Circumnavigator* (New York: Thomas A. Crowell, 1964), 6.

Tudor, this unobtrusive woman named Philippa of Lancaster was to become the mother of a great empire."[20]

The royal couple was estranged at first, João pursuing his many military campaigns against the Castilians and the Berbers, who invaded southern Portugal periodically from their stronghold in Ceuta on the North African coast. Meanwhile, Philippa presided over the court in João's name and proved to be both wise and generous. While she had João's mistress immured in a convent, the prisoner was treated with respect. Queen Philippa even adopted João's two illegitimate sons and raised them with her own offspring—thereby laying the foundations for the bastard House of Bragança, which would figure quite prominently in subsequent Portuguese history.

From the outset, King João faced a serious challenge from the Portuguese noblemen who had supported him, accustomed as they were to regard the monarch as but the primus inter pares. According to A. R. Disney, "Consequently, João's rule was characterized by his on-going campaign to consolidate and enhance royal authority. Over time he was able to strip some noblemen of their estates and titles and force others into exile. By the end of his reign most of the truly powerful noblemen in Portugal, including João's sons, were of royal appointment."[21]

Queen Philippa introduced many enlightened practices from Flanders and England. In 1396, the Portuguese concluded a diplomatic and commercial treaty with the English that has endured with some modifications down to the present. The queen enjoyed the support of the burghers and the new aristocracy created out of João's supporters. She also befriended the Jews and earned their loyalty. Then, in 1411, Portugal and Castilla signed a peace treaty that brought an end to the decades of hostilities between them. However, by this time, Portugal was on the verge of bankruptcy caused by the seemingly endless wars. There was civil unrest and even the prospect of revolution.

Philippa conceived an audacious plan. Either by crossing Fez (Morocco) in North Africa and then the (fabled) Christian kingdom of Prester John to the south or by circumnavigating the continent,

20. Ibid., 7.

21. A. R. Disney, *A History of Portugal and the Portuguese Empire: From the Beginnings to 1807*, 2 vols. (Cambridge: Cambridge University Press, 2011) 1:126.

Portugal could redirect Venice's lucrative spice trade with the Orient and thereby spare itself economic ruin. In the face of skepticism and interminable debate, she dispatched spies to North Africa to take the measure of its defenses. One of the reports she received documented the arrival in Ceuta of a vast caravan laden with gold from Timbuktu. Until that time, European bankers had assumed that the gold they needed for the Oriental trade (and that they purchased under unfavorable conditions in several North African cities) came from India.

Armed with this new information, Philippa convinced Florentine bankers to underwrite a military campaign against Ceuta. King João thought the venture to be both risky and foolhardy. However, Philippa patiently gained support for it from churchmen, some nobles, and her three eldest sons. The king relented, and the necessary naval buildup began. The strategy included a disinformation campaign designed to make the Berbers believe that Portugal was aligning with Castilla for a push against the Kingdom of Granada. While the invasion of North Africa in 1415 was at first star-crossed and on the verge of failure, the invaders prevailed.[22]

Philippa died on the eve of the departure of the Ceuta expeditionary force. King João I (1384–1433) would survive her for many more years before finishing a reign that spanned half a century. It was under his guidance that Portugal matured into a serious player in European and world affairs. Payne concludes, "Though its population was no more than one and a half million, it had achieved strongly institutionalized government, a sense of national unity, a basis for modest economic development, commercial and maritime forces eager for a more expansive role in the world, a reorganized military aristocracy seeking new fields for adventure, and firm, calculating leadership able to guide the energies of its followers into major enterprises abroad."[23]

João I died in 1433 and was succeeded by his son Duarte (1433–1438). Duarte was married to Leonora of Aragón, daughter of King Fernando I (1412–1416). Upon his untimely death, she became regent for their royal successor, six-year-old Afonso. Leonora was suspected by much of the aristocracy due to her ties to the Ara-

---

22. Parr, *Ferdinand Magellan*, 11–15.

23. Payne, *A History*, 1:130.

gonese court and Castilian nobles who had recently seized control of that kingdom. So Prince Henry, her brother-in-law, negotiated a coregency between her and his brother, Prince Pedro. That did not go well, and Leonora was forced to flee to Castilla. From there, she organized opposition against Pedro's regency until her death in 1445. Pedro systematically repressed her supporters, forcing many to flee and redistributing their property and titles to his own loyalists. However, some of his arbitrary policies incited growing opposition within Portuguese society, and in 1446, Afonso turned fourteen and thereby became eligible to assume the kingship. The following year, he married his cousin Isabella, Pedro's daughter. By 1448, Pedro was forced to resign. When his enemies convinced the young monarch to review and possibly reverse many of Pedro's endowments, the ex-regent organized a rebellion that was readily defeated. (Pedro died in battle.)

King Afonso's rule would last nearly forty-three years (1438–1481). Throughout it, the monarch bestowed noble privilege almost recklessly. The chief beneficiaries were his uncle, Prince Henry, and the successive dukes of Bragança. There was even invention of new titles to confer—such as marquis, baron, and viscount. Also, under Afonso, the previous aversion of the Portuguese monarchy to becoming involved in the dynastic entanglements of the Castilian court was relaxed. In 1447, Isabella, a daughter of Afonso's uncle, Prince João, married the Castilian king, Juan II. Then, in 1455, Afonso's sister Joana married the Castilian king, Enrique IV. On two separate occasions, an aging Afonso himself proposed marriage to the future Queen Isabella, King Enrique's younger half sister. (She refused—instead marrying Ferdinand of Aragón in 1469.)[24] Then, in 1474, shortly before his death, Enrique conferred his kingdom upon his daughter Juana (born of his Portuguese wife, Joana, but possibly not the king's child). It would be the accusation of the designated successor's illegitimacy that informed Isabella of the competing claim to the Castilian throne.

---

24. William H. Prescott, *History of the Reign of Ferdinand and Isabella the Catholic*, 3 vols. (Philadelphia: J. B. Lippincott and Company, 1873), 1:181, 1:196–97.

Ethnic Relations in Medieval Iberia

For the nearly eight centuries after the first Muslim invasion of Iberia in 707 until their definitive defeat in 1492, relations between the peninsula's various Islamic and Christian dynasties (and its influential minority, the Jews, as well) ran the gamut. As we have seen, at times, there were marital alliances across ethnic and religious boundaries; at others, Christians and Muslims were battlefield adversaries. There were periods of tolerance and others of persecution of Christians (the so-called Mozárabes) and Jews under Muslim rule, and the same could be said for the Christian monarchies with respect to their minority populations. Islamic Sevilla and Christian Toledo each had their glorious epochs as beacons of enlightened thought and religious universalism. The introduction of the notion of a "crusade" against Islam was imposed upon Iberia at the end of the eleventh century from trans-Pyrenean Europe,[25] and particularly by the papacy as a part of its wider strategy regarding liberation of the Holy Land. Payne notes:

> For Alfonso VI of Castile, dealing with the Muslims was mainly a political, not a religious, enterprise, and in the thirteenth century, the tomb of Fernando III was inscribed with the title "king of the three religions." In some of the campaigns of the twelfth and thirteenth centuries, French crusaders either quarreled with or deserted their Castilian and Aragonese allies because of the latter's refusal to slaughter conquered Muslims. Ramón Llull and the Dominicans of Valencia proposed to educate and convert, not expel or even subdue, Muslims of neighboring regions. While Jewish communities were totally expelled from every other part of western Europe, they continued to flourish and multiply in the Hispanic kingdoms.[26]

The Navarrese, too, accommodated their influential Jewish community and were twice admonished by thirteenth-century popes for doing so.[27]

Nevertheless, it could be said that the religious borderland status of Muslim Al-Andalus and Christian Iberia meant that each had

---

25. Ibid., 1:136.
26. Ibid., 1:136–37.
27. Bard, *Navarra*, 68.

a sharply drawn religious other—an influence that underscored and thereby enhanced each protagonist's own orthodoxy. Indeed, Hispanic believers remained the most orthodox (that is, the least given to theological questioning and heresy) within Islam and Christianity, respectively. The presence of an influential Jewish minority within both Al-Andalus and the Christian kingdoms also meant that Iberia was the prime context within which the world's three major monotheistic religions competed for the status of God's chosen recipients of divine revelation. As a consequence, given the right circumstances, ruling Muslims and Christians were both prime candidates for religious intolerance—a potential that grew incessantly on the Christian side as it successfully prosecuted the Reconquest to regain control of the entire Iberian Peninsula.

Anti-Semitic violence broke out during the 1330s in Navarra[28] and then spiked in the massive pogrom of 1391 in southern Castilla. The circumstances of the Jews within Christian Iberia had indeed become quite precarious. In the aftermath of the pogrom, Jews were pressured to convert to Christianity, and about half (or more than one hundred thousand persons) did so, while others, the so-called Sephardic Jews, fled abroad. However, according to Payne:

> The paradox of the history of Castilian Jewry was that mass conversion was not a step toward solving the religious problem but only made it more intense. The Conversos, as the converts were termed, usually advanced further in wealth and status in their new situation as Christians. Intermarriage of wealthy Conversos with the aristocracy became increasingly common, and the number of descendants of formerly Jewish families placed in influential positions in or out of government was impressive. Suspicion and hatred of Conversos grew more intense as their wealth and influence increased.[29]

Therefore, by the time of the Catholic Monarchs, many Jews had accumulated great wealth and were well connected within the power structures of both state and church. Their heavy involvement in tax collection incurred the resentment of the common people, and their willingness to serve as moneylenders to the crown incurred the wrath

---

28. Ibid., 68–69.
29. Payne, *A History*, 1:208.

of Castilla's powerful aristocracy. Possibly a quarter of the Catholic bishops were of at least part Jewish descent. In sum, there was much envy of such Jewish success, as well as concern over its implications for the society's ostensibly predominant Christian nature.[30] An obsession bordering on paranoia emerged regarding the belief that many of the Conversos were actually crypto-Jews who continued to practice their religion in secret. The dilemma was perhaps best personified by the fanatical Dominican Tomás de Torquemada, the prelate charged, as the first inquisitor general, with implementing the Spanish Inquisition, which was designed to ferret out and punish such heretics.[31] Yet Torquemada was himself of Jewish descent. Indeed, it is likely that even (Spanish) Pope Alexander VI was of Jewish origin.

Things came to a head with stunning alacrity after the Catholic Monarchs triumphed over the Muslims of Granada in 1492.[32] While some of the defeated were transported to North Africa, those who wished to remain as subjects of the Christian rulers were allowed to do so and were even able to practice their religion. As a largely agrarian population, they were not felt to pose a threat.[33] The Jews were another matter altogether, and that same year they were ordered to convert to Christianity immediately or leave. The new wave of Sephardim resettled in several Middle Eastern and European countries, including tens of thousands in Portugal alone.[34]

---

30. Ibid., 1:207–12.

31. Under Torquemada, it is estimated that two thousand Conversos were burned at the stake and fifteen thousand received lesser punishments. Ibid., 210.

32. An eyewitness of the Christian forces at the siege of Granada, the Italian Pietro Martire d'Anghiera, wrote to the archbishop of Milan, asking, "Who would have believed that the Asturians, Gallegos, Basques, and the inhabitants of the Cantabrian mountains, men accustomed to deeds of atrocious violence, and to brawl over the slightest occasions at home, should mingle amicably not only with one another, but with Toledans and the wily and jealous Andalusians; all living together in harmonious subordination to authority, like members in one family, speaking the same tongue, and nurtured under a common discipline?" Quoted in Thomas, *Rivers of Gold*, 34.

33. It would not be until more than a century later, in 1617, that Spain's remaining Muslims were given the ultimatum of choosing between the alternatives of conversion to Christianity or expulsion.

34. Julio Caro Baroja, *Los judíos en la España moderna y contemporánea*, 3 vols. (Madrid: Ediciones ISTMO, 1961) 1:190–203. Portugal's tolerance would soon be tested when the conversion-or-expulsion option was extended to Portuguese Jews in 1497. In 1506, Lisbon experienced its own pogrom, and a series of anti-Semitic measures were passed into law (rescinded almost immediately, in 1507, however).

2

Iberian Explorations

And then there was the critical question of Atlantic expansion and exploration. Both the Andalusian ports of Castilla and the southern reaches of Portugal flanked the outlet of the western Mediterranean into the Atlantic and together constituted Europe's best-situated launching area for exploration of the South Atlantic and beyond.

Portugal's capture of Ceuta conferred upon her much prestige in European circles. More importantly, Portugal now controlled both shores of the critical Strait of Gibraltar—which meant that its exploration of the African coast and the South Atlantic could now commence unimpeded. The key figure in the new Portuguese initiative was Philippa's son, Henry—a cenobite and grand master of the Order of the Knights of Christ, a physicist and skilled mathematician. Prince Henry the Navigator, as we recall him, vowed to his mother while she lay dying on the eve of the Ceuta campaign that he would devote his energies to discovering her imagined route to the Indies.

The efforts to further Portuguese hegemony in North Africa proved both costly and ineffective. So it was that Henry turned his attention to southerly exploration of the African coast. He dispatched annual probes that gradually expanded Portuguese knowledge of the hostile coastline. However, the limited nautical and navigational technology of the age made progress painfully slow.

But then, in 1425, a sea captain was blown out to sea by a storm off Cape Bojador and discovered the island of Madeira. It proved to be of immediate and multifaceted importance. It gave the Portuguese a strategic base from which to provision and launch further explorations to the south. Its benign climate facilitated agriculture, particularly the cultivation of sugar, which was still deemed a scarce spice in European markets. It was forested and therefore provided the nearly deforested Portugal with an ample source of timber for shipbuilding and house construction.[1]

In 1431, Portugal's good fortune was multiplied with the discovery and colonization of the Azores; two years later, Cape Bojador was rounded successfully. In 1434, King João I died and was succeeded by Afonso V (1438–1481). Between 1441 and 1447, there were no fewer than twenty Portuguese exploratory probes of the African coastline. And by the time of Henry's death, his captains had discovered the Cape Verde Islands.

Nevertheless, on balance, Prince Henry failed to discover a sea route to the Indies. Sierra Leone was the southernmost limit of his explorations, and the pinnacle of his African success was the founding of an entrepôt at Arguim, thereby providing Portugal with lucrative trade in African gold, ivory, and slaves imported through the Portuguese African port of Lagos. The Lagos Company became a monopoly of the Knights of Christ. Prince Henry also assembled an extraordinary international team of physicists, mathematicians, and navigators (in the village of Vila do Infante) that effected many innovations designed to enable long-distance exploration of the world's oceans. According to Charles McKew Parr, "Henry's monumental contributions to celestial navigation, to cartography, and to naval architecture still stand as milestones after five hundred years."[2]

In addition to discovering Madeira, the Azores, and the Cape Verde Islands, Henry's captains found what came to be known as the Sargasso Loop (prevailing southerlies a short distance off the African coast and northerlies farther out to sea). The knowledge of this phenomenon was critical to any further European probes of the South Atlantic, and it remained a closely guarded state secret for several decades.[3]

But then, according to Parr,

> With the death of Prince Henry in 1460, there died also the obligation to carry out the pledge to Philippa, herself now dead for nearly half a century. The crusading scientific urge to seek the land of Prester John

---

1. Charles McKew Parr, *Ferdinand Magellan, Circumnavigator* (New York: Thomas A. Crowell, 1964), 19–20.

2. Ibid., 17.

3. Ibid., 25.

and to find the sea route to India was dead. The technical research junta at *Vila do Infante* was dissolved, the village itself abandoned, and African scientific exploration ceased. Only the profitable slave caravels continued their voyages from Lagos to the depot of Arguim on the African coast, where, in huge barracks, the Arab slavers delivered the Negro captives to await transport to market.[4]

In 1470, exploration resumed under the aegis of Ferdinand Gomes, a wealthy Lisbon merchant. He was accorded a monopoly on Arguim's trade, with the condition that he further southern exploration of the African coast by three hundred miles annually. Eventually, one of his caravels reached Guinea, thereby providing Portugal with direct access to its gold mines while circumventing Morocco's control over their output. Portugal was able to issue its own new and valuable gold coin—the cruzado. This attracted the attention of many of Europe's major bankers, notably, Florentines and Genoese. It also drew French and English privateers, initiating contraband traffic often backed secretly by wealthy Northern European merchants. In 1474, King Afonso V placed African affairs under his nineteen-year-old Crown Prince João, and the following year, the monarch declared a crown monopoly over this commerce—administered through a newly created Casa da Guiné.

When, in 1475, Afonso V invaded Castilla to support his niece Juana's claim to the Castilian throne, he also married her. The Portuguese and Juana's supporters fared badly in the conflict. Spanish galleons made for the Guinea coast and inflicted such heavy damage upon Gomes's vessels that he petitioned to be released from his African contract.[5] The Portuguese were forced to sue for the peace that was framed by the Treaty of Alcáçovas (1479). Under its terms, Portugal recognized Castilian sovereignty over the Canary Islands (first discovered by Portugal in 1336 and contested since then by the two Iberian powers), whereas Castilla recognized Portuguese claims to Madeira, the Azores, and the Cape Verde Islands and agreed that the Portuguese had an exclusive right to further exploration of the African coast.[6]

---

4. Ibid., 27.

5. Ibid., 27–28.

6. "In 1480, the crown officially adopted a policy of absolute secrecy concerning knowledge gained from Portuguese explorations and completely excluded subjects of other powers, on pain of death." Stanley Payne, *A History of Spain and Portugal*, 2 vols. (Madison: University of Wisconsin Press, 1973), 1:197.

In 1481, King Afonso died and was succeeded by his son, João II (1481–1496). The new monarch was regarded with trepidation by the nobility. Of stronger character than his father[7] and a veteran observer of the perennial disputes between the town councils and abusive nobles, he immediately convened Parliament to listen to grievances. While confirming his respect for the nobility's traditional rights, he announced that they were all subject to reconfirmation—and only after the aristocrats' pronouncement of unequivocal loyalty to the crown. While there was outward conformity, almost immediately, plots were hatched to remove the young monarch, led by the powerful Duke of Bragança, with some encouragement from the Catholic kings.

Meanwhile, in 1482, João II completed fortification of an entrepôt on the island of Sâo Jorge da Mina off the Guinean coast and established a corresponding Mina House in Lisboa to administer the African slave trade while retaining the crown monopoly on ivory and gold. He also launched renewed explorations of the African coast with the express intention of finding a sea route to India.[8] In effect, he eclipsed the Lagos Corporation and earned the enmity of the Knights of Christ. They gave their allegiance to the king's adversaries, the Braganças.

In 1483, the king learned of their plot and arrested and beheaded the Duke of Bragança, causing two of his brothers to flee to the court of Castilla. João seized their entire patrimony. Almost immediately, there was another antiroyalist conspiracy, this time planned by the bishop of Evora and the Duke of Viseu, brother of João's queen, Leonor. According to Disney,

> Viseu was a young man of great ambition, but little sense. A passive sympathizer of the Bragança conspiracy, he had been duly cautioned; but the warning clearly fell on deaf ears. Viseu was nursing several per-

---

7. A. R. Disney describes João as a religious person with "a strong belief in the majesty of kingship, a deep sense of responsibility to his subjects and a commitment to doing justice. . . . Determined, hard-working and politically shrewd, João brought a new steel to royal government. Fernando and Isabel of Spain with somewhat grudging admiration referred to him simply as 'the man', and Machiavelli allegedly used him as a model for the archetypal Renaissance ruler portrayed in The Prince." A. R. Disney, *A History of Portugal and the Portuguese Empire*, 2 vols. (Cambridge: Cambridge University Press, 2011) 1:133–34.

8. Payne, *A History*, 1:197; Parr, *Ferdinand Magellan*, 28.

sonal grievances—such as the king's refusal to grant him the mastership of Santiago, which João had decided to reserve for his own son, Prince Afonso. The conspirators' plan was to assassinate both João II and Afonso, then elevate Viseu to the throne. Once he had become king, Viseu would recall the Bragança exiles, marry a Castilian princess and return to the pro-seigneurial policies of Afonso V.[9]

In September 1484, an informed João summoned Viseu to his private chambers and stabbed the hapless duke to death. Most of Viseu's followers were decimated, although the king was considerably more magnanimous to the duke's younger brother, the fifteen-year-old Manoel—second in line to inherit the throne behind Afonso. Manoel was allowed to retain his patrimony and title as Duke of Beja.

Columbus and Portugal

João II sought to exclude all foreigners from Portugal's maritime explorations. Nevertheless, such an autarkical policy was impractical. It ran against the grain of the overextended Portuguese monarchy's dependence upon foreign (German and Italian) financial backing and the need for foreign scientific expertise. Nor did it preclude potential foreign explorers from leveraging the Portuguese and Castilian/Spanish crowns against one another.

The best-known of these was the Genoese navigator Cristoforo Colombo. In 1481, he had commanded a Portuguese vessel carrying materials to Guinea for construction of the São Jorge da Mina fortification and thereby gained knowledge of the winds and currents along the African coast. In 1484, Columbus sought the support of King João II for a transatlantic search for a westerly direct sea route to the Orient. It was withheld, since the king's advisers believed that the Italian had underestimated the Earth's circumference. At the time, Lisbon was awaiting news of Diogo Cão's (unsuccessful) attempt to round southern Africa (1482–1484).

After his failure to secure Portuguese backing, in 1486, Columbus journeyed to Córdoba, where Castilian Queen Isabella was holding court as she prepared her final assault upon the Muslims of Granada.

---

9. Disney, *A History*, 1:135.

He gained a royal audience in 1487, but her advisers were equally skeptical of his calculations of the Earth's circumference. Nevertheless, her influential chaplain, Bishop Juan Rodríguez de Fonseca, recommended that Columbus be given a stipend, if only to keep him from renewing his overtures to Portugal.

There was another development that would prove decisive. West African malaguetta peppercorns ("grains of paradise") became available in large quantities through the Guinean trade and were sold by the Mina House into the European market, a development that shook the Venetian and Florentine spice merchants to their core. The Hanseatic League, through the House of Fugger, dominated the Venetian trade, and their key competitors were Medici bankers. Portuguese King João II welcomed the opportunity afforded by this rivalry.[10] Indeed, in 1485, Jakob Fugger himself traveled to Lisboa to engage the monarch. While there, he committed his extensive resources to further Portuguese Atlantic explorations and was able to secure a near monopoly on the malaguetta trade.[11] He opened an office in Lisboa in 1486 under the direction of his Sevilla[12] manager, Cristóbal de Haro.

This particular Haro family, while likely from the Riojan town of that name, was unrelated to the early lords of Bizkaia. Rather, they were probably Conversos from the La Mota Jewish quarter in Haro.[13]

---

10. Payne considers João II to be "shrewd and farsighted" and "one of the ablest European rulers of the century." He had been made de facto ruler by the elderly Afonso V and negotiated the Treaty of Alcáçovas in 1479, whereby Castilla recognized Portugal's monopoly on the African coastal trade and exploration. Payne, *A History*, 1:197.

11. The king invited Fugger to a meeting at the residence of his personal physician, Maese Rodrigo, a Sephardic Jew. Several geographers and cartographers were in attendance, as well as two Sephardic astrologers. The discussion regarded the report of two Portuguese monks back from Jerusalem who claimed to have learned from some religious pilgrims of a sea route around southern Africa. In promising his support for exploration, Fugger was excited by the prospect of discovering an alternative route to the Orient that might afford him direct access to its spice trade. Paul Gallez, *Cristóbal de Haro: Banqueros y pimenteros en busca del estrecho magallánico* (Bahía Blanca: Instituto Patagónico, 1991), 22–23.

12. By the late fifteenth century, Sevilla had emerged as the world's most important concentration of Jews, many of whom were influential persons engaged in the professions. The city's Converso financiers were now on a par with the Venetian, Florentine, and Genoese bankers within European high finance. Ibid., 25.

13. Ibid., 24. Haro, the largest town in the Rioja during the thirteenth century, had approximately one thousand Jews at that time. When the Castilian king, Alfonso VIII (1158–1214), accorded Haro a fuero, or municipal charter, it gave the town's Jews several privileges for hav-

It seems that Cristóbal and Diego de Haro were sons of Juan Alonso de Baera and that they came under the protection of the powerful constable de Haro, who shielded them during a mid-fifteenth-century anti-Converso purge. They resettled near Burgos, their benefactor's residence, and assumed his surname out of gratitude.[14]

Cristóbal de Haro carried out Jakob Fugger's mandate to sponsor continuing Portuguese initiatives in search of a sea route to the Orient. After such probes into the unknown, Portugal's Atlantic explorers could then put in at Guinea on the way home to take on the cargo that more than compensated the House of Fugger for its advances. The first expedition was the voyage of Bartolomeu Dias, who left Lisboa with two caravels in August 1487, vowing not to return until he discovered the southern African cape and the sea route to India. Among the crew was Bartolomeo Colombo, Christopher Columbus's brother.[15]

In December 1488, while Christopher Columbus was again in Lisbon awaiting a royal audience to renew his petition, Bartolomeu Dias returned to Portugal after successfully circumnavigating the Cape of Good Hope. With this success, Portugal had established the possibility (albeit not as yet the reality) of a sea link between Europe and the Orient. Once again Columbus was passed over. Nevertheless, in Lisboa, he and his brother continued their study of world maps, both ancient and modern, further informing and firing their imaginations regarding the possibility of a westerly transatlantic sea route to India.

Twice rejected in Lisbon, Columbus ultimately found his benefactress in Queen Isabella of Castilla. How could she not be taken with the vision of transatlantic exploration? She was, after all, the great-

---

ing assisted him in his war against Navarra. Consequently, the Jews of Haro did not suffer the pogrom of 1391, but their numbers declined drastically as a result of persecutions during the fifteenth century. When Haro's Jewish community was censused in 1492 as a part of the expulsion of unconverted Sephardim, it included forty-eight taxpayers in possession of fifty-five houses, all in La Mota. "Jewish Virtual World: Haro, Spain," Jewish Virtual Library, http://www.jewishvirtuallibrary.org/jsource/judaica/ejud_0002_0008_0_08437.html.

14. Parr, *Ferdinand Magellan*, 172.

15. Ibid., 34.

niece of Prince Henry, the Navigator.[16] This time, in 1492, Bishop Fonseca urged his monarch to accept the proposal. Columbus also had the backing of influential Conversos at court.[17] Columbus's years of difficulty in securing royal sponsorship were not due exclusively to skepticism of his estimates of the Earth's circumference. There were also his incredible demands. He wanted to be accorded immediately the rare and prestigious title of "admiral" and then that of "viceroy" and hereditary governor of any lands that he might discover. He insisted upon a tenth of all the valuable goods found, bought, sold, or exported from them. He also reserved the right to invest up to one-eighth of the expenses of future expeditions with a commensurate claim upon their returns. King Fernando was simply astounded at the Genoese's audacity.[18]

The Iberian Competition

On his return to Europe from his first voyage, Columbus's landfall was Portugal, where he was immediately ushered before King João. The monarch was extremely courteous as he predictably informed Christopher that the lands he had discovered must certainly belong to Portugal under the terms of its existing treaties with Castilla. Columbus was also received by Queen Isabella, daughter of the Catholic Monarchs. King João offered Columbus horses for his journey to Spain, but the admiral preferred to go by sea. Then, after Columbus departed,

> on March 13, King João interrogated extensively the two Portuguese who had been with Columbus and who had remained in their native land. He decided immediately to send a fleet under Francisco de Almeida to search for the lands found by Columbus. One Portuguese chronicler, Rui de Piña, says that some courtiers of João suggested that Columbus

---

16. Hugh Thomas, *Rivers of Gold: The Rise of the Spanish Empire, from Columbus to Magellan* (New York: Random House, 2003), 34.

17. Some historians believe that Columbus himself had some degree of Jewish ancestry. Gallez, *Cristóbal de Haro*, 34.

18. William Thomas Walsh, *Isabella of Spain: The Last Crusader* (New York: Robert M. McBride, 1930), 338–39.

should be murdered on his way to Spain so that they could take advantage of the success of the expedition.[19]

In 1493, Bishop Fonseca was placed in charge of organizing Columbus's second voyage. Critics at the time were said to have commented that "organizing fleets is more the business of Bizkaians than of bishops."[20] Indeed, Fonseca commissioned a Basque, Juan de Arbolancha, to assemble six vessels in the Bizkaian port of Bermeo. However, when they put in at Cadiz, they were diverted by royal order to transport the defeated Muslim king of Granada and his followers to North Africa. Thus, the "Basque fleet" never realized its intended New World mission. This also meant that Basques would be underrepresented in the list of the approximately twelve hundred men who participated in Columbus's second voyage.[21] There were only twenty-two Basques in all, including Pedro de Arana. (Another of the admiral's "relatives"?) Upon reaching the New World, Columbus discovered that his first colony had been wiped out to the last man—including Diego de Arana. Not surprisingly, some Basque mariners accompanied Columbus in each of his three voyages after the initial one to the New World.[22]

On balance, none of the admiral's subsequent voyages were positive experiences. In Fonseca, he now had an envious and powerful adversary. His interviews with the Portuguese monarchs en route to Spain after his initial discovery had aroused some doubts in Castilian circles regarding Columbus's loyalties. The admiral's efforts would also meet with insurrection in the New World by both his ostensible Indian allies and some of his colonists. At one point, he was relieved of his New World command and possessions and ordered back to Spain to face trial. Nor were his efforts to find the westerly trade route to the Orient successful. Rather, he managed to map only a

---

19. Thomas, *Rivers of Gold*, 101.

20. Bartolomé de las Casas, *Historia de las Indias*, 3 vols. (Mexico City: Fondo de Cultura Económica, 1951), 1:300.

21. José Manuel Azcona Pastor, *Possible Paradises: Basque Emigration in Latin America* (Reno: University of Nevada Press, 2004), 476.

22. Carlos Clavería Arza, *Los vascos en el mar* (Pamplona: Editorial Aramburu, 1966), 125–27.

relatively small stretch of what would prove to be a formidable continental barrier.

Despite Columbus's pretensions to hold a monopoly on New World exploration, others received authorization to explore parts of it. At the beginning of May 1499, Peralonso Niño departed Spain with permission to pearl along the northern South American coast. He had captained the *Santa María* in Columbus's first voyage and had participated in the second and third—he knew the area well. His expedition was both short and extremely profitable.

That same year, Alonso de Hojeda, a man who had been on Columbus's second voyage and who was a protégé of Bishop Fonseca, was authorized to explore the coast of what would become present-day Venezuela. He departed Spain on May 18, 1499, accompanied by the Italian navigator Amerigo Vespucci and the cartographer Juan de la Cosa.[23] Amerigo, of course, leant his name to the continent and was said to have called the area Venezuela, or "Little Venice," after seeing a village of Indians who had built their dwellings on stilts over water. When the expedition arrived at Hispaniola, there was violence, including some fatalities, when Columbus's supporters objected to Ojeda's usurpation of their leader's exclusive exploration rights.

In 1500, Rodrigo de Bastidas, backed by nineteen Sevillan investors, left for northern South America with two caravels. According to Hugh Thomas, "Half of his sailors were Sevillanos, half Basques."[24] Juan de la Cosa was along, as was Vasco Nuñez de Balboa—the man destined to be the first European to spy the eastern Pacific Ocean. This expedition accumulated some gold and emeralds and was probably the first to reach Panama. Bastidas was shipwrecked on Hispaniola

---

23. One Juan de la Cosa made the first map of the world (or mappa mundi) in 1500 after returning from Columbus's second voyage. There is controversy over whether he was Basque (in which case, his name may have been Lakotza) or a native of from Santoña, Santander—in any event, located a few miles west of Bilbao and quite influenced by it. There was a Juan de la Cosa on Columbus's first voyage, but again, it is not entirely certain that he was this same man. See Antonio Ballesteros Beretta, *El cántabro Juan de la Cosa y el descubrimiento de América* (Santander: Diputación Regional de Cantabria, 1987) and Jon Bilbao *Vascos en Cuba (1492–1511)* (Buenos Aires: Editorial Ekin,1958), 49–54. Hugh Thomas treats him as being from Santoña and as the single individual who participated in the two voyages of Columbus and that of Ojeda. Thomas, *Rivers of Gold*, 188.

24. Thomas, *Rivers of Gold*, 191.

and endured a trying trek to its European settlement. He lost most of his treasure along the way, but arrived back in Spain with some of it.

After returning to Spain from his first expedition, Ojeda immediately received permission for a second one. This time, he partnered with investors, including two Andalusian merchants—Juan de Vergara[25] and García de Campos. Their four vessels left in early January of 1502, a few months before Columbus's fourth voyage. The expedition founded a settlement on the Guajira Peninsula in present-day Colombia, the first European settlement on the American mainland. However, there were immediate hostilities with the natives, and after three months, Vergara and Campos detained Ojeda and abandoned the settlement. Ojeda was imprisoned on Hispaniola between 1502 and 1504, until Bishop Fonseca secured his release.

Within the infrastructure that Columbus established in the Caribbean, there were some key Basque participants. Several were in the ranks of the European insurrectionists. One of them from the second voyage, Fernando Guevara, fell out of favor with the rebel leader, Francisco de Roldán, over an Indian woman and was incarcerated. By then, Columbus had negotiated a fragile peace with Roldán, so when Guevara's Basque compatriot, Adrián de Mujica, came to his aid, he was arrested and executed by Columbus.[26]

Another notable Basque on the second voyage was Francisco de Garay. In 1497, he and an Aragonese partner, Miguel Díaz de Aux, were charged by Hispaniola's first governor, Columbus's brother Bartolomeo, with building the colony's first city—Santo Domingo. They discovered an enormous gold nugget that made them the two richest men on the island. Francisco's luxurious residence in Santo Domingo was the city's first to be constructed of stone. Garay was later made the governor of Jamaica, where he founded settlements and an extensive livestock industry.[27]

---

25. Some sources refer to him as a Gipuzkoan merchant. In any event, he was of Basque descent.

26. Laurence Bergreen, *Columbus: The Four Voyages* (New York: Viking, 2011), 263–66.

27. Thomas, *Rivers of Gold*, 176, 206, 266. Garay became an extremely wealthy pig raiser, at one time requiring the services of five thousand Indians for their care. Donald. E. Chipman, *Nuno de Guzman and the Province of Panuco in New Spain 1518–1533* (Glendale: Arthur H. Clark, 1967), 46–47.

Also of interest was the abortive attempt to found a Bizkaian colony in the Caribbean:

the plan [was] established by the Bizkaian Luis de Arriaga in 1501 and approved by Queen Isabella to populate Hispaniola with two hundred families from Bizkaia. The colonists' mission was to found four settlements of fifty members each. In exchange they would receive a hacienda on the condition that they remain in their respective settlements for five years and pay their taxes to the Crown. Although the plan was never carried out, it was undoubtedly the first large-scale scheme of Iberian migration to America.[28]

In light of all this activity, Spain faced a serious challenge in building a fleet equal to the opportunities afforded by the New World. The Catholic Monarchs turned to Bishop Fonseca, and he

was helped in this by Captain Diogo Barbosa, a Portuguese exile with experience in maritime administration. Diogo Barbosa brought in naval architects and shipwrights from Portugal, and soon Juan [Fonseca] was launching seaworthy caravels. He also recruited artillerists from Germany to teach naval gunnery to his captains, and persuaded Jewish astronomers and map makers to come from Lisbon, under his protection, to improve the charts and nautical instruments for his navigators. He opened a royal school of navigation in Seville under the direction of his Florentine friend, Amerigo Vespucci, with authority to examine the qualifications of all pilots, and to withhold or grant licenses to them.[29]

Vespucci was an agent of the Medicis, and Fonseca awarded them trade privileges. It would now be common for some of the vessels in Spanish commercial fleets to fly Medici banners.

While Columbus would die believing that he had discovered lands off the coast of China, there was a growing awareness that Spain had thus far encountered a "New World," rather than a sea route to the Orient. Peralonso Niño stated that his expedition had sailed along the coast of a little-understood continental mainland.

---

28. Azcona Pastor, *Possible Paradises*, 24.

29. Parr, *Ferdinand Magellan*, 189.

As successive Spanish[30] and Portuguese[31] expeditions mapped parts of the South and Central American coastlines, it was becoming increasingly evident that Columbus had but scratched the surface of a continuous continental barrier that posed a far more formidable obstacle than had Africa to the Portuguese earlier. If Spain wished to engage in Asian maritime commerce, it had first to find either a southern or northern passage through or around an immense American land mass.

Over time, Bishop Fonseca would become the (corrupt) gray eminence behind the Spanish throne, the key administrator of its voyages of exploration and New World initiatives, and the richest man in the realm. Particularly insidious were his murky dealings with the Inquisition as the archdeacon of the diocese of Sevilla. When Torquemada launched his anti-Semitic purge, allies of the Jews importuned the Catholic Monarchs to soften the proceedings. They appointed the bishop of Sevilla as an appeals judge. The bishop delegated this authority to Fonseca. Many frightened Conversos sought him out, and he exacted a high price for intervention (which in any event oftentimes proved ineffectual in the face of the Inquisitorial juggernaut). Fonseca was also well placed to assist Muslims seeking exit permits. Parr notes that the bishop no doubt learned much about the existing organization and economics of the spice trade, not to mention the geography of southern Africa and the Middle and Far East, from his spoliation of beleaguered Converso and Muslim merchants.[32]

In 1503, the Catholic Monarchs established the Real Casa de Contratación de Indias (The Royal House of Indies' Commerce), also known as the Casa de Antillas (House of the Antilles), modeled on Portugal's Casa da India. Fonseca was appointed its first chief administrator and "prince president" of what would become the Supreme Council of the Indies. Queen Isabella died in 1504, and King Ferdinand essentially turned the crown's colonial affairs over to Fonseca. He accumulated a vast fortune, much of it in New World properties, plantations, and slaves—no doubt abusing his offices to sell favors. In

---

30. Hugo O'Donnell, *España en el descubrimiento, conquista, y defensa del Mar del Sur* (Madrid: Mapre, Editorial, 1992), 30–38.

31. Gallez, *Cristóbal de Haro*, 44–45, 54–76.

32. Parr, *Ferdinand Magellan*, 186–87.

order to blunt challenges to his authority, Fonseca tended to appoint beneath him weak and inept administrators. At the same time, he brooked no challenges from independent explorers. When Columbus pressed his demands, the bishop became the arrogant Genoese's implacable foe—the admiral ended up destitute and embittered after serving a prison sentence. When, after discovering the Pacific Ocean, Vasco Nuñez de Balboa tried to set up an independent government in Panama, Fonseca had him executed as a traitor.[33]

The bishop's power was not unlimited, however, and he was not without his detractors. The grand defender of the Indians, Bartolomé de las Casas, denounced Fonseca for his corruption, naked greed, and total indifference to the egregious abuses inflicted upon New World native populations. This prompted the protective religious orders charged with proselytizing the Indians to push back against Fonseca.

More tellingly, perhaps, were the mixed results of the bishop's machinations within Iberian affairs—particularly regarding royal marital alliances and succession to the Spanish thrones. Arranged marriages were a critical component in statecraft, providing the cement for international bonding—even between potential rivals and enemies. Two of the daughters of Ferdinand and Isabella would marry King Manoel I of Portugal, and a third, Catherine of Aragón, married King Henry VIII of England and bore him the future Queen Mary I.

Fonseca was particularly instrumental in negotiating the critical unions of two of the Catholic Monarchs' children—Spanish heir apparent Prince Juan of Asturias and his sister Juana to Archduchess Margaret and her brother, Archduke Philip of Flanders—the offspring of the Holy Roman emperor, Maximilian. Fonseca made four trips in all as a Spanish royal emissary, and while in Northern Europe cemented close ties with the House of Fugger. After much intrigue and considerable historical vagary (including the premature death at age twenty-one of Prince Juan), Philip became king of Castilla, which made it likely that his son, Charles (King Ferdinand's grandson), would one day become the monarch of Spain. Relations between son-in-law and father-in-law were strained. Philip had the backing of much of the Castilian aristocracy and powerful Cardinal Ximenes

---

33. Ibid., 190.

de Cisneros—opposed as they were to Ferdinand, an Aragonese "foreigner," assuming the kingship of Castilla. He did all that he could to isolate his wife, Juana, from her father, and his son Charles from his grandfather, as well. King Philip died three months after ascending the Castilian throne, quite possibly having been ordered poisoned by King Ferdinand.

Charles was but six at the time of his father's death and became the ward in Flanders of his aunt, Archduchess Margaret. Philip's will appointed William du Croy, the Lord of Chièvres, as the boy's tutor. Fonseca had the complete confidence of both Margaret and William and provided them with intelligence regarding Spain, even while serving as the trusted aide of King Ferdinand. Given that Ferdinand's daughter, Juana, was unbalanced (she is known to history as "Juana la Loca" or "Crazy Juana"), the surviving Catholic Monarch served as his grandson's regent in Spain until the boy should come of age. Fonseca was placed in charge of sequestering Charles's unbalanced mother, which he did for many years thereafter.

It was with the boy's third preceptor that Fonseca would encounter difficulty. According to Parr:

> This was the Dutch priest Adrian Dedel, Dean of the University of Louvain, who had taught at the University of Utrecht and was author of a book on philosophy. He was a man of simple honesty, uncompromising in his hatred of laxity in the clergy. He therefore always held aloof from Bishop Fonseca, resisted his advances, and more than once rebuked him for hypocrisy. Years later, when Adrian became Pope, he intervened to rescue the victims of Juan's tyranny and caused his political downfall. . . . The only books that Charles liked were on the history of government, for his inclination was towards statesmanship. Therefore Dean Adrian employed his friend, the great Dutch scholar Erasmus, to compose for Charles a book of advice on Christian kingcraft. This might be compared with Machiavelli's contemporary handbook *The Prince*, which it resembled only in general topic, as Erasmus's advice was quite different from that of the worldly Italian.[34]

On January 1, 1515, fifteen-year-old Charles, Archduke of Austria, became the ruler of the Low Countries. His grandfather, Ferdinand II, died a year later. By then, the Aragonese king was thoroughly

---

34. Ibid., 201, 202.

disaffected with both Charles and his aunt, Margaret. Indeed, Ferdinand had contracted (quite tardily) marriage with a French princess simply in order to produce a different heir, but their son died in childbirth. The king then resolved to make Charles's younger brother, Ferdinand, his successor, but relented under the pleadings of Cardinal Cisneros, whom he appointed as interim regent of Castilla

Thus began a period of extreme intrigue in the circle around Charles. Fonseca had a foot firmly planted on both sides of the divide, professing allegiance to Cardinal Cisneros while, at the same time, retaining his close ties with Chièvres. The latter saw his influence over Charles coming to an end and resolved to enrich himself by any means, an undertaking that suited Fonseca just fine. Cardinal Cisneros was both upright and patriotic, so Chièvres made certain that the only news and recommendations that reached the young pretender concerning Spain was authored by Fonseca. Cisneros had Charles named king of Castilla and wanted him to come to Iberia immediately, but Chièvres did all that he could to delay the event so that the two intermediaries could siphon off as much wealth as possible during the indeterminate state of affairs.

In September of 1517, Charles finally landed in Asturias with a large force of mercenaries. The Spanish regent, Cardinal Cisneros, set out to meet his young ruler and render an account of his stewardship. On the road, the prelate died—with all of the symptoms of having been poisoned. It would be the bishop of Burgos, Juan Fonseca, who knelt before the monarch, assured by Chièvres that it was to Fonseca that the young man owed his crown.

Fonseca thus became the virtual ruler of Castilla and Aragón—at this juncture in league with Chièvres, the newly appointed chancellor of the realm. They embarked upon every imaginable form of corruption, particularly that of selling offices and titles—many to absent Flemish lords. The clergy became thoroughly incensed when Chièvres had his nephew named bishop of Toledo, the wealthiest and most influential of all Spanish dioceses. In the process, the new kleptocracy so antagonized virtually every sector of Spanish society that Fonseca brought back from Sicily a contingent of loyal troops and then placed his brother Antonio in command of the entire army.

On January 12, 1518, the Holy Roman emperor, Maximilian I, died. Charles was then encouraged to compete against England's

Henry VIII and France's François I as his grandfather's successor—the selection to be determined by a corruptible group of electors. Charles's successful bid was financed by Jakob Fugger from his vast resources. The House of Fugger would henceforth experience both the joys and sorrows of being the emperor's personal banker. There were the obvious concessions and privileges accorded to an insider; there would also be the formidable drain generated by Charles's perennial deficits and boundless ambition.

Gertrude von Schwarzenfeld subtitled her biography of the complex emperor *Father of Europe*.[35] For our purposes, this captures nicely Charles's Eurocentric preoccupation, which assumed both Machiavellian temporal and Erasmusian spiritual expressions.[36] Upon the accession of Charles to the imperial throne, France was now virtually surrounded by the Habsburg Empire, and England faced a mighty continental foe. Both would mount military challenges to Habsburg hegemony, including sponsorship of corsair assaults upon Spain's maritime commerce after 1522. King François "declared that he would like to see the clause in the will of Adam that excluded France from the division of the world."[37]

The same year, 1517, in which Charles first set out for Spain, Martin Luther posted his theses on a church door in Wittenberg. In 1521, the youthful Charles signed the Edict of Worms, condemning Luther and thereby laying the foundations of the Protestant Reformation and the ensuing Wars of Religion. One of their consequences was the rebellion and rise of Protestant Holland, which would later mount its own ascendant maritime threat to Catholic Spanish and Portuguese naval and commercial hegemony in the Atlantic. In Eastern Europe, Charles also faced increasing danger from an expanding Ottoman Empire and in the Mediterranean from North African pirates.

Thus, by the time the eighteen survivors of Magellan's expedition straggled into the Andalusian port of Sanlúcar de Barrameda in September of 1522, having crossed the Pacific while becoming the first to circumnavigate the globe, Emperor Charles V was already com-

---

35. Gertrude von Schwarzenfeld, *Charles V: Father of Europe* (Chicago: Henry Regnery, 1957).

36. Ibid., 36–45.

37. Thomas, *Rivers of Gold*, 516.

mitted to the struggle for political control of Europe, leadership of the Counter-Reformation, and defense of the Occident against the Turks. Because Spain's maritime capacity was increasingly committed to the political contest in Atlantic and Mediterranean waters, the priorities for whatever could be spared were protection of the vulnerable Indies fleet and maintenance of crown authority in the Americas. While Magellan "discovered" the southern passage, its extreme southerly location added thousands of miles to the westerly sea route from Europe to the Orient, and the strait's inclement climate and currents would prove daunting obstacles to any sort of reasonable maritime commerce. Consequently, possible maritime hegemony over the remote Pacific became of lesser concern, at least for the time being. Indeed, as we will see, the initiative for subsequent Spanish Pacific exploration would become as much the initiative of New World viceroys as of Old World monarchs.

The Iberian Model of European Expansion

There was enormous similarity and overlap in the two Iberian exploratory thrusts into the South Atlantic and beyond. While the competition between Portugal and Spain (and particularly Castilla) in this regard dates from the early fourteenth century, it certainly heated up after Columbus's landmark first voyage. Both monarchies were imbued with a sense of urgency, yet neither possessed the wherewithal to make exploration and maritime commerce a crown monopoly. Both therefore relied somewhat upon their own Conversos, but particularly on foreign bankers—the rival Fuggers and Medicis. The financiers made significant loans to cash-strapped monarchs while also carving out privileged positions for their own merchant ships within many expeditions.

Such entrepreneurship extended down to the level of the seamen who crewed the vessels. Few were "shanghaied" or otherwise forcibly conscripted; rather, they were recruited with the promise of a fractional share in any benefits. While both monarchies did their best to limit participation in the expeditions to its own nationals, that was clearly impractical. Recruitment of persons willing to take a leap into the unknown was never easy, particularly after many an expedition limped back to its home port having lost a significant percentage of its vessels and personnel along the way. The Genoese, in particular, provided vision, expertise, and personnel to both Iberian monarchies. The participation of foreigners is best illustrated by that of the Columbus brothers—at some point, they sailed under *both* Iberian flags.

Another clear source of tension for both monarchies was the personality of the explorer himself—with Columbus setting the tone. Most proved to be men of unconventional vision and vast personal ambition. All were potential rebels and renegades. Viewed from the perspective of the Iberian royal courts, there was always considerable ambivalence regarding those who planted the country's flag half a world away. As we have seen and will see further, the very success of an explorer made him an object of suspicion (and envy), a man to be reined in as best as possible by the colonial bureaucracy and possibly even tried in the court system for alleged abuses. Given the elements in play, possibly the remarkably similar responses by the two Iberian powers were inevitable, but the resulting administrative systems certainly leant themselves to corruption and the settling of old scores.

There was one seemingly small difference in the administrative philosophies of King Manoel and Bishop Fonseca, the architects of the two respective Iberian colonial policies. While both tried to undermine their underlings, Manoel provided favored treatment to the Knights of Christ. Thus, while a mariner in his service theoretically gained a share in an expedition's spoils, in order to dispose of it back in Portugal, he required a license that was often the object of extortion by some bureaucrat (or even several) of the Knights of Christ. While there was considerable cupidity in Sevilla, as well, Bishop Fonseca and his cronies dared not squeeze their seaman. In Castilla, there was a long-standing tradition that commoners had rights that needed to be respected. As a consequence, there was a flow of disaffected mariners from Portugal to Spain, rather than in the other direction—all of which helped Fonseca's agenda while undermining Manoel's.

That having been said, during the early decades of the sixteenth century, Portugal had the clear upper hand. From the time of Columbus's first voyage until Magellan's penetration of the strait that bears his name, Spanish exploration was characterized by a series of failed attempts to discover the New World's southern passage. It was during that period that Portuguese successes in both Africa and Asia effectively co-opted the Venetian monopoly over the spice trade. By 1510,

Portugal had entered upon what would prove to be a three-decades-long golden era of commerce with the Orient.[38]

Stanley Payne lumps together the Spanish and Portuguese initiatives and then characterizes them as follows:

> The expansion of Spain and Portugal overseas in the fifteenth and sixteenth centuries was one of the most important achievements in world history, an enterprise for which Hispanic people had been prepared by their past and by the changes and opportunities attending the close of the Middle Ages. The medieval heritage of a military society, frequently thinking in terms of divine warfare and crusading, used to living on the boundaries of Latin Christendom and ever pressing back those boundaries, provided cultural and psychological training that was no doubt indispensable for the role played by the Hispanic peoples in the expansion of Europe. Desire for glory and riches had been a major incentive in the Reconquest since the eighth century, but fifteenth-century society had become more self-conscious about such goals and had better information about how to attain them.
>
> . . . For centuries the expansion of the faith was inextricably intertwined with military glory and economic profit. Because of this it is idle to ask, as is frequently done, whether the Portuguese pioneers and Castilian conquistadores were motivated more by greed or by religious zeal.[39]

Thus, from the outset, there was a peculiarly Iberian model of European expansion, a pattern that informed the subsequent two and one-half centuries of Spanish exploration of the vast Pacific.

---

38. Eventually, however, Portugal undermined the value of its position by flooding the European market with spices. Also, much of the wealth from the trade was dissipated in Lisbon's conspicuous consumption, rather than reinvested in the requisite infrastructure of empire. By the mid-sixteenth century, Portugal's thalassocracy was withering and both its Muslim opponents and the Venetians had recovered their former trade with the Orient. Payne, *A History*, 1:232.

39. Ibid., 1:88.

3

Ferdinand Magellan

The famed Portuguese explorer Ferdinand Magellan (Fernão Magalhães) himself was both a precipitate and an incarnation of Iberian
history. He was descended from a Burgundian ancestor who came
to Iberia as a Christian crusader against the Moors and who was
rewarded with an estate near Braga in the Minho region of northern
Portugal. Magellan's father, Ruy, was clearly a protégé of beleaguered
King João. The Portuguese king and queen were estranged, and each
maintained a personal court and retinue. Hers was by far the most
stable and sedentary. (The king had many enemies and moved about
the country frequently with his own security force.) The queen's court
received pages, such as the Minho contingent—Ruy Magellan's two
sons, Diogo and Fernão, along with their cousins, Francisco and João
Serrão.

Charles McKew Parr describes the curriculum as follows:

Apart from the acquisition of courtly accomplishments, the pages were
required to study map-making, the rudiments of astronomy, and celestial navigation. In no other country at this time were such courses given.
The King himself saw to it that these subjects were taught by experienced navigators and that the boys were thoroughly grounded in the
practical elements of maritime science, for he foresaw the future need
for well trained commanders.[1]

In 1490, King João II arranged the marriage of the frail fifteen-
year-old crown prince, Afonso, to Isabella, the eldest daughter of the
Catholic Monarchs. Since the latter seemed unlikely to produce a
male heir (and never did), the young prince, had he survived, would

---

1. Charles McKew Parr, *Ferdinand Magellan, Circumnavigator* (New York: Thomas A.
Crowell, 1964), 44.

ultimately have ruled all four Iberian kingdoms. However, within that same year, Afonso died under mysterious circumstances[2] while horse-back riding—possibly assassinated by the Braganças or even by the Spaniards. (The prince's Castilian valet and riding companion on the day of his death disappeared.) The king then initiated a campaign to elevate his favorite, an illegitimate son, Jorge, as his successor. He bestowed many titles upon the boy.

In 1493, the king sent Jorge to the queen's court, and the two Magellan brothers formed a natural alliance with the heir apparent, who was but a year younger than the twelve-year-old Ferdinand. All were under the tutelage of the queen's brother, Duke Manoel de Bragança, who had spent most of his boyhood as a refugee in Spain and had been educated at the Castilian court. He was but eight years older than Diogo, the eldest Magellan brother. For whatever reason—possibly an indiscretion by the Magellan boy, maybe incompatible personalities, or out of simple political antipathy—Duke Manoel took an immediate dislike to Ferdinand, and the feeling was mutual.[3]

Ferdinand had come to court in 1492 and was no doubt electrified by the 1493 arrival in Portugal of Columbus en route to Castilla on his return from his first voyage. The Magellans and their Serrão cousins all harbored dreams of going to sea. King João interviewed the Genoese (who believed that he had indeed discovered a westerly route to the Orient) and managed to dissimulate his extreme disappointment and displeasure over the Spanish triumph—after all, it had been his own ill-advised decision not to back the explorer. The Portuguese king immediately made plans to launch a westward expedition, and tensions rose between Portugal and Spain—outright warfare did not seem out of the question.

It was then that Pope Alexander VI, a Spaniard, intervened in order to prevent unbridled competition and/or hostility between the two Iberian kingdoms. In 1494, he brokered the Treaty of Tordesillas, which divided the entire world between Spain and Portugal into distinct and mutually exclusive spheres of influence. The pontiff was thereby rewarding the two countries that had expelled the Muslims from European territory and that seemed poised to circumvent Arab

---

2. Ibid., 46.
3. Ibid., 45–48.

and Ottoman control of the middle segment of the lucrative Mediterranean spice trade, as well.

While the competition (and at times outright antagonism) between Spain and Portugal could become palpable, they also shared common projects and even a common identity.[4] The Tordesillas Line drew the boundary at 370 leagues west of the Cape Verde Islands. Eventually it would provide Portugal control over Brazil, the western parameter of its around-Africa route to the Orient, while allocating the remainder of the (still unrecognized as such) American islands and continents to Spain. Given that the capacity to calculate longitude had yet to be perfected, just where the boundary fell in Asia was uncertain. Doubt regarding the future status of the Moluccas, the fabled "Spice Islands," was sufficient to sustain Spanish interest in the Columbian project.

The immediate effect of the Tordesillas Line was to place the Pacific off-limits to European exploration. The Portuguese in Southeast Asia had little incentive to expand their activity eastward into what would surely prove to be Spanish waters. At the same time, Europe's other sixteenth-century maritime powers—the French, the English, and eventually the Dutch—were effectively precluded from Pacific exploration by nominal (albeit far from impermeable) Portuguese control of the African circumnavigation route. From a Spanish viewpoint, the search for the southern passage would prove to be both difficult and protracted.

There was the other possibility, namely, that of finding a northern passage through Arctic waters. It had the attraction of providing the shortest possible route from Europe to Japan and China. Indeed, after the interview with Columbus, King João sent out expeditions to explore Greenland, Newfoundland, and Labrador and even dispatched another north to the Arctic and then eastward in search of a possible sea route to China through the Arctic Ocean. It was all to no avail.[5]

---

4. Indeed, when Alexander VI accorded Fernando of Aragón the title "King of Spain," the Portuguese protested that they were as much a part of "Spain" as were the Castilla and Aragón of the Catholic Monarchs. Stanley Payne, *A History of Spain and Portugal*, 2 vols. (Madison: University of Wisconsin Press, 1973), 1:243.

5. Paul Gallez, *Cristóbal de Haro: Banqueros y pimenteros en busca del estrecho magallánico* (Bahía Blanca: Instituto Patagónico, 1991), 38.

Meanwhile, it had also become evident that King João's plans for Jorge were unrealistic. They were opposed by his queen, who championed her brother Duke Manoel's claim to the throne. Leonor received the support of the Catholic Monarchs. Given that Pope Alexander was a Spaniard, there was little likelihood of Jorge's illegitimacy being erased through papal decree. So King João acceded to the inevitable and designated Manoel as his successor. In 1495, João died at age forty, "a sad and lonely figure." There is even speculation that he might have been poisoned by his queen.[6]

Soon thereafter, King Manoel I (1495–1521) married Isabella, Afonso's widow, thereby ostensibly consolidating Luso-Castilian reconciliation. However, their respective interests would quickly prove to be irreconcilable. The ascendancy of King Manoel and the resulting rehabilitation of the Braganças were sad tidings for the Minho pages. The Bragança nobles as a whole were a landed aristocracy with little interest in King João's maritime agenda, although Manoel would quickly reverse this policy shift, and by 1496, he had restored the Mina House and was supportive of the planning for a new Portuguese expedition to the South Atlantic. As for the Minho pages, they managed to hang on at court, but were assigned clerical positions in the Mina House. For the time being, they would be facilitators of, rather than participants in, Portugal's maritime ventures.

Manoel was also beseeched by his Spanish parents-in-law to reverse Portugal's open-door policy regarding exiled Sephardim Jews. Indeed, in 1496, the Portuguese king was persuaded by the Catholic Monarchs to institute his own expulsion of those who refused to convert to Christianity, spurred on by the growing unease in the general populace over the increasing numbers and influence of the Sephardim in the country. It seems likely that Cristóbal de Haro's privileged status was compromised (at least to some extent) by this growing anti-Semitism.

Prior to this time, the House of Fugger had enjoyed a near monopoly of Portugal's African commerce. But now the Florentines, in the guise of the Marchioni bankers, mounted a challenge. They won over (or bribed) Dom Álvaro Bragança, the king's uncle and influential

---

6. A. R. Disney, *A History of Portugal and the Portuguese Empire*, 2 vols. (Cambridge: Cambridge University Press, 2011) 1:136–37.

advisor. Dom Álvaro headed a promaritime faction within the royal council that provided the Florentines with an inside track as Portugal renewed its African trade and exploration.

It was then that a Genoese navigator, Giovanni Gabotto (John Cabot), passed through both Sevilla and Lisbon, seeking support for a voyage of exploration in search of the northern passage. Rejected in Iberia, Cabot went on to London and was received by an interested King Henry VII. After all, discovery of a northwest passage would provide England with a shorter sea route to the Orient than the Portuguese trans-African one. Cristóbal de Haro happened to coincide with Cabot in London and while there agreed to underwrite the (ultimately unsuccessful) Cabot expedition—thereby cementing the permanent animosity of King Manoel.[7]

In the summer of 1497, the Portuguese monarch commissioned Vasco da Gama to sail to India with a fleet of four ships. Along the way, da Gama would overcome much adversity and lose two of the vessels. In September of 1499, he returned with a modest cargo of spices. One of the two ships was flying the flag of the Florentine House of Marchioni.[8]

Also, while he may not have sponsored Cabot, after Columbus's successes, King Manoel was obviously interested in discovering his own North Atlantic sea route to the Orient. In 1499, João Fernandes Lavrador reached Greenland and sighted the coast of Labrador (subsequently named for him). Then, between 1499 and 1502, two Portuguese brothers, Gaspar and Miguel Corte-Real, made two voyages to Greenland and Newfoundland, mapping hundreds of miles of the Labrador coast.

King Manoel wrote to his Spanish in-laws informing them of the expedition's success and foreseeing that the axis of trade with the Orient would now shift to Portugal. Given that it was yet to be determined where the Tordesillas Line fell in the East Indies, it scarcely dissuaded the Catholic Monarchs from continuing to pursue their own search for a westward sea route to the Spice Islands. Meanwhile, the Portuguese immediately set about preparing a larger expedition to India. Haro tried unsuccessfully to help finance it; Ferdinand Magel-

---

7. Gallez, *Cristóbal de Haro*, 38.
8. Parr, *Ferdinand Magellan*, 51.

lan tried to enlist, but was rejected. One of the thirteen vessels flew the Marchioni flag. Over the next few years, it would seem that the Fugger financier and the page shared the common lot of being out of favor. They must have shared chagrin "when each year a returning fleet discharged the home-coming adventurers covered with nautical distinction and laden with incredible gains."[9]

Over time, however, the fortunes of both would change. Despite any antipathy that King Manoel might hold toward Cristóbal de Haro, it was convenient to have the House of Fugger as a counterweight to the growing influence of the House of Marchioni. Indeed, for the first decade and a half of the sixteenth century, Cristóbal continued at his post in Lisboa as an active player in Portugal's spice trade with Africa, India, and beyond, channeling a portion of it through Fugger's Augsburg and London facilities, as well as through the House of Haro in both Antwerp and Sevilla.[10]

Cristóbal also became a key underwriter of Portuguese expeditions to the New World. He continued to believe in the importance of a westward route to the Orient, as did King Manoel and the House of Marchioni, for that matter. We are told:

> Dom Manuel, even after da Gama's route to India had been firmly established, did not neglect the possibility of finding a western route across the Atlantic to India. On March 15, 1501, he sent a fleet of four ships . . . to explore along the coast of Brazil en route to India. With this fleet Dom Alvaro Braganza sent along, as captain of a caravel, Dom Diogo Barbosa, who became an advocate of a western route to India. . . . Cristóbal de Haro also was a believer in the possibilities of a western route, and he persuaded Dom Manuel to let him send, on May 3, 1501, Captain Cristóbal Jacques with three caravels to explore the southern Brazilian coast.[11]

King Manoel also dispatched fruitless explorations to the northeastern Atlantic in search of a northern passage.

Before the sea route to India could be firmly established, it was first necessary to defeat the Muslims who exercised considerable political and economic control of both India and parts of Indonesia. In

---

9. Ibid., 52.
10. Gallez, *Cristóbal de Haro*, 39.
11. Parr, *Ferdinand Magellan*, 53.

1503, Vasco da Gama destroyed an Arab naval force in Indian waters, and Portugal thereby "blasted its way into the spice trade."[12] Consequently, "In 1503 the King changed the name of Mina House to India House, to indicate that its administration no longer was restricted to the West African coast, but now embraced the entire field of overseas colonization."[13]

In the Service of Portugal

The goal of discovering a westerly route to the Orient remained a Portuguese priority:

> De Haro still persisted in his westward ideas, and in 1503 the King permitted him to send Captain Gonçalo Coelho with six *naos* to thrust far down the coast of South America. This large, well organized fleet carefully explored the Patagonian coast and may have discovered the mouth of the strait which later was penetrated by Magellan. It is indeed quite possible that Ferdinand Magellan himself may have been so placed, in the colonial bureau in which he was employed, as to have learned of it. Upon the return of this expedition to Lisbon, all reports of its findings were suppressed. If it did discover the westward strait, the King probably decided it was not to his interest to disclose its existence since it would be advantageous to Spanish commerce. At all events, on November 15, 1504, Dom Manuel issued a decree that ordered complete secrecy, under pain of death, of all maps, logs, reports, and any other details of southeastern or northeastern navigation. He evidently thought he would eventually have Spanish competition in the Orient via the western route, and hence, in 1505, he determined to desist from further efforts westward and to entrench himself in the possession of the eastward route.[14]

The latter decision provided the Minho trio with their opening. King Manoel ordered that six permanent Portuguese bases be established—three on the East African coast and three along western India. Francisco de Almeida was given command of a fleet of twenty-two ships, fifteen hundred soldiers, four hundred artillerymen, and a

---

12. Payne, *A History*, 1:199.

13. Parr, *Ferdinand Magellan*, 54.

14. Ibid. The fact that the South American coastline curves ever westward in descending from Brazil meant that the strait, the critical southern passage, would likely fall within the Spanish orbit of influence as defined by the Treaty of Tordesillas.

group of experienced civil servants from India House who would take charge of the on-site administrative details. The Magellan brothers (Diogo, now twenty-six years old, and Ferdinand, twenty-four) and Francisco Serrão (also twenty-four years of age) were all able to join the administrator ranks—their noble status making them supernumeraries and their personal biographies members of the (extended) royal household.

The makeup of the Almeida expedition was quite reflective of the Portugal of the day. The key military personnel were drawn from the powerful Knights of Christ. All of the caravels flew their banner of the red crucifix on a white background, underscoring that the expedition was also in a very real sense a crusade intended to conquer or convert Arab and pagan infidels alike. Ten of the twenty-two vessels were private—including one each belonging to the Houses of Fugger and Marchioni and two to individual Converso merchants.[15] Taken together, they bespoke the crown's continuing reliance on foreign financiers, on the one hand, and powerful Jewish merchants, on the other.[16]

The Minho trio spent twenty-seven months in East Africa while participating in military campaigns against the Arabs. Ferdinand Magellan clearly stood out, since he would serve as lieutenant to two of the most influential Knights of Christ commanders and was given command of his own small vessel. Ferdinand comported himself well in combat, acquiring considerable wealth as his share of the booty.[17]

These bold moves in the Indian Ocean, conceived as they were to establish Portuguese hegemony over the spice trade, provoked what would prove to be the ultimate confrontation between Portugal and the Arabs, their Indian allies, and the Venetians. There was considerable

---

15. Ibid., 62.

16. Regarding the latter, Portuguese Christian society was coming to mirror Spanish ambivalence over doubts regarding the sincerity of its Jewish converts, as well as resentment over their financial and political influence. Indeed, while Almeida was en route to East Africa, in 1506, there were massive anti-Semitic riots in Lisbon that resulted in the deaths of many Jews and destruction of their property on a mass scale. The response of the alarmed King Manoel was to liberalize the laws concerning the Conversos while taking measures to protect them from further assaults. The new policy was informed more by the crown's clear reliance upon the resources and expertise of the Converso community than by any sort of moral concern over its fate.

17. Ibid., 82–83.

skirmishing along the coast of western India for several months while the Egyptians and Venetians prepared a war fleet in Egypt. Magellan commanded a small caravel that was engaged in many naval actions during this period. On February 2, 1509, Almeida triumphed over the Egyptian fleet at the decisive battle of Diu.[18] It forever changed the fortunes of the Portuguese, Venetians, and Egyptians—not to mention millions of East Africans and Indians.

King Manoel was notorious for interfering with and undermining the authority of his key subordinates, particularly the successful ones. So Almeida was soon replaced as governor general in India by Afonso Albuquerque. Magellan, ever the loyalist, resented the treatment of Almeida and quickly fell afoul of his replacement. It was the latter who was the real architect (1509–1515) of Portuguese hegemony (limited as it was) in Asia. In 1510, he captured and fortified Goa, which became the capital of Lusitanian activity in the Orient. In 1511, the Portuguese seized Malacca on the Malay Peninsula, which gave them domination of the route to Indonesia and the opportunity ultimately to establish alliances in the politically fissiparous Moluccas. In 1513, Albuquerque secured commercial rights to Macao from China. He was so successful that Stanley Payne labels him as "one of the greatest, perhaps the most extraordinary of all, of the Hispanic conquerors" and then provides a synopsis of the differing challenges faced by the Portuguese and Spaniards in their respective imperial initiatives:

> The military success of small Portuguese forces on the other side of the world, virtually cut off from reinforcements, in a hostile environment populated by scores of millions of potential foes, was in some ways more remarkable than the sixteenth-century Spanish conquests in the Western Hemisphere. In India the Portuguese had to face not religious ascetics of Hindu culture but members of dominant military castes. The giant war junks of China and Java were frequently larger than Portuguese ships and sometimes as strongly constructed. Unlike Amerindians, Asians were capable of laying cannons which far surpassed those of the Portuguese in size. Nor can it be contended that Arab merchants,

---

18. Ibid., 88–93.

Hindu princes, Mongol emperors, and Malay sultans were awestruck or nonplussed by the sudden appearance of a handful of Europeans.[19]

Both Ferdinand Magellan and Francisco Serrão played important roles in the expansion of Portugal's influence in the Far East. Each commanded vessels and participated in numerous sieges and other military actions; Magellan was wounded seriously. Each undertook an exploratory initiative outside the framework of official policy or sanction. Serrão ended up in Ternate in the Spice Islands, where, for years, he maintained what was almost tantamount to a private fiefdom while pleading in vain with the officials in Malacca and Governor General Albuquerque in India to send him reinforcements. He even importuned his Malacca-based cousin, Ferdinand Magellan, to send a caravel with the assurance that he would leave Ternate with a large cargo of spices worth a fortune.

Magellan and the caravel that he was commanding disappeared from Malacca for many months. When he reappeared, it was to argue that he had been exploring beyond Ternate in the remote East Indies (some historians surmise that he reached the Philippines) and believed that much of the region fell within the Castilian orbit as guaranteed by the Tordesillas Line. It was not a conclusion that would endear him to either Governor Albuquerque or King Manoel. In 1513, Ferdinand returned to Portugal after eight years in the Orient, bereft of both fortune and influence and accompanied only by his faithful Malaccan slave, Enrique.[20]

The next three years were probably the most frustrating in Magellan's life. In Portugal, he found everything changed. The India House had evolved into a vast, impersonal, self-serving bureaucracy thoroughly controlled by the Knights of Christ. Magellan scarcely even knew anyone there any longer. He returned briefly to Minho to his family's properties and was received chillily by his relatives. His personal wealth became encumbered in a lawsuit. Through the intervention of a friend, João of Lisbon, Ferdinand enlisted in a Moroccan campaign and acquitted himself well. However, while there, he made

---

19. Payne, *A History*, 1:200.
20. Parr, *Ferdinand Magellan*, 84–127.

powerful enemies who then attempted to have him court-marshaled.[21] João of Lisbon was unable to intervene, because he was off commanding an expedition to Brazil, financed by none other than Cristóbal de Haro, which was yet another attempt to find the southern passage. While the legal proceedings were a draining experience, Ferdinand was able to prevail on his own.

His nadir was undoubtedly the day that he made a public appeal to King Manoel for personal advancement within the royal household and support for an expedition to relieve his cousin in Ternate. Ferdinand offered to bring back a shipload of spices that would become entirely the monarch's property. The king denied the requests and berated Magellan. When a frustrated Ferdinand asked if he might therefore serve another master, King Manoel told him to suit himself and then physically turned his back on the devastated supplicant. According to Parr:

> Dom Manuel no doubt felt justified in his refusal to give Magellan a promotion, and he found ample reason for the rejection of his application to return to the East. It will be remembered that both Governor General Albuquerque, in India, and General Pedro de Sousa, in Morocco, had written the King complaining of Magellan. He was identified with the two Serrãos and with the group headed by Duarte Barbosa, who were suspected of secret Spanish relations. Moreover, Magellan had embarrassed the King by his persistence in averring that Maluco [the Moluccas] lay in the zone of Castile.[22]

There seems little doubt that King Manoel was also settling some old scores dating back to the days when the Magellans were under his tutelage as pages at the court of his sister, Queen Leonor.

In any event, Magellan was now completely ruined in Portugal, as were his chances of returning to the Portuguese Far East. He retired to the obscurity of a mariners' tavern in Porto to weigh his limited options, which would likely entail entering into the service of a foreign nation—Spain being the most promising prospect. In Porto, Ferdinand was reunited with Ruy de Faleiro. The Faleiro brothers had been fellow pages at court with the Magellans. The Faleiros both excelled in astronomy and navigation. By this time, Ruy's brother,

---

21. Ibid., 131–46.
22. Ibid., 147.

Francisco, was already living and working in Spain and had published the first book in Spanish on navigation.[23] Ruy, having been passed over recently for the post of royal astronomer, was himself disaffected with King Manoel.

Upon his return to Portugal, João of Lisbon approved of Magellan's inclination to go to Spain and divulged to him all that he had learned about the southern South American coast. He had sailed around Cape Santa María and into the vast estuary of the La Plata River—which he mistook for the southern passage. According to Parr:

> Additionally, he also told Magellan that Cristóbal de Haro had accumulated considerable navigational data concerning the American coast from several previous voyages of exploration and discovery, and this was now on deposit in the King's chartroom in Lisbon. These secret expeditions, he said, had gone much farther south along the continent and had reported a sharp westward trend of the coast. Its contours had reminded him of the line of the eastern coast of Africa below the equator, with which both he and Magellan were thoroughly familiar. John of Lisbon therefore thought it probable that, if the strait at Cape Santa Maria should not prove navigable, he could navigate around the unknown extremity of the continent, just as Bartholemew Dias had sailed around the southern tip of Africa.[24]

João of Lisbon even managed to arrange for Magellan to gain access to the sensitive chartroom, where he was able to copy critical documentation.

In the Service of Spain

In 1516, Bishop Fonseca and Diogo Barbosa sent Juan Díaz de Solís to South America in search of the southern passage. Díaz de Solís, too, sailed around Cape Santa Maria and into La Plata River, where he was killed (and eaten) by the natives. At about this same time, Magellan received a visit from Duarte Barbosa. Shortly before Ferdinand left India, they had become fast friends in the subcontinent.

---

23. Ibid., 150.
24. Ibid., 151.

Duarte was the "nephew"[25] of Diogo Barbosa (the ship's captain in Portugal's 1501 expedition to Brazil). Diogo had subsequently entered the service of Spain's Casa de Antillas under the command of Bishop Fonseca and was currently governor of the Castle of Sevilla (through marriage) and the knight commander of the arsenal. The latter appointment made him the key official in the implementation of voyages of discovery.

Duarte had returned to Portugal in the hope of receiving a royal appointment, but like Magellan, he was identified with the wrong faction, and his career was blocked. While on a visit to see his uncle, he learned of Bishop Fonseca's resolve to follow up on the Díaz de Solís initiative—always in search of the westerly sea route to the Spice Islands. Both Barbosas believed that it was best to recruit a Portuguese commander. Duarte approached João Serrão, who was already a ship's captain in Spain. João deferred to his brother Francisco (who was in Ternate in the Spice Islands and obviously unavailable) and then to Ferdinand Magellan as two men better acquainted than was he with the area east of Malacca.

João Serrão was in correspondence with Magellan, but could not afford the risk of crossing the frontier. Duarte, who was not as yet in the employ of Spain, could. It was Barbosa who returned to Porto to recruit Ferdinand. Given the international diplomatic implications, Duarte first obtained general permission to recruit him from Bishop Fonseca and the then Spanish regent, Cardinal Cisneros. Magellan agreed to their proposal with the proviso that Ruy de Faleiro be included. Magellan also resolved to recruit several disaffected Portuguese pilots. Faleiro remained behind awhile longer; Magellan and his pilots snuck out of Portugal and made for Sevilla.[26]

It was there that Magellan entered immediately into the household of Diogo Barbosa. Indeed, it seems likely that a part of the negotiation with Duarte included an arranged marriage with Diogo's daughter Beatriz. She and Ferdinand were married but a few weeks after his arrival in Sevilla. So at a stroke, Diogo became both Magellan's patron and his father-in-law.[27]

25. Again, it is quite possible that Duarte was actually Diogo's illegitimate son.

26. Parr, *Ferdinand Magellan*, 150–53.

27. Ibid., 210–11.

It was about this same time that Cristóbal de Haro's fortunes in Portugal took a serious turn for the worse. In 1516, he sent his ships to India to receive their usual cargo of spices, but in Malabar, the local commander seized everything, and the fleet returned empty-handed. When Haro protested, the king feigned ignorance and promised to investigate, even though the seizure was unthinkable without the complicity of the crown. Despite the evident royal involvement, a few months later, Cristóbal dispatched seven trading vessels to Guinea that were then destroyed by the Portuguese navy, but only after their cargoes of European trade goods had been off-loaded.[28]

So it was that in 1517, Haro fled Portugal for Sevilla. His brother, Diego, arranged to transport the House of Haro's movable wealth surreptitiously by mule train through the Algarve, while Cristóbal galloped off on the quicker main route to Spain. At each way station, he purchased all of the available mounts in order to frustrate any pursuers. He arrived at Sevilla in the middle of the night and went straight to the residence of Bishop Fonseca. The two men conferred until morning, during which time Cristóbal likely divulged many Portuguese secrets. A furious King Manoel had all of the House of Haro's remaining property in Lisbon confiscated.[29] Paul Gallez speculates that Cristóbal's possession of the sensitive knowledge about the southern passage had sealed his fate in Portugal. He was, after all, of Castilian origin and therefore of questionable loyalty. Indeed, it may be that the only thing that prevented his assassination was the power and wealth of the House of Fugger.[30] Haro wanted vengeance for his treatment by King Manoel. What better way than to assist the Spaniards in undermining Portugal's near monopoly of the spice trade? While the House of Fugger had just lost much of its influence in Lisbon, it already had a relationship with the soon-to-become Holy Roman emperor, Charles V.

Barbosa was not dissuaded by the Díaz de Solís failure and continued with plans for a new expedition in search of the southern passage. Its private investors were to include Bishop Fonseca and a well-placed colonial official, Juan de Aranda. Recruitment of Magellan by Bar-

---

28. Ibid., 80.
29. Gallez, *Cristóbal de Haro*, 82.
30. Ibid., 80.

bosa had been a part of that strategy. But there was a different candidate for command of the next expedition—another disaffected Portuguese captain, Estevâo Gomes. Indeed, there had been initial steps to appoint him, but then Diogo Barbosa insinuated that Gomes might actually be a Portuguese agent, and Cardinal Cisneros refused to give the critical approval.

Shortly thereafter, the cardinal died, and Fonseca was anxious to proceed with the new expedition. Cristóbal de Haro knew both Gomes and Magellan, so his opinion in this matter was of obvious interest to the bishop, who had not had the time even to interview Magellan as yet. Haro recommended Gomes, who had actually worked for him earlier in Portugal as a ship's pilot. While he felt that Ferdinand was competent and did not dislike him personally, the banker underscored Magellan's headstrong personality, the history of his difficulties with royal authority, and his unbounded ambition. Cristóbal believed (quite correctly, as it turned out) that Magellan's demands regarding participation in any spoils of discovery (economic and political) would be far more exorbitant than those of the more tractable and complacent Gomes.

There then ensued a most tangled series of events. Barbosa had the little-known Magellan apply to the Supreme Council of the Indies for permission to command a royal westerly expedition to the Moluccas, confident that the petition would likely be denied, which it was. This provided the opening for Diogo to propose a private initiative (one that would still require royal approval) to be financed by himself and his secret partner—head councilor of the Council of Indies, Juan de Aranda. The latter was the insider conduit to the aloof prelate, and the plan was to offer personal participation in the venture to Bishop Fonseca.

Ruy Faleiro rejoined Magellan in Sevilla and took an immediate dislike to Aranda. Ruy proved to be jealous, petulant, and quite unreasonable regarding any sharing of the authority and benefits of the expedition. Fortunately for all concerned, Aranda was more tolerant, and when new developments at court made it necessary for them all to travel to Valladolid to make their case, Aranda even paid the expenses of the impecunious Faleiro, his brother Francisco, and

Magellan. Aranda demanded that he receive one-fifth of the explorer's would-be benefits, a demand that triggered a row and stalemate with Ruy Faleiro.[31]

It was February of 1518—the young monarch and his Flemish retinue had been in Castilla for but five months. However, Charles was already beginning to assert his opinion and will. Aranda's concerns were quite justified, since Cristóbal de Haro and Bishop Fonseca had just secured a mandate, dated February 10, 1518, from the king's council, approving an expedition to the Moluccas to be commanded by Gomes.[32] According to Parr, "Aranda knew very well the unscrupulous character of the crafty Bishop. He feared that Fonseca had decided to abandon his Seville partners in favor of an alliance with Cristóbal de Haro, who could be infinitely more helpful to him in putting into effect the plans he had already worked up with Aranda and Barbosa."[33]

This threat to their plans brought Ruy Faleiro around, and he ultimately agreed to accord Aranda a one-eighth share in the expedition. And then, "on February 23rd, a formal legal contract was drawn up to this effect which is still preserved in the records. Ferdinand's signature to this document appears not as Fernão Magalhães, the Portuguese form of his name, but Fernando Magallanes, the Spanish form, indicating that his nationality was now Spanish, and that he was no longer a subject of Dom Manuel of Portugal."[34]

Given the House of Fugger's existing relationship with the king, Fonseca asked Cristóbal de Haro to explain the project to Charles in order to secure the required royal approval of it. De Haro agreed, but suggested that Gomes come along and present the venture as his own idea, thereby somewhat dissimulating Fonseca's and Haro's private investment. This proved to be a mistake. The rustic and inarticulate Gomes conveyed the impression that he was a disaffected Portuguese

31. Ibid., 212–14.

32. The council was composed of Chièvres, Charles's chancellor, Adrian of Utrecht, and Fonseca. Bishop Fonseca's status as the only Spaniard on the council meant that the others (not to mention Charles) had to depend upon his local knowledge, which made him primus inter pares. Chièvres and the royal treasurer, Jean Le Sauvage, were to be accorded secret participation in the benefits of Gomes's expedition.

33. Gallez, *Cristóbal de Haro*, 215.

34. Ibid.

traitor proposing to organize and command an end run around King Manoel and into the Portuguese sphere of interest, in clear violation of the Treaty of Tordesillas.

This gave both Charles and his chancellor, Adrian, the future pope, serious pause. The latter viewed Manoel as an ally in Christian evangelization, having recently been accorded by Pope Leo X the exclusive right to Christianize the Orient. Charles was far from amused by the blatant disregard of the prerogatives of a fellow ruler. Furthermore, two of his sisters, Isabella and María, had been King Manoel's queen consorts, María having just died in 1517. Five months after this meeting with Gomes, and faced with rising hostility in Castilla, Charles would arrange a marriage between his niece, Eleanor, and King Manoel—a strategic move designed to preclude Portuguese support for a Castilian rebellion. So Charles had little reason to so blatantly antagonize Manoel.

Clearly, it was necessary for the bishop and the banker to regroup. Fonseca recalled that Juan de Aranda was besieging him for an audience to propose the Magellan/Faleiro initiative. Haro allowed that maybe he had erred in recommending Gomes over Magellan. Aranda, Magellan, and Faleiro met with Fonseca and won him over. Magellan and Faleiro made their geographical arguments, backed by charts, maps, and a globe. Bishop Fonseca then secured Chièvres's (self-interested) support, and they both lobbied Adrian. Chancellor Adrian was favorably impressed by Magellan's Christian piety. If he was no ardent supporter of the plan, at least his potential opposition had been neutralized.

As was the custom, Charles was provided with a précis of his petitioner, in this case prepared personally by Chièvres:

> Chièvres brought out Magellan's noble ancestry, his personal participation in the earlier, heroic Portuguese battles in India which had already begun to assume legendary proportions, the exciting shipwrecks which he had experienced, and the fact that Magellan had returned to Portugal a poor man after seven years of continuous warfare, while most of his fellows had amassed fortunes. That he had been severely wounded three times while fighting the Mohammedans and that he had recent experience in Morocco were also recorded.[35]

---

35. Ibid., 219.

In sum, the document depicted Magellan as "a gallant knight, a Christian crusader, and a navigator of scientific competence."[36] Chièvres prepared Magellan for his royal audience by suggesting that he emphasize to King Charles that he was no traitor, since King Manoel had dismissed him with permission (at least sort of) to serve a foreign master. He was also to say that he had strong evidence the Moluccas were within the Spanish orbit as demarcated by the Tordesillas Line. The point was to obviate at the outset the two prime objections against Gomes. And it worked. Magellan and Charles hit it off immediately. For added measure, Fonseca brought in the respected Cristóbal de Haro to endorse the plan.

While the wily banker knew that the point was to convince the king, and not himself, Haro still had his reservations regarding Magellan. He knew that all of Ferdinand's knowledge of the South American coastline was second-hand. Haro felt that his own vast network provided him with sounder knowledge of the Far East than that demonstrated by the petitioner. Furthermore, he was accustomed to treat commanders of his vessels as salaried employees, rather than as stakeholders, and he was simply appalled by Magellan's terms. He listened to the request for greater rewards than Portugal had accorded to Bartholomeu Dias, Vasco da Gama, or Afonso de Albuquerque. Nevertheless, Cristóbal played his part well.

In a profound sense, Ferdinand Magellan and Cristóbal de Haro shared a similar purpose—both were anxious to use the southern passage to reach the Orient. Magellan anticipated realizing the promised great wealth proffered by his cousin, Francisco Serrão, in Ternate, while Haro sought to undermine Portugal's near monopoly of the spice trade. Both harbored personal resentment and grievances against the Portuguese monarch and were itching to make King Manoel pay dearly for their ill treatment. Both sought personal enrichment, not to mention power and a place in history, by pioneering the westerly sea route to the Orient. King Manoel was about to feel the effects of the extraordinarily long reach of both his persistent ex-subject and the House of Fugger.

Under the original plan that had been submitted by Magellan to Cardinal Cisneros, Diogo Barbosa was to have defrayed all costs of

---

36. Ibid.

the venture, including outfitting the vessels and securing their trade goods, in return for the exclusive right to trade with the Moluccas. The new proposal submitted to King Charles called for crown financing, conceding a share of one-twentieth of any and all the profits to Magellan and Faleiro while according them equal cocommand (with title of "captains general"), as well as a ten-year exclusive (and hereditary) privilege to organize future Spanish exploration of the Orient. Fonseca liked aspects of the new proposal, since it removed Diogo Barbosa's control and placed the venture squarely in the bishop's hands—subject only to the liens of Magellan and Faleiro.

It was evident that Charles was prepared to approve Magellan's project on the spot, and while Fonseca and Haro would have liked to quibble over details, there was a sense of urgency. Undoubtedly, the Portuguese would protest.[37] So the bishop and banker urged Charles to accept Magellan's terms as presented—confident that they could subsequently undermine them. Of thetwenty-two thousand ducats to fund the expedition, the crown put up the majority. Cristóbal de Haro provided two thousand, and he and Bishop Fonseca between them agreed to pay for the ships' provisions and the goods for trading with the natives.[38]

A confident Magellan obtained five rather worn vessels and set about immediately repairing and fitting them with cannon, since a sea battle with the Portuguese somewhere along the way seemed possible, even likely. Duarte Barbosa was sent to Bilbao to secure cannons, arms, and armor for the fleet. A Basque, Captain Artieta, went to Bizkaia, accompanied by Duarte Barbosa, to obtain ships' stores from several chandlers.[39] Artieta purchased the *Trinidad*, the expedition's flagship, in Bilbao. It is also said that the *Victoria*, the vessel destined to become the first to circumnavigate the globe, was constructed in 1515 in the Basque town of Zarautz.[40]

---

37. Indeed, the Portuguese ambassador in Sevilla did so and also advised his monarch to interdict the Spanish initiative by offering Magellan a high post back in Portugal. King Manoel's advisors refused this advice.

38. Hermann Kellenbenz, *Los Fugger en España y Portugal hasta 1560* (Salamanca: Junta de Castilla y Léon, Consejería de Educación y Cultura, 2000), 215.

39. Gallez, *Cristóbal de Haro*, 228.

40. Victor María de Sola, *Juan Sebastián de Elcano: Ensayo biográfico* (Bilbao: La Editorial Vizcaína, 1962), 165.

It was now that Fonseca and Haro conspired to reconfigure the expedition to suit their own purposes. The first order of business was to isolate Magellan. Without really showing his hand, the bishop adroitly managed to embroil Juan de Aranda in a punishing lawsuit (presided over by Fonseca himself) regarding the councilor's presumed conflict of interest in having secured a personal contract for one-eighth of the proceeds of the expedition. Aranda's career was effectively destroyed; he was removed from the Council of the Indies, and his contract was voided. Fonseca then hoodwinked the mercurial and obstreperous Ruy Faleiro with the promise of sole command of a second, follow-up expedition, in return for relinquishing his contractual claim on the first. Faleiro withdrew from the venture—thereby creating a key vacancy in its leadership.

Fonseca's next move was to engineer an artificial funding crisis by presenting the crown with the bill for its four-thousand-ducat commitment. Treasurer Sauvage (Fonseca's coconspirator and Chièvres' partner in looting the Spanish treasury of a hundred thousand ducats monthly) informed his monarch that there was no available money to meet the commitment. However, Cristóbal de Haro and the House of Fugger possibly could be prevailed upon to assume the crown's commitment. The banker, of course, agreed and personally undertook the preparations for the expedition, as well. Both he and the bishop became major investors in the project. Fonseca dissimulated his conflict of interest by employing surrogates and associates. He entered a subscription of fifty thousand maravedís in the name of his illegitimate son, Juan de Cartagena. Meanwhile, Haro invested both the House of Fugger's and his own resources. Given his experience with Oriental trade, he included his personal stash of ingots and iron bars to be traded for spices in the Moluccas. So at a stroke, the crown had been excluded from direct participation in the profits, and Diogo Barbosa (whose power base rested in his influence on the council and the Casa de Antillas) had been effectively isolated.

The two cabalists then sought to undermine Magellan's authority within the command of the five-vessel fleet. The captain general was obviously going to command the flagship, the *Trinidad*, with Ruy Faleiro as a coequal at that point, and Ferdinand intended to handpick the commanders of the others. But then Fonseca convinced the king that there should be a Spanish commander, as well, with equal authority, and Charles signed a letter to the board of the Casa de Antillas to that effect, ordering it to make the appointment and suggesting they consider Juan de Cartagena. The nominee possessed only one real credential—he was Fonseca's "nephew."[41] Magellan intended to utilize the Portuguese pilots who came with him to Spain. But then Fonseca prevailed upon him, in the spirit of reconciliation, to accept the appointment of Estevâo Gomes as his chief pilot. In concurring, Ferdinand was unaware that Gomes, his distant relative and ostensible colleague, was actually quite jealous and embittered. Estevâo was now in league with Fonseca and Haro, charged with engineering a mutiny on the high seas.

It was but a small matter to insinuate, by means of royal orders,[42] other key personnel who would affect the expedition—all with large salaries. Fonseca managed to remove the treasurer of the Casa de Antillas, Doctor Matienzo, a close friend of Diogo Barbosa, replacing him with the bishop's loyalist, Luis de Mendoza. There would no longer be any official fiscal scrutiny of or opposition to de Haro's agenda. Juan de Cartagena was given command of a vessel and named to the important post of *vedor general* (overseer) of the fleet. His personal friend, Antonio Quesada, was named captain of another ship. Antonio de Coca, a Fonseca family bastard (son of the bishop or possibly of his brother Antonio), was made comptroller of the fleet. Gerónimo Guerra, either "nephew" or adopted son of Cristóbal de Haro (a supposed bachelor), was made an accountant. Finally, the Spaniard Gonzalo Gómez de Espinosa was made the sergeant-at-arms, or chief police officer, of the expedition. This, however, would turn out badly for the bishop and banker, since Magellan immediately recognized Espinosa's importance and successfully cultivated his loyalty.[43]

It was also about this time that an Italian, Antonio Pigafetta, showed up in Sevilla with Charles's royal recommendation that he

---

41. It is quite likely that he was the bishop's illegitimate son. It was common custom at that time to refer to bastard sons as nephews, particularly those sired by clergymen.

42. It seems likely that Fonseca employed a combination of persuasion and dissimulation in his dealings with Charles. The bishop may well have authored many key documents and then included them among many others awaiting perfunctory royal signature. This tactic would have been facilitated by the monarch's reliance upon Fonseca in dealing with an increasingly restive Spain while pursuing his own external agenda to become the Holy Roman emperor.

43. Parr, *Ferdinand Magellan*, 227–34.

be included in the expedition. It seems likely that he was the eyes and ears of Venice—supported by Cristóbal de Haro, given the House of Fugger's extensive involvement in that city-state. Pigafetta sailed on the flagship and became an ardent admirer of Magellan. He would provide the best account of the voyage.

The apparent coup de grâce came when Fonseca convinced Charles that there were too many former Portuguese nationals of dubious loyalty involved and secured a royal order limiting them to a total of five. However, while it might seem that by now the triumph of the bishop's and the banker's "anti-Magellan coup" was complete, there was one caveat. Ferdinand retained the king's respect and admiration. In a face-to-face meeting, the captain general convinced Charles to rescind the order. Magellan was originally authorized to name twenty-four Portuguese to the expedition—twelve to be nominated by him and the other dozen by Charles himself to underscore his support of the captain general. Magellan then blithely ignored his monarch's quota and hired thirty-seven Portuguese nationals in all.[44]

Key Portuguese players in the expedition were Magellan's nephew, Álvaro de Mesquita (who came from Portugal to join the venture); a page, Cristóbal Rabelo; the captain general's friend and relative by marriage, Duarte Barbosa; Estevâo Gomes (who, in the event, was no supporter); Magellan's cousin, João Serrão; and Enrique, Ferdinand's slave. There were also some Portuguese pilots, most notably João Lopes Carvalho. In general, recruitment for the voyage proved difficult, and the ultimate makeup of the 265-member expedition was thoroughly international. In their number was a contingent of thirty-five Basques, representing about 13 percent of the total.[45]

The expedition's Basque destined for historical greatness was Juan Sebastián de Elcano (Elkano). His earlier career is somewhat

---

44. Ibid., 245–50.

45. J. Ignacio Telletxea Idigoras, "Vascos y mar en el siglo XVI," in *Itsasoa: El mar de Euskalerria, La naturaleza, el hombre y su historia*, vol 4, ed. Enrique Ayerbe (Donostia-San Sebastián: Eusko Kultur Eragintza Etor, 1988) 175; and Segundo de Ispizúa, *Historia de los vascos en América* (Bilbao: Impr. J. A. de Lerchundi, 1914), 196–200. We know the birthplace of thirty-three of these men. Twenty-one were from Bizkaia, including seven from the small coastal town of Bermeo. There were also nine Gipuzkoans and three Navarrese. P. Pablo Pastells, *El descubrimiento del Estrecho de Magallanes: En conmemoración del IV centenario*, 2 vols. (Madrid: Sucesores de Rivadeneyra, 1920), 1:207–27).

shrouded, although he seems to have been born into the petty nobility of the Gipuzkoan coastal town of Getaria, to a family of modest circumstances. He learned his seamanship in the Cantabrian Sea, possibly working in the fishing fleet and/or through involvement in the contraband trade with neighboring France. In 1507, at the age of twenty, Elkano was a sailor on one of the many ships transferring a victorious Spanish army from Italy to Valencia. Two years later, he was the master of one that carried the crusading force led by Cardinal Cisneros against the North African stronghold of Oran.

In the aftermath of the Oran triumph, the pope blessed Spanish King Fernando's new crusade. The call for vessels went out, and Gipuzkoa alone supplied about one hundred, one of which was now owned and captained by Elkano. The Spaniards conquered Tripoli, but then suffered reversals. When the crown failed to pay the campaign's costs in a timely fashion, the young Elkano was unable to meet his financial obligations. He ended up losing title to his two-hundred-ton ship to merchants associated with the Duke of Savoy. That, in turn, placed him on the wrong side of the law—the sale or transfer of a Spanish vessel to any foreigner was prohibited.[46] He was liable for the amount of the transfer, subject to confiscation of half of his property, and at risk of further trial and punishment.[47]

It seems that Elkano disappeared for a while and became a fugitive. However, by 1519, he was in Sevilla, and his sailing experience landed him a high position in Magellan's fleet as master (second in command) of the *Concepción*, captained by Gaspar de Quesada.[48] According to Mairin Mitchell,

At this time the majority of the officials of the Casa de Contratación were Basques, a fact partly due to their aptitude for accountancy. The Treasurer was a Bizcayan, so was the principal technical adviser on artillery; the chief factor, the chief contador (accountant) and six other con-

---

46. Spain possessed superior naval technology vis-à-vis that of other European countries, with the possible exception of the Portuguese. Consequently, it was treated as a carefully guarded state secret. Maurice G. Holmes, *From New Spain by Sea to the Californias 1519–1668* (Glendale: Arthur H. Clark, 1963), 139–41.

47. Mairin Mitchell, *Elcano: The First Circumnavigator* (London: Herder Publications, 1958), 35–39.

48. Carlos Clavería Arza, *Los vascos en el mar* (Pamplona: Editorial Aramburu, 1966), 133–34.

tadores were from Elcano's own Province of Guipuzcoa. Earlier, one of them, Ibarrola, had served in the Casa de Contratación for many years; he was related to Juan Sebastian, and he was also a great friend of the Treasurer, who was Magellan's principal sponsor at the Casa, and on the closest of terms with the Captain-General of the fleet now in preparation. Ibarrola therefore, as a kinsman of Elcano, and as possessing a friend in common with Magellan, was doubly qualified to help Juan Sebastian to get appointed to one of the five ships.[49]

Recruiters of mariners from the Casa de Contratación focused upon the Basque Country, and with the prospect of serving under Elkano, a contingent of at least two dozen men signed on together.[50]

Despite all of the machinations of the banker and bishop, the character of the expedition was greatly influenced by the agendas of the increasingly assertive young monarch:

> Don Charles was sincerely resolved to respect the rights of Dom Manuel to the exclusive colonial exploitation of the area assigned to Portugal by treaty, but he was equally determined to assert his own rights. On February 20, 1519, he sent Dom Manuel an amicable personal letter assuring him that Ferdinand Magellan's armada would continuously remain in Spanish waters and would in no manner trespass in the Portuguese zone. This ingenuous communication from his candid brother-in-law made Dom Manuel furious because of its calm assumption that Maluco lay on the Spanish side of the division line. International conditions had changed, and Dom Manuel did not hold the diplomatic whip hand over this exasperating boy as he had held it over his grandfather, Don Ferdinand of Aragon. The French war was over, and both Sicily and Navarre now were safely Spanish; hence Portugal could no longer play France against Spain. Ambassador Alvaro de Costa had little means of applying pressure upon Don Charles, whom he now belatedly realized was wholeheartedly in favor of the expedition. Its adventure appealed to the King's youthful, action-starved spirit, but he was also aware that its success would make his rule popular with the Spanish people, and its financial returns would help pay off the heavy debts he was incurring in the electoral campaign for the crown of the Holy Roman Empire.[51]

---

49. Mitchell, *Elcano*, 42.
50. Parr, *Ferdinand Magellan*, 249.
51. Ibid., 241.

It required an inordinate year and a half to prepare the expedition, far more time than for any other Spanish expedition to date. Of no small import were the shady machinations of the Portuguese consul in Sevilla, Sebastían Álvarez. He cynically stirred up popular demonstrations and opposition among Spanish pilots against the "foreign" (that is, Portuguese) character of the venture. He played to the cupidity of officials of the Casa de Antillas, not to mention Chièvres and Sauvage themselves, with bribes that fostered delay and ensured that there would be shorting in the provisioning of the fleet. Indeed, in August of 1519, a frustrated Charles simply ordered the fleet to sail without further delay. At the solemn mass of farewell held in Triana, the captains vowed to follow the course ordained by Magellan and obey him in everything. Yet according to Pigafetta, "Three of the commanders [Mendoza, Cartagena, and Quesada] who took this solemn oath were already secretly committed to mutiny against him and to murder him as soon as the occasion might permit. Don Antonio wrote in his journal at this time, 'The captains hate him exceedingly, I do not know why unless because he was Portuguese and they Spanish.'"[52]

Magellan was forced to halt the fleet in Sanlúcar de Barrameda—having discovered that supplies listed in the ships' ledgers were simply missing.[53] It would take another month before the captain general was prepared to put out to sea, which he did on September 20, 1519.

At Sea at Last

From the outset, Magellan walked the thinnest of lines between his support and his many adversaries. In addition to the internal sedition represented by Fonseca's and Haro's agents, as he departed Spain, the captain general had to be on guard against Barbary pirates and a possible Portuguese fleet sent to interdict the expedition. In point of fact, there were rumors that King Manoel had dispatched three fleets—one to stop Magellan south of the Canary Islands, another to bar his possible change of course to reach the Orient by rounding

---

52. Ibid., 256.
53. Ibid., 253–55.

South Africa, and a third to the Spice Islands themselves to confront Magellan should he manage to complete his westerly voyage.

The fleet reached the Canary Islands without incident, and while there, Magellan received word from Diogo Barbosa that it was now common knowledge in Sevilla that the three captains planned to mutiny and kill him should he resist. There was also an excellent chance that through their agents, the Portuguese knew the precise course that Magellan had presumably agreed to follow before departing Spain and were preparing their ambush. It was even possible that Fonseca was in league with the Portuguese under an accord whereby Magellan and his inner circle would be arrested and removed to Lisbon for trial while the expedition under Cartagena would be allowed to proceed, but with limited objectives.

In any event, Magellan managed to outmaneuver the attempts of Cartagena to goad him into a confrontation over his change of course south of the Canary Islands. Ferdinand hugged the African coast and then deliberately sailed into an area of notorious doldrums. There the fleet was becalmed for three weeks, and the men suffered considerably from heat and reduced rations. However, Magellan had thereby eluded the Portuguese (who gave up their search) and had frustrated the plans of his duplicitous captains. Rather than falling for their bait after the blatant insubordination that was designed to bring matters to a head between the three captains and their captain general, Ferdinand lured his adversaries into a meeting at which they showed their cards. Magellan had prepared his response. When Cartagena openly blurted out his demand that Magellan relinquish command, at Magellan's signal, the vessel's master at arms, the *alguacil mayor*, Espinosa, entered the room with guards and arrested the belligerent captain for mutiny.

Captain Luis de Mendoza, a member of the anti-Magellan cabal, pleaded for Magellan to let him have custody of Cartagena. This was agreed, but a short time later, Cartagena was able to organize another near mutiny in league with Antonio de Coca and a worldly lay priest, Father Pedro Sánchez de Reina, who went from ship to ship entertaining the seamen and subtly fomenting dissent against the captain general's leadership and judgment. It was unclear how Reina joined the expedition—he may have even been planted by Sevilla's Portuguese consul Álvarez.

At this point, Magellan faced a clear dilemma. After all, Cartagena and de Coca were the illegitimate offspring (scions, as it were) of Bishop Fonseca, arguably the most powerful man in Spain. Prudence dictated that they simply be relieved of their commands and remanded to Mendoza's custody.

Magellan had to deal with other challenges while his fleet was refurbished in Santa Lucia Bay (the bay of present-day Rio de Janeiro). The expedition had skirted the northern reaches of Brazil, that part of the territory where the Portuguese were most active. At Santa Lucia, the fleet was able to replenish its stores of food and water, not to mention relax and enjoy the sexual favors of the native women. It was there that Duarte Barbosa became overly embroiled in the fun. He became if not insubordinate, at least lax, in following out Magellan's orders—thereby undermining his commander's confidence in him.

Magellan now made the mistake of elevating his relative Álvaro de Mesquita to the position of second in command and captain of his most formidable vessel, the *San Antonio*. In the event, Mesquita would prove to be weak, indecisive, and simply not up to such a challenge. With some difficulty, Magellan, concerned that the Portuguese would somehow learn of his presence and come running, managed to extricate his expedition and sail south. Still, while he remained nominally in control, as the fleet departed Santa Lucia Bay, Magellan was even more isolated than ever on his flagship, the *Trinidad*.[54]

After a series of miscalculations that prompted the captain general to linger in the estuary of the Río de la Plata in order to probe it thoroughly, thinking it was the likely mouth of the southern passage,[55] Magellan ordered the fleet farther south and into the mouth of the approaching Antarctic winter. He hoped to traverse the passage soon and quickly, aspiring to reach the tropical Spice Islands within a few weeks of having done so. But after weeks of frigid and stormy weather, Magellan led his grumbling men into a barren bay that he

54. Ibid., 265–85.

55. This episode undermined both Magellan's self-confidence and that of his men. Since Magellan was supposedly in possession of critical Portuguese intelligence regarding the southern South American coast, it seems likely that the former probes, such as that sponsored by Cristóbal de Haro and the later one led by Juan Díaz de Solís, had regularly confused the vast estuary of the Río de la Plata with the Strait of Magellan.

named Puerto San Julián. It was his intention to winter there before proceeding farther south in the spring.

While the most adequate bivouac encountered thus far south of Río de la Plata, San Julián was cold and bleak. Magellan held a meeting of the delegates of his grumbling crewmen during which the majority opinion was to return to Brazil to lay over in the far more appealing setting of Santa Lucia Bay. The captain general argued persuasively that after wintering in San Julián, the expedition would surely discover the passage quickly and reach the Moluccas. He appealed to their oath to Charles and played upon their Castilian pride. While Magellan was thereby able to secure the grudging acquiescence of the rank and file, he knew that the real source of sedition, the Fonseca faction, was another matter. He therefore convened a meeting of his council of officers at which their spokesman, Luis de Mendoza, demanded that Magellan return north, if not to Santa Lucia Bay, then at least to the Río de la Plata, to establish winter quarters. An obstinate Magellan advised them that their counsel was simply advisory and refused to follow it.

In anticipation of possible insurrection, Magellan ordered Álvaro de Mesquita to place the *San Antonio* on the highest alert. Mesquita believed that to be an overreaction, and he ignored the command. Two nights later, while the captain slept, a boarding party led by Captain Quesada, Juan de Cartagena, Antonio de Coca, and Juan Sebastían Elkano boarded the *San Antonio* and were welcomed by their coconspirators, Jerónimo Guerra and his followers. The mutineers were confronted by the shipmaster, the Basque Juan de Elorriaga. He ordered the intruders to leave while also directing his boatswain to arm the crew and secure the forecastle. Quesada drew his knife and stabbed Elorriaga six times, leaving him for dead on the deck. The mutineers then locked Mesquita in Guerra's cabin. Elkano was placed in charge of the appropriated vessel's powerful artillery battery.

At this point, three of Magellan's five ships—the *San Antonio* (now commanded by Quesada), the *Victoria* (under Mendoza), and the *Concepción* (captained by Juan de Cartagena)—were in the hands of the mutineers. Albeit disloyal, Estêvão Gomes, the chief pilot on the flagship *Trinidad*, was scarcely in a position to foment sedition, surrounded as he was by Magellan's supporters. The captain general could also count on the loyalty of the *Santiago*, commanded by his cousin, João Serrão.

Magellan now calculated that Luis de Mendoza and the other Fonseca men would try to take over the fleet, with killing him their main objective, but that they would exercise care so to avoid as much physical damage to the expedition as possible. They were unlikely to attack the shallow-drafted *Santiago*, since it was the fleet's best vessel for inshore activity in uncharted shallows. Nor were the expedition's principal financial backers, the bishop and the banker, likely to be amused if the *Trinidad* were damaged or destroyed.

Magellan dispatched Espinosa and five unarmed seamen to the *Victoria* with a letter from Magellan. They were allowed on deck, and Espinosa informed Mendoza that the important communication was for his eyes only. At this point, the mutineer rashly invited the *alguacil mayor* and one of his companions to his cabin. After reading and rejecting a letter that simply demanded his surrender, Mendoza reached out to hand it back to Espinosa, who plunged his poniard into the rebel's throat. Espinosa then waved a white flag from the cabin's window, the signal to send a boarding party of marines commanded by Duarte Barbosa. The startled crew of the *Victoria*, unaware that Mendoza was dead, were quickly overwhelmed and ordered to move the ship next to Magellan's flagship. João Serrão moved the *Santiago* closer, as well, and the captain general had blocked the exit to San Julián Bay. The remaining two rebel vessels were trapped.

After Mesquita refused to intercede with Magellan on the mutineers' behalf, Quesada prepared for battle. The *San Antonio* received a broadside at close quarters from the *Trinidad*, and it was then boarded by a party led personally by Magellan. He walked up to the armored Quesada and demanded that he surrender, which he did. Espinosa was dispatched to the *Victoria* to receive the surrender of the abject Juan de Cartagena.

The mutiny was over. Magellan then convened a court-martial, presided over by neutral officials—and no doubt with an eye toward future investigations and proceedings back in Spain. The court found the officers Cartagena, Quesada, Mendoza, de Coca, and Elkano guilty of treason while convicting forty seamen of mutiny, as well. Mendoza's body was hanged, drawn, and quartered—its parts being displayed prominently as a warning. Quesada was sentenced to decapitation. When no one else would carry it out, the unpleasant assignment was given to his secretary, Luis de Molina, in return for a pardon for his part in the conspiracy.

Magellan was leery of executing Cartagena, Coca, and Guerra because of their kinship with Fonseca and Haro. The other mutineers were condemned to death, but the expedition could scarcely afford to lose such manpower, and the sentences were commuted to hard labor. They were organized into gangs assigned to the most menial of tasks under Mesquita's now stern supervision. Parr states, "The inclusion of del Cano among the castigated rebels, while Cartagena was exempted, particularly aroused the indignation of the group of Basques among the seamen, for del Cano belonged to the petty nobility of Vizcaya and was looked up to by his compatriots."[56] Meanwhile, Juan de Elorriaga would linger for two months before dying of his wounds—visited daily in the sickbay by Magellan. While the fleet lingered at Port San Julián, the feckless Juan de Cartagena and Father Reina were emboldened by the usual grumbling to incite yet another mutiny. It was quelled easily and resulted in another court-martial of its leaders and their definitive detention.

Running short of supplies and believing that the passage was nearby, Magellan himself became restless and decided to dispatch João Serrão and the *Santiago* in search of the strait. Serrão struggled southward for sixteen days, making but sixty miles before discovering an attractive anchorage at the mouth of what he christened Río de Santa Cruz. Ironically (and unknowingly), he was now within two days of the passage, at 52 degrees south latitude. Serrão resolved to turn back to convince Magellan to move his winter quarters to the new site, but upon leaving Santa Cruz, he was shipwrecked almost immediately. Only one man was killed, however, and two others were sent on a harrowing journey on foot back to Port San Julián in search of aid. A rescue force reached Serrão, and after a month's absence, he and his crew were reunited with Magellan.

Serrão convinced his captain general to move the expedition to Santa Cruz. As the fleet left Port San Julián, Juan de Cartagena and Father de la Reina were put ashore with provisions and weapons. While a more lenient measure than execution, it was as likely to result

56. Parr, *Ferdinand Magellan*, 301.

in death. The two unfortunates were on their knees and pleading for mercy as the fleet disappeared to the south. Magellan established a new winter base at Río de Santa Cruz, and he was even able to salvage much of the *Santiago*'s cargo—including Cristóbal de Haro's valuable copper ingots and iron bars.

It was then that the captain general faced yet another serious challenge. Estevâo Gomes argued that the expedition was now so far south that it could set out on an easterly course across the Atlantic and arrive at the Moluccas without fear of confronting Portuguese patrols at sea. Short rations and scurvy were becoming prominent issues, so many of the officers, including Duarte Barbosa and João Serrão, were tempted by this plan. Magellan was opposed and argued in favor of proceeding south, but with the concession that if they failed to find the passage by 75 degrees south, they would strike out eastward across the Atlantic. Gomes then overplayed his hand by suggesting that they retrieve Juan de Cartagena and put him in command. He reasoned that certain fame and fortune awaited them if the fleet returned to Spain with the spices gathered by Francisco Serrão and commanded by Fonseca's protégé. Gomes had displayed his disloyalty to his fellow Portuguese, Magellan, and his plan was simply too duplicitous for the captain general's supporters—who now accepted (albeit reluctantly) Magellan's proposal.[57]

Finding the actual strait a few days later proved to be an emotional rollercoaster. While Magellan lingered therein, before striking out into what he labeled the "Pacific Ocean," he assigned the *San Antonio*, under Mesquita's command, to explore the southern fringe of the passage. It simply disappeared and was never seen again by Magellan, who suspected (accurately) a new insurrection that was probably dealt with poorly by Mesquita. Indeed, Magellan suspected (again presciently) that the mutineers had set out for Spain, where they would spread as much calumny as possible against him. He now knew that the only choice was to complete the mission as ordained by his monarch. Success would be his best defense and exoneration. In anticipation of likely formal court proceedings once back in Europe, the captain general began to seek consensus and then document it in reaching his critical decisions.

---

57. Ibid., 300–306.

In the event, the Pacific crossing proved to be a near disaster. Like his contemporary navigators, Magellan was unable to calculate longitude and could therefore only guess at the length of the voyage that lay ahead. Again, like all before him, he underestimated the size of the Earth. To make matters worse, he had lost his major hoard of supplies when the *San Antonio* defected. Magellan had his two commanders, Duarte de Barbosa and João Serrão, inventory their stores, and the results were disheartening. So as not to alarm the men further as they probed the unknown, Magellan swore his captains to secrecy. Theirs would have to be a leap into the void with the hope that they could live off the sea and the fruits of any islands that they might encounter. Unfortunately, the fleet sailed 20 degrees north before heading west from the Chilean coast. Had Magellan begun the Pacific crossing a few degrees south, he could have island-hopped across much of the vast ocean.

The fleet left the Strait of Magellan on November 28, 1520, and would not arrive in the Philippines until March 16, 1521—a voyage of more than three and a half months. Save for a couple of landings on uninhabited atolls, where Magellan was able to secure a little fresh water and cure the flesh of fish and seabirds, and one major bloody confrontation with natives in Guam that resulted in the desperate Europeans looting a village's food stores, the expedition was constantly at sea. Nineteen of the crew died of scurvy, and all were greatly incapacitated. According to Parr,

> Under the heat of the Equator, almost all of the crew and many of the men-at-arms were down with scurvy. Stricken men lay groaning wherever there was a bit of shade, and those still on their feet tottered and staggered. The sick had such swollen joints that they shrieked when they had to move a hand or foot. Ulcers broke out all over their bodies. Their gums were puffed out and their teeth were covered by the pulpy growth; when they tried to eat, their teeth loosened in the sockets and fell out. Their palates became so enlarged and sore that men died of starvation rather than swallow what food was available. The fetid breath of the sufferers was almost unbearable, and this, together with the putrifying odors from the bilge, made the ship's atmosphere nauseating even to those hitherto inured to it.[58]

---

58. Ibid., 330.

In addition to the generally low morale, Parr states, "The Gallegos and Basques resented the assumption of superiority by the Castilians, and the French and Flemings, being northerners, banded together against the southerners, the Iberians and Italians."[59]

There seems little doubt that Magellan was looking for the Philippines. Having once been there, he knew their latitude and roughly that of the Moluccas, as well, yet he steered a course about 10 degrees north of the latter. He may have intended to establish a fortified Spanish presence in the archipelago to be used as a base from which to proceed to the Moluccas and subjugate their rulers to King Charles. His first landing, on the island of Samar, proved most promising. He was reasonably well received by its ruler. There was abundant gold and Chinese porcelain, the latter evidence that they had indeed reached the Orient. With proper rest and abundant and proper food, Magellan's men recovered their strength quickly—Juan de Coca was the exception; he died a week after the fleet reached Samar, thereby removing the last of the expedition's Fonseca inner circle.

Magellan was informed of much larger and heavily populated islands to the north. While Duarte Barbosa and João Serrão both urged him to set sail immediately for the Moluccas and the expedition's main objective—Francisco Serrão's spices—Magellan insisted on exploring the Philippines further. No doubt he was motivated by the clause in his contract with the king that made him outright governor of any two of the islands of his choosing that he should discover.

Guided by the rajah of Samar, the fleet reached the rich and populous island of Cebu. And it was there that the fatal complications began. Magellan's slave, Enrique, was now able to communicate in his native Malay—the lingua franca of Southeast Asia. And then Magellan, when accorded a royal audience, encountered an Arab trader at the court. There could no longer be any doubt that they were in the Orient. The captain general was successful in cowing the rajah into accepting both Charles and Jesus—aided by the Moor, who spoke of the terrible wrath of the Portuguese against those who had resisted their king's sovereignty and deity.

---

59. Ibid., 324.

Magellan would undergo an immediate and puzzling personality transformation. He suddenly became a religious zealot who, along with his devout chaplain, Father Valderrama, set about sermonizing and baptizing pagans by the thousands. Meanwhile, the more venal crewmen set up shoreside stalls to traffic in gold and other trade goods. Many (led by Duarte Barbosa) became involved in the constant partying with women and palm wine that belied their leader's ascetic Christian message. Several of the other rajahs in the area opted for the carrot of Magellan's monarch and deity, rather than feel the stick of their wrath. However, there was one notable exception, a long-standing adversary of the now Christian rajah, and Magellan decided to make an example of him.

Inexplicably, perhaps now convinced that he was on a divine mission and therefore protected by God himself, Magellan insisted on heading an expeditionary force of volunteers—not the trained men-at-arms under Espinosa's command. In doing so, he was counter-manding Charles's specific order that the captain general should never expose his person in combat. He also ignored the admonitions of Duarte Barbosa and João Serrão not to involve the expedition in what was tantamount to a civil war. The captain general then rejected the offer of a thousand warriors made by his Christian rajah ally. Rather, Magellan insisted that he and his court witness from a safe distance the meting out of Christian punishment to a recalcitrant infidel. In short, the hubristic captain general inexplicably simply ignored the wisdom of his own extensive military experience. In any event, he clambered ashore with a ragtag force of a few dozen men to confront an army of several thousand and was killed in the surf as he and a few hapless survivors retreated toward their longboats.

This rather bizarre and ignominious demise belied a most extraordinary career. According to American historian Edward Gaylord Bourne:

> Columbus and Magellan are the great figures of this heroic age in American history. But though their lives overlapped a quarter of a century, they really belong to different ages. There was nothing of the prophetic mysticism [at least until the very end] in the make-up of the great Portuguese. Magellan was distinctly a man of action, instant, resolute, enduring. The first voyage across the Atlantic broke down the barriers of the ages and was a sublime act of faith; but the first navigation of the

Straits of Magellan was a far more difficult problem of seamanship than crossing the Atlantic. More than half of the English and Dutch navigators who later attempted it towards the end of the sixteenth century gave it up and turned back. Columbus's voyage was over in thirty-five days; but Magellan's expedition had been gone a year and weathered a subarctic winter before its real task began—the voyage over a trackless waste of waters exactly three times as long as the first crossing of the Atlantic. For these and other similar reasons it seems to be the mature judgment of the historians of the discoveries that Magellan is to be ranked as the first navigator of ancient and modern times, and his voyage the greatest single human achievement on the sea.[60]

Again Bourne opined,

The scientific results of Magellan's voyage were far more important than the political advantages derived from it. Once for all it gave a practical demonstration of the sphericity of the earth that convinced the ordinary mind unreached by the scientific proofs. It revolutionized all ideas as to the relative proportions of the land and water of the globe, and dissipated the traditional error on which Columbus's voyages and his whole geographical system were based, that the area of the land far exceeded that of the water. The vast width of the Pacific revealed that America was a new world in a more comprehensive sense than had been suspected.[61]

After Magellan

Duarte Barbosa was then elected by the crew as their new captain general. One of his first acts was to maltreat Magellan's slave, Enrique, who then retaliated by providing the rajah with critical intelligence regarding the Europeans' weaknesses. The Christian rajah was no longer impressed by the omnipotence of either Spaniards or their god. He set his trap as Duarte made his preparations to leave for the Moluccas. Dangling the promise of a treasure in gold and jewels assembled as an offering to be sent to King Charles, Barbosa was induced to accept the invitation for him and many of his officers to attend a farewell dinner on shore. João Serrão was suspicious and reluctant to go,

---

60. Edward Gaylord Bourne, *Spain in America, 1450–1580*, vol. 3 of *The American Nation, a History: From Original Sources by Associated Authors*, ed. Albert Bushnell Hart, 28 vols. (New York: Harper, 1904), 127–28.

61. Ibid., 132.

but was then accused of cowardice by Duarte and relented. Antonio Pigafetta, the expedition's chief chronicler, remained behind, having been wounded in Magellan's fatal folly. The uninvited Elkano was on board, as well.

It was then that they observed the *alguacil*, Espinosa, and the pilot, João Lopes Carvalho, hastily returning alone from the dinner, having intuited an ambush. A short time later, there were cries of distress from the palace, and the Spanish vessels fired broadsides into the town. A helpless João Serrão, surrounded by several native guards, appeared on the dock and pleaded with Carvalho to dispatch the copper ingots and two small cannon that he had agreed to give to his captors as a ransom for his freedom. He informed Carvalho that all of the other crewmen (save for the slave Enrique and Father Valderrama), including Duarte Barbosa, were dead. Carvalho demurred, possibly calculatedly, in the realization that Serrão would be his key rival in the subsequent election of a new captain general. Carvalho declared that it was too risky to chance a shore landing and he set sail—abandoning Serrão to his fate.[62]

Carvalho was indeed elected the leader on the assumption he would know how to lead the expedition to Ternate and then back to Spain. In the event, that proved beyond him. He decided to scuttle the worm-eaten *Concepción*, dividing the remaining 109 men between the other two vessels. The *Victoria* was now under Elkano's command.

Carvalho then embarked on a rather sinister piratical campaign throughout the Philippines and beyond, during which the fleet preyed on any other vessel that it came across. Finally, the disgusted men deposed their captain general in favor of Espinosa. For the following four months, he worked his way toward the Moluccas, asking for directions in various ports along the way. They arrived at Ternate only to discover that it was now under Portuguese control—both Francisco Serrão and his rajah were dead. The Spaniards sailed on to Tidore, where they found an ally in its rajah. Espinosa then built a strong shoreside fortification, underscoring the standoff between the rival Spanish and Portuguese claims to the region.

Espinosa decided to leave the Moluccas. However, when he encountered some difficulty with the *Trinidad*, he ordered Elkano and

62. Parr, *Ferdinand Magellan*, 363–68.

the *Victoria* to leave without him. The *Victoria* set sail on December 21, 1521, with a contingent of sixty, including thirteen islanders from Tidore.[63] They were negotiating hostile Portuguese waters as they skirted India and the Cape of Good Hope, never daring to land and therefore subject to great privations. By the time they arrived in the Cape Verde islands, on July 9, 1522, an additional twenty-eight men had perished. The Portuguese authorities managed to capture and imprison thirteen of the crew, including two Basques who had gone ashore in search of food and water. After it became evident that the governor would not release the captives, Elkano set sail, and on September 6, 1522, the *Victoria* reached the Spanish port of Sanlúcar de Barrameda with eighteen Europeans (three Basques, including himself) and four islanders on board, as well as a modest cargo of spices that was impounded immediately by Cristóbal de Haro to satisfy the expedition's financial obligations.

Elkano and two of his men were summoned to Valladolid and were received by Emperor Carlos V. As Magellan had feared, the *San Antonio* did return to Spain after disappearing. Its pilot, Estevâo Gómes, wrested command from Álvaro de Mesquita in Tierra del Fuego, wounding and imprisoning his captain. Back in Europe, the hapless Mesquita was turned over to the authorities, while Guerra and Gómes mounted their denunciations of Magellan. Gómes and Mesquita were both imprisoned (Guerra was not, given his influential protectors), pending a formal investigation. The stakes were high, since the two evident mutineers now argued that they were forced to act by the captain general's arbitrary departures from his royal mandate, the implementation of incompetent commands, and Mesquita's complacent execution of them. There ensued an inquiry in which fifty-five of the *San Antonio*'s crew gave testimony. All were not in the opposition to Magellan, so the picture that emerged was quite confusing and contradictory. Gómes, along with five of his associates, received a prison sentence, although he was quickly released and given a new naval command. By the time Elkano arrived in Spain and was summoned to court to give his version of the Magellan expedition, the importunate Mesquita, although released from prison, had been

---

63. Clavería, *Los vascos*, 134.

stripped of all of his possessions.[64] All of the verdicts were handed down by Bishop Fonseca himself.

In Valladolid, Elkano was queried closely by the authorities regarding the voyage, and particularly its insurrections. He denounced his captain general harshly, accusing him of lack of consideration for his men, irreverence toward the monarch's instructions, and harboring an anti-Castilian and pro-Portuguese bias, as best expressed in the conferral of command upon his relatives, Álvaro de Mesquita and Duarte de Barbosa. Elkano neglected to mention his own part in the *San Antonio* mutiny on the high seas and his subsequent command of the mutineers' cannon.[65]

Out of gratitude, the emperor gave the survivors a quarter of the one-fifth share in the cargo that accrued to him.[66] Elkano requested that he be named commander of any subsequent voyages to the Moluccas. This was denied, since the king had already commissioned a second expedition under the command of García Jofre de Loaísa. However, Elkano was to serve as captain general on the return voyage. (The plan called for Loaísa to remain in the Moluccas as the Spanish governor.) Furthermore, Elkano would assume Loaísa's post, should his commander die on the outward journey.[67] Charles also conferred upon Elkano a pension of five hundred gold ducats annually, to be paid to his impoverished relatives, and the right to incorporate into his family escutcheon the image of a globe bearing the inscription *Hic primus circundedit me* (You were the first to circle me). Elkano asked for and received a pardon for the crime of having sold a Spanish vessel to a foreigner. Since the royal treasury was strapped, the pension was to be paid by the Casa de la Especiería (House of Spices),[68] a new monopoly on trade with the Indies sited in La Coruña and owned by Bishop Fonseca and Cristóbal de Haro. In the event, the pension was never paid during Elkano's lifetime and then became the object of interminable, if fruitless, litigation by his estate.

---

64. Eustaquio Fernández de Navarrete, *Historia de Juan Sebastián del Cano* (1872; Bilbao: Amigos del Libro Vasco, 1985), 111–12.

65. Ibid., 113.

66. Ibid., 110–11.

67. Manuel Lucena, *Juan Sebastián Elcano* (Barcelona: Ariel, 2003), 210–11.

68. Ibid., 114.

According to Parr, it is likely that Elkano and the other mutineers destroyed Magellan's papers and diaries in order to silence the captain general's account of the voyage.[69] We know details of it largely from the testimony of the mutineers themselves and from the chronicle of Antonio Pigafetta. The Italian was granted a private royal audience with Charles, at which (Parr speculates) he gave the king his full version. It seems, however, that Pigafetta was ordered to expunge some of his observations of the various mutinies—just by whom is uncertain. With Magellan unable to defend himself, and most of his Portuguese intimates dead, the Fonseca-Haro faction had the courtroom to themselves.

Arguably, Espinosa might have provided a credible countervailing version of the Magellan expedition, but circumstances sidelined him, as well. By the time he repaired the *Trinidad*, the monsoons had shifted, and he could no longer follow in the wake of the *Victoria*. He headed north, into the China Sea, in search of easterlies that would carry him to New Spain. Proper understanding of that alternative lay in the future, and Espinosa was no navigator. After much hardship and the deaths of thirty-three of his fifty-three men, the twenty survivors limped back to Ternate and surrendered to the Portuguese. It was not until 1526 that he was released by them and allowed to return to Spain, well after the official investigations were concluded.[70]

Meanwhile, before the launching of the Loaísa expedition, Portugal challenged the claim that the Moluccas fell within the Spanish orbit as defined by the Tordesillas Line. A joint commission of inquiry began nearly two months of hearings in Badajoz on April 11, 1524. The proceedings alternated between the Spanish city and Elvas, in Portugal. Both sides named a formidable team of councilors. Castilla was represented by nine experts—including Hernando Colón (Christopher Columbus's son), Sebastiano Caboto (son of John Cabot and now in the service of Spain), and Juan Vespucci (Amerigo's nephew and the subsequent author, in 1526, of a famed world map). The Spanish claim was based upon a map prepared (probably in 1523) by Elkano. He was a key member of the Spanish delegation.

---

69. Parr, *Ferdinand Magellan*, 376.

70. Ibid., 368–71. A grateful Charles made Espinosa a nobleman and gave him a generous pension. In 1529, he was appointed to a high naval post.

The Portuguese side was led by the renowned figure Diogo Lopes de Siqueira, the former governor of India that Magellan had once served so loyally.[71]

There was also certain intrigue surrounding Elkano's person. He asked for and, on May 20, 1524, received two bodyguards from Charles after informing his monarch that his life was threatened. Some historians think that Lisbon might have sent assassins to block Elkano's input from the proceedings,[72] but others suspect that kinsmen of María Vidaurreta, the woman with whom he had an illegitimate child, were trying to force the now celebrity to marry her.[73] The Portuguese refused to accept Elkano's map as definitive, and the proceedings terminated without any kind of agreement. The Loaísa expedition had been placed on hold pending the outcome of the Badajoz negotiations, and preparations for it now commenced in earnest.

By this time, the influence of Cristóbal de Haro at the Spanish court was paramount. By 1519, the emperor Carlos's trusted secretary was Maximilian Transsylvanus, Diego de Haro's son-in-law. Creation of the Casa de Especiería in Asturias itself reflected its more convenient location (compared with Sevilla) with respect to trade with the Low Countries. Of the required funding of 16,601,558 maravedís for the Loaísa expedition, the crown put up 10 million. Cristóbal de Haro became the point person in the financing of the remainder. He induced Jakob Fugger and his associates to provide 3,750,000. Cristóbal himself invested 806,250 and attracted an additional 733,125 from other Spaniards (including one of his sons). Cristóbal de Haro was charged with oversight of the preparations for the fleet.[74]

---

71. Mitchell, *Elcano*, 108–11.

72. Ibid., 115.

73. Lucena, *Juan Sebastián Elcano*, 211.

74. Kellenbenz, *Los Fugger*, 216–18. The banker would continue to be a major financial force at court for years to come. In 1528, when the crown needed financing of 113,000 ducats to send an expeditionary force of two thousand infantrymen to Flanders, it was Cristóbal (and both Italian and German bankers recruited by him) that provided the letters of credit. Then, in the summer of 1529, when King Carlos needed a loan of 1,5 million ducats, Haro was again on the point for the House of Fugger. Ibid., 83–85. Meanwhile, he negotiated for the Fuggers' control of crown income from some of its *juros* (proprietorships) and *maestrazgos* (mastership over the territory of a military order) through outright purchase or as collateral on loans. Ibid., 192–97.

Meanwhile, there were serious developments in the New World
New World that would affect Pacific explorations for years to come.
In 1519, a resident of Cuba and former mayor of the island's second
largest town, Hernán Cortés, received permission to launch a land
exploration on the adjacent continent. By then, Spanish colonists
were reasonably well ensconced on several Caribbean islands, and
there was a clear understanding that a continental barrier separated
them from the Orient—hence the launching of Magellan's expedition
that same year in search of the southern passage. However, the mainland itself remained pretty much a terra incognita that had barely
been investigated. Cortés was proposing only the third mainland
expedition to date and was a heavy financial investor in it. But then,
just as he was prepared to depart, Cuba's governor, Diego Velázquez
de Cuéllar, annulled the expedition's license. So it was an impulsive
Hernán Cortés who disobeyed an official order to the contrary and
invaded Mexico, landing at the site of the future Veracruz. This made
him a potential rallying point for a New World challenge to absolute
crown authority over colonial political and economic affairs. Indeed,
an alarmed Governor Velázquez in Cuba and Bishop Fonseca in Spain
tried to bring Cortés to heel with a military force and an assassination
attempt—both unsuccessful.[75]

Cortés was not the only explorer to launch an expedition to the
American mainland in 1519. Inspired by the report of Juan de Grijalva's explorations along the Gulf Coast of northern Mexico, Francisco
de Garay, governor of Jamaica, sent his own four ships (under the
command of Captain Alonso Álvarez de Pineda) to explore the entire
coastline from Florida to Veracruz. Indeed, Pineda arrived at the latter a few days after Cortés had thence initiated his conquest of central
Mexico. Hernán had destroyed his own vessels in order to prevent his
men from defecting, and he now faced a possible threat to his rear
guard. He rushed back to Veracruz and met with Pineda's three-man
delegation, which sought to negotiate the northern limit of Cortés's
claims along the Gulf Coast. Rather than accede, Cortés arrested the
men, then tricked Pineda into sending ashore another party of twelve,
four of whom were also seized. The remaining eight returned to their

---

75. Parr, *Ferdinand Magellan*, 190.

ship, and Pineda sailed away. From his seven captives, Hernán learned of Pineda's explorations and Garay's ambitions.

Cortés resolved to establish his presence and claim to the entire Gulf Coast as soon as possible after first defeating the Aztec Confederation and then resuming his march to Tenochtitlán. By 1521, Cortés was in control of central Mexico and was constructing his own port of Veracruz. Meanwhile, in 1520, Governor Garay, "on good terms with Bishop Fonseca,"[76] petitioned the crown for creation of the province of Pánuco to the north of Veracruz and asked to be made its *adelantado*, or military governor. He also dispatched Pineda to the area to found a colony at the mouth of the Pánuco River. He planned to provision it monthly from Jamaica with supply ships. The first mission, under the command of Diego de Camargo, reached the colony just prior to an Indian attack in which Pineda and forty colonists were killed. The more than sixty survivors, now under Camargo, made their way to Veracruz, arriving there in very poor condition. Camargo expired soon thereafter, and his followers entered Cortés's ranks. Unaware of any of this, Garay continued attempts to resupply his Pánuco colony. The next captain to arrive at the Pánuco River was Garay's long-term associate Miguel Díaz de Aux. He found no sign of life in the destroyed colony and took his fifty men to Veracruz. They, too, entered Hernán's service.[77]

Faced with Cortés's fait accompli, the crown sought to limit its scope. On June 4, 1521, it created the province of Pánuco and named Francisco de Garay as its first *adelantado*, with authorization to colonize that region. When he learned of this, Cortés was quick to order his representatives at court to seek revocation of or limitations upon Garay's grant. By late 1522, Hernán was making his own plans to occupy the Pánuco.[78]

At the same time, Hernán's stunning accomplishments could scarcely be ignored. They had revealed the mineral wealth and agricultural potential of the American mainland. Spanish imaginations

---

76. Samuel Eliot Morison, *The European Discovery of America*, vol. 2, *The Southern Voyages, A.D. 1492–1616* (New York: Oxford University Press, 1974), 517.

77. Donald E. Chipman, *Nuno de Guzman and the Province of Panuco in New Spain 1518–1533* (Glendale: Arthur H. Clark, 1967), 46–53.

78. Ibid., 56–58.

were now inflamed by rumors of fabled civilizations and fabulous mineral wealth to both the vague north and south of central Mexico. There was also the immediate attraction of its salubrious highlands, which offered a vast new frontier to the established Estremaduran ranching complex—native region of Cortés and many of his conquistadors. The lowlands held out the prospect of eventual tropical plantations, which, among other products, might provide serious competition to Portuguese Madeira's near monopoly on the European sugar market.

Consequently, in October of 1522, a rebellious Cortés received formal royal recognition of his Mexican conquests. He was appointed governor and captain general of the new viceroyalty of Nueva España. However, Charles V also sent out a treasurer, an accountant, a trade agent, and an inspector to look after his interests—Cortés had now been effectively incorporated into Spanish officialdom.

The following year, the king ordered Cortés to explore both the North Atlantic and North Pacific in search of the Strait of Anián—the fabled northern passage that would provide Europe with its shortest route to the Orient. By then, Hernán had already founded a shipyard at Zacatula, about 170 miles to the north of the future settlement of Acapulco. The intent was to construct both caravels and bergantines for Pacific exploration.[79] Then, in 1525, the emperor ordered Cortés to send an expedition to the Orient to search for Magellan's lost *Trinidad.*[80]

It was not until 1523 that Garay was able to undertake a colonizing initiative in the Pánuco. It would seem that he needed financial assistance, since he enlisted the support of Diego Colón and Governor Velázquez. No doubt the latter welcomed the opportunity to thwart his old nemesis, Cortés. However, by 1523, Hernán had established his own settlement on the Pánuco River. Garay learned of it only upon his arrival in Cuba en route to Nueva España. He now

---

79. Holmes, *From New Spain by Sea*, 48–51.

80. Ibid., 53–54. Cabot never made it to the Moluccas. In Brazil, he learned of fabled Inca wealth and spent considerable time exploring the Río de la Plata and ascending the Paraná in search of a way to it. His fixation with the area led to a mutiny that he was able to suppress. He established the first European settlement in both Uruguay and Argentina, both subsequently destroyed by the Indians. On July 22, 1530, Cabot arrived back in Sevilla with a single ship, twenty-four crewmen, and fifty slaves that he purchased in Brazil.

requested that a prominent official in the West Indies, Alonso de Zuazo, go to Mexico to mediate between himself and Cortés. The Garay and Cortés supporters were also pressing their patrons' conflicting claims at the Spanish court. The upshot was a royal order that stated that the activities of neither man should infringe upon those of the other until there was resolution of their dispute. In effect, both were able to pursue colonization schemes in the Pánuco, although it remained under Garay's jurisdiction and was not yet formally a part of Nueva España.

In June of 1523, ignorant of the royal decree of the previous April, Garay departed from Cuba with eleven ships and six hundred men. Intending to settle along the Pánuco River, he mistakenly entered the similar Palmas River, instead. He acceded to his men's desire to explore it in search of minerals, but a four-day expedition found the area to be depopulated and worthless. Garay decided to send his ships to the Pánuco River, under the command of the experienced Juan de Grijalva, while he led a large party there overland. By the time it arrived at Cortés's settlement, he and his men were in sad shape. While they were reasonably well attended by Pedro de Vallejo, leader of the Cortés settlement, Garay's men were disarmed. Grijalva refused to turn over his vessels, but some of his crew mutinied, and the others refused his order to fire upon them. So Grijalva surrendered to Vallejo and was imprisoned.

Word of Garay's arrival had been sent to Cortés in Mexico City, and he immediately dispatched a military force to the Pánuco to confront the interloper. It was under the command of Cortés's long-standing comrade in arms, Pedro de Alvarado. Scarcely had the mission left Mexico City when Hernán received his copy of the royal order regarding the Pánuco. He immediately dispatched an emissary to Alvarado to head off any bloodshed. Garay was shown the order, and he and his councilors decided that they must leave the Pánuco River to settle elsewhere. His men were unwilling to continue, and Garay, Grijalva, and a handful of Velázquez supporters were put on a boat to Cuba, while Garay was invited by Cortés to come to Mexico City. Hernán proved to be Garay's gracious host from October to December as the two men worked through the details of an agreement that divided the Pánuco between them. They also agreed that the *adelantado*'s son would marry the conquistador's daughter. They attended Christmas Eve midnight mass together and then had breakfast at Cortés's home. Garay immediately fell ill and was dead two days later.[81]

---

81. Chipman, *Nuno de Guzman*, 67–73.

4

Andrés de Urdaneta

The second expedition to the Moluccas, headed by García Jofre de Loaísa,[1] and consisting of 450 men sailing in seven vessels (four of which were constructed and outfitted in Bizkaia), left La Coruña on July 24, 1525. Elkano, as pilot major and captain of the *Sancti Spiritus*, was second in command, as well as the venture's chief navigator. Given that the expedition was highly focused on the Basque Country and considerable recruitment was effected there, this would prove to be the most "Basque" of any of Spain's Pacific explorations. There were at least eighty-two Basques in the lists of participants, and the lists are incomplete, prompting the historian Juan Gil to round off the number in the Basque contingent at a hundred.[2] These included two of Elkano's brothers, one of whom served as the ship's master of the *San Gabriel* and the other as the pilot of the *Sancti Spiritus*. Elkano's brother-in-law, Santiago de Guevara, became the captain of the *Santiago* during the voyage.[3] Segundo de Ispizúa notes that many who joined the expedition were recruited by Elkano himself.[4]

One Basque lad was destined for particular greatness. Andrés de Urdaneta was born in 1508 on the farm Oyanguren, located about two kilometers from the Gipuzkoan town of Villafranca. In 1525, Elkano

---

1. García Jofre de Loaísa's Iberian origins and early career are somewhat murky. Segundo de Ispizúa, citing Fray Rodrigo de Aganduru's *Historia general de las islas occidentales al Asia adyacentes*, written in the early seventeenth century, notes that Loaísa was "a Bizkayan gentleman—Basque, although born in Ciudad Real." But this may well be a stretch. Segundo de Ispizúa, *Historia de los vascos en América*, 6 vols. (Bilbao: Impr. J. A. de Lerchundi, 1914–1919), 1:242.

2. Juan Gil, "El entorno vasco de Andrés de Urdaneta," in *Andrés de Urdaneta: Un hombre moderno*, ed. Susana Truchuelo Garcí (Lasarte-Oria: Ordiziako Udala, 2009), 327.

3. María Estíbaliz Ruiz de Azúa y Martínez de Ezquerecocha, *Vascongados y América* (Madrid: Editorial MAPFRE, 1992) 57; Gil, "El entorno vasco," 329.

4. Ispizúa, *Historia*, 1:241.

recruited the seventeen-year-old as his page, signing as personal guar-
antor of a salary advance to his protégé.[5]

It was one of the charges of the Loaísa expedition to map prop-
erly the passage through the Strait of Magellan. Basques were paramount in this endeavor. The youthful Urdaneta was already honing
his budding observational and navigational skills, and Martín de Uriarte, the Basque pilot of the flagship, provided the first systematic
charts. According to Samuel Eliot Morison, "Martín de Uriarte had
time to write a *derrotero* (sailing directions) for the Strait, which he
took back to Spain. It was grossly inaccurate, recommending several
harbors that had neither holding ground nor protection, and describing others that nobody can identify, but no better guide was available
until the next century."[6]

When the *Sancti Spiritus* was shipwrecked in the Strait of Magellan, and he was forced to abandon the marooned survivors to go in
search of assistance, Elkano chose Urdaneta as his sole companion.
While traversing the strait, the *San Gabriel* slipped away from the rest
and made for home. The remaining vessels entered the Pacific without
incident, but five days later were dispersed by a storm, and three of
them were lost to Loaísa. The two caravels, the *Santa María del Parral*
and the *San Lesmes*, were never heard from again, although it seems
that the former might have crossed the ocean on its own to Mindanao
in the Philippines.[7]

The *Santiago*, now captained by Elkano's brother-in-law, Santiago
de Guevara, sailed northward to Nueva España (Mexico) to request
that relief for the battered expedition be dispatched from there. On
board the *Santiago* was another Gipuzkoan, the twenty-seven-year-
old priest Juan de Areyzaga, from the coastal town of Zumaia. He
would later recount to Gonzálo Fernández de Oviedo, author of the
monumental *Historía general y natural de las Indias*, the voyagers on

---

5. Mairin Mitchell, *Friar Andrés de Urdaneta, O.S.A.* (London: Macdonald and Evans, 1964), 4, 13, 27.

6. Samuel Eliot Morison, *The European Discovery of America*, vol. 2, *The Southern Voyages, A.D. 1492–1616* (New York: Oxford University Press, 1974), 481.

7. Fernando Guillén Salvetti and Carlos Vila Miranda, "La desdichada expedición de García Jofre de Loaísa," in *Descubrimientos españoles en el Mar del Sur*, 3 vols., Amancio Landín Carrasco et al. (Madrid: Editorial Naval, 1992), 1:213–14.

the *Santiago*'s many travails before reaching Tehuantepec. Areyzaga also claimed to have communicated with Patagonian Indians in his native Basque language.[8]

Meanwhile, on April 3, 1526, another expedition departed Sanlúcar de Barrameda, bound for the Strait of Magellan and the Moluccas beyond. It consisted of two hundred men and was headed by Sebastian Cabot, by now a Spanish captain general. Much earlier Sebastian may have accompanied his father John, both serving England, in the unsuccessful 1497 search in Terranova for the northern passage. In 1508–1509, Sebastian headed his own repeat expedition for the English crown and erroneously claimed to have found the passage—he had likely discovered the entrance to Hudson Bay, instead.

Loaísa himself succumbed to scurvy in the mid-Pacific on July 20, 1526, and was succeeded by Elkano—who also died of the disease shortly thereafter (August 4). Eleven days before his death, Elkano made out his last will and testament, witnessed by seven persons. All were Basques, including his young protégé. Urdaneta was named coequal heir of Elkano's share in the benefits of the expedition, along with the deceased's brother-in-law, Guevara, and his nephew Esteban.

In October of 1527, Cortés dispatched three ships to the Moluccas under the command of Álvaro de Saavedra. In addition to determining the fate of the *Trinidad*, they were to ascertain that of the Loaísa and Cabot expeditions, as well.[9]

Elkano's Legacy

Elkano's will and testament is a window upon the pious mentality and social relations of his day. It distributes his assets among his immediate family and kinsmen. It reflects charitable concerns in bequests for widows and orphans. Virtually every church and chapel in his natal

---

8. Areyzaga's biographer, José de Arteche, provides a discussion of the philological and linguistic literature that makes this possibility less far-fetched. José de Arteche, *Cuatro relatos* (Pamplona: Editorial Gómez, 1959), 53–59. Indeed, there have been several scholarly attempts to detect links between Basque and many Amerindian languages. To date, however, Basque remains as its own language family—that is, without clearly demonstrable connections with any other human tongue.

9. Maurice G. Holmes, *New Spain to the Californias by Sea, 1519–1668* (Glendale: Arthur H. Clark, 1963), 53–54.

town and a select few in neighboring towns receive their due. The church of the Virgin of Itziar, patroness of mariners, is singled out for special treatment. As had Columbus in his will, Elkano remembered the monastery of the Virgin of Guadalupe in Extremadura—another protectress of mariners.

Elkano then directs his attention to his monarch in order to list his assets. He states that he is owed 1,750 ducats by the king to be paid by the House of Spices. One thousand ducats was his salary as chief pilot and captain of the *Sancti Spiritus*. Cristóbal de Haro had advanced Elkano fifty thousand maravedís, which he used to meet certain obligations, against said salary, and the remainder represented the Basque's personal stake in the profits from the sale of the expedition's cargo. He had also borrowed an additional eleven or twelve thousand maravedís from the banker. Elkano notes that both of his debts to Haro are documented formally and should be paid by his estate.[10]

The figure of Elkano lends itself to multiple interpretations. For many, he was Magellan's loyal confidante who, upon his commander's death, assumed control and completed the first circumnavigation. Hugh Thomas refers to him as "immortal"[11] and as "a resourceful Basque sailor. . . whose place in history is secure."[12] To be sure, he is viewed as a hero of the greatest magnitude in the Basque Country,[13] with corresponding recognition in monuments, plaques, and building names. Yet some historians are more reserved in their praise, underscoring that he had been one of the conspirators in a mutiny against Magellan. Indeed, Elkano received a death sentence that was commuted only out of the sheer necessity of allowing the repentants to resume their places in the expedition's lean ranks. In the judgment of historian J. C. Beaglehole, Elkano was "a good pilot but a faithless man," one of three ringleaders who actually led the assault on Magel-

---

10. Eustaquio Fernández de Navarrete, *Historia de Juan Sebastián del Cano* (1872; Bilbao: Amigos del Libro Vasco, 1985), 321–26.

11. Hugh Thomas, *The Golden Empire: Spain, Charles V, and the Creation of America* (New York: Random House, 2011), 54.

12. Hugh Thomas, *Rivers of Gold: The Rise of the Spanish Empire, from Columbus to Magellan* (New York: Random House, 2003), 499.

13. Mitchell, *Friar Andrés*, 27 –28.

lan's flagship.[14] Nor was his performance during the Loaísa voyage particularly distinguished.

Curiously, there is a sense in which the images of Magellan and Elkano are as linked in death as were their lives—reflected in a duel between their respective biographers over their characters and accomplishment as the first to circumnavigate the world. On Magellan's side, there are Antonio Pigafetta, Charles Mckew Parr, and Stefan Zweig. The chief spokesman for Elkano is Victor María de Sola.[15] Parr is at pains to stress that Magellan was the first circumnavigator, because even though he died in the Philippines while serving the Spanish flag, he had already arrived there years earlier in the service of Portugal. Parr concludes his treatment of Elkano as follows:

> For propaganda purposes, the Emperor made the most of the exploit of circumnavigation. He had del Cano acclaimed as the circumnavigator, endowed him with a pretentious coat of arms, and gave him a handsome pension. However, perhaps because of Don Antonio's confidential report to him, Don Charles refused del Cano's petition to be made a Knight of Santiago, as Magellan had been. He also quietly rejected several other pleas from del Cano for favors. Cristóbal de Haro was taken in by the plaudits, or perhaps he simply found it politic to join them, and therefore had del Cano appointed chief pilot of the second *Armada de Maluco*. Del Cano suffered catastrophic losses when he tried to duplicate the achievement of Magellan in the *paso*. Worn out by a task too immense for his powers, he collapsed and died at sea.[16]

Samuel Eliot Morison concludes:

> Juan Sebastián de Elcano received full honors for sailing *Victoria* home, which caused his part in the San Julián mutiny to be overlooked and forgiven. A younger man than Magellan . . . he had commanded a ship

---

14. J. C. Beaglehole, *The Exploration of the Pacific* (1934; London: Adam and Charles Black, 1966), 25.

15. Without trying to be a scold, I would note that the Sola account relies most heavily upon Pigafetta, Parr, and Zweig—particularly on Parr. Whole passages of the latter's work are virtually lifted and translated into Spanish without scholarly attribution. The only time Parr's name comes up is when he says something critical of Elkano and then only as introduction to Sola's rebuttal. It is all most reminiscent of Mairin Mitchell's translations of Arteche (see the Introduction, note 2), who, in turn, cherry-picked Ispizúa. After crafting this section of the present book, I empathize with all of those fellow authors, however, because we are all reduced to repeating tales that were themselves generated long ago out of fragmentary evidence.

16. Parr, *Ferdinand Magellan*, 371.

bigger than any of Magellan's before the great voyage. Nobody ever denied the high quality of his seamanship. But what of his personality? Neither Pigafetta nor the Portuguese author of the Leiden Narrative, both of whom sailed from Tidore to Seville, ever mentions him. Possibly they had not forgotten the mutiny at San Julián; more probably they had suffered personal slights. Since Magellan forgave Elcano for his part in the mutiny, so should we; but it is hard to overlook his lying at Magellan's expense about the mutiny of San Julián in 1527. Anyway, as captain of *Victoria* he never wavered on the difficult voyage home.[17]

In 1938, Stefan Zweig published his biography of Magellan in German, but it came out simultaneously in English translation and had its greatest impact among the English-speaking readership. Indeed, there is a kind of subtext in the debate that, from the Anglo side, might be characterized as an anti-Spanish and pro-Lusitanian bias. The former seems nourished, perhaps unconsciously, by Spain's "black legend" treatment in British historiography—itself a function of the infamous Inquisition, Spain's point position in the Counter-Reformation, and the several wars between the two nations over the past several centuries. The latter is consonant with the key role of British royal figures in Portuguese affairs and the several commercial treaties, military alliances, and lack of warfare between Portugal and Great Britain during the past half millennium.

Zweig gives Elkano his due, if in an offhanded manner: "This homeward journey of the battered galleon [the *Victoria*] round the second half of the globe, after thirty months had been spent on the first half of the journey, was one of the most heroic deeds in the history of navigation; and del Cano now compensated for his behaviour to Magellan by admirably fulfilling the will of the dead leader."[18] Nevertheless, in Zweig's account, it would be Elkano who usurped the credit that rightfully belonged to the intrepid Portuguese captain general:

It is the inevitable tendency of the world to reward the man who has the luck to finish a job, and forget those whose preliminary expenditure of blood and of mental labour prepared it and rendered it possible. On this occasion the distribution of honours and rewards was peculiarly

---

17. Morison, *The Southern Voyages*, 457.

18. Stefan Zweig, *Magellan: Pioneer of the Pacific* (London: Cassell, 1938), 269.

unjust. The very man who wanted to hinder Magellan's deed at the decisive moment, the sometime mutineer Sebastian del Cano, annexed all the glory, all the honours, all the dignities.[19]

Zweig concludes his book by observing:

Disastrous had been the atmosphere of misfortune diffused by Magellan. Whoever befriended him and helped him, became involved in his dark career; whoever trusted him paid heavily for the trust. This great and dangerous deed had, like a vampire, destroyed the welfare of its promoters, and snatched the lives of many of them. Faleiro, Magellan's partner, having returned to Portugal, was imprisoned; Aranda, who had smoothed Magellan's path, was subjected to a shameful enquiry and lost his money. Enrique, whose freedom Magellan had promised, was treated as a slave immediately after his master's death. But the man who opposed him, Sebastian del Cano, was able to grasp all the glory and all the profit which should have gone to the faithful and the dead.[20]

The Rise of Andrés de Urdaneta

In early September of 1526, the Loaísa expedition, now under the command of the Bizkaian Toribio Alonso de Salazar, reached Guam in the Marianas. However, he, too, died of scurvy, to be succeeded under unusual circumstances by a Gipuzkoan Basque, Martín Iñiguez de Carquizano. When the men were asked to choose between him and Hernando de Bustamante, at one point during the count of the paper ballots, Carquizano, fearful of losing, tossed them all into the sea. Opinion was clearly divided into two antagonistic factions—the Basques evidently siding with Carquizano. The tenuous compromise was to appoint both men to a joint command.[21]

The expedition finally arrived in the Moluccas, only to be confronted by the Portuguese. Carquizano convened the officers and argued successfully, over Bustamante's lone objection, that if their dealings with the Portuguese were to be effective, the expedition needed a supreme commander—namely, himself. Urdaneta clearly garnered Carquizano's highest respect. Once in the Moluccas, and

19. Ibid., 287.
20. Ibid., 291.
21. Mitchell, *Friar Andrés*, 30.

fearing imminent attack by the Portuguese, the commander dispatched seven emissaries to the important island of Gilolo to seek an alliance with its king. Despite his tender age of eighteen, Urdaneta was appointed coleader of the successful mission. Carquizano next sent Urdaneta on a similar diplomatic assignment to the island of Tidore. It also resulted in a commitment by the native ruler to the Spanish cause.[22]

Meanwhile, the governor in Ternate communicated with Carquizano, claiming that the Moluccas were Portuguese under the Treaty of Tordesillas. He ordered the Spaniards to leave the area immediately. Carquizano replied, "Write, and go on writing, but we are coming, not going."[23] In anticipation of a battle, Carquizano divided his men into three companies, giving command of one of them to Urdaneta. In January of 1527, the Portuguese destroyed the *Santa María de la Victoria* at Tidore, the last remaining vessel of the expedition, ushering in a standoff between the Ternate-based Lusitanians and the Spanish garrisons at Gilolo and Tidore. Carquizano mandated construction of a small boat at both strongholds, placing Urdaneta in charge of the Gilolo project. He then named the young man commander of an exploratory expedition charged with obtaining navigational and cartographic understanding of the Moluccas, an experience that would further sensitize him to their prevailing winds and currents.

The Spaniards barely avoided capture by the Portuguese upon their return to Gilolo. Urdaneta effected an escape to Tidore, where the position of the besieged Spanish garrison was equally precarious. On March 27, the Portuguese approached in two boats, and Carquizano ordered Urdaneta to confront them in a canoe armed with a cannon. The Portuguese withdrew, and Urdaneta tried in vain to overtake them. He ordered a volley, and the gun's fuse accidentally ignited a barrel of powder. Fifteen of the natives in the crew were killed. Urdaneta, his clothing on fire, jumped into the sea. The Portuguese observed the disaster and made for the survivors, trying to outpace the Spanish boat that was also converging. According to Urdaneta's own account,

22. Ibid., 30–32.
23. Ibid., 35.

I started to swim towards the praus from Gilolo, little by little, with the use of my hands keeping myself on the surface of the water, so that the Castilians who were in the praus saw me and made the Indians come to my rescue, and I begged Our Lord that they might reach me before the enemy, who were firing on me, could injure me. I was so badly burnt that it was twenty days before I could go outside the house of an Indian on Gilolo where I stayed.[24]

He was disfigured for life.

There then ensued an uneasy truce between the Spaniards and Portuguese, each awaiting reinforcements. In 1527, the Spanish crown planned an expedition to the Moluccas under the command of another Portuguese captain in its service, Simón de Alcazaba. Cristóbal de Haro was again requested to secure the funding from Fugger and other Germans, as well as Spanish commercial interests. This time, given the political and military standoff between the Iberian powers in Asia, he was unsuccessful, and the venture was cancelled.[25] In the interim, in the Moluccas, there were even exchanges of friendly visits. Relations again chilled, though not to the breaking point, when, in May of 1527, a new Portuguese governor arrived and demanded that the Spaniards leave the Moluccas immediately.

Carquizano now dispatched Urdaneta to Gilolo to deal with factionalism that had broken out within the ranks of the Spaniards. While he was there, a Portuguese boat seized two canoes of native fishermen, killing their occupants. Urdaneta overtook the aggressors in a light canoe, swam to their boat, and demanded the names of its crew, which he subsequently recorded from memory on a palm leaf.

Eight days later, the ruler of Gilolo seized some vessels from Ternate with Urdaneta's assistance. The rajah ordered that forty of the captives be decapitated to avenge his fishermen. The incensed Portuguese governor informed Carquizano of the outrage, but without referring to the earlier massacre. Assuming Urdaneta to be guilty, his commander condemned him to death in absentia. When he learned of this, instead of accepting the protection on offer from the rajah, Urdaneta resolved to travel to Tidore to plead his case. The rajah

24. Ibid., 40–41.

25. Hermann Kellenbenz, *Los Fugger en España y Portugal hasta 1560* (Salamanca: Junta de Castilla y Léon, Consejería de Educación y Cultura, 2000), 221.

insisted on sending his nephew along, who then supported Urdaneta's account of the sequence of events by referring to the Basque's list of names extracted earlier from the Portuguese transgressors. A relieved Carquizano embraced Urdaneta and promised him future rewards and honors.[26]

Relations between the Spaniards and Portuguese reverted to their former hostilities and intrigue. At one point, the latter tried unsuccessfully to contaminate the former's water supply. Then, in July of 1527, an ostensibly peaceful Portuguese emissary managed to poison Carquizano himself. Once again succession was in doubt when another Carquizano, nephew of the deceased commander, opposed the candidacy of Bustamante. Eventually, the chief pilot, Hernando de la Torre, became the compromise commander. He immediately named Urdaneta treasurer of the expedition.

Given that the Portuguese had a secured sea route to their homeland and powerful bases in Malacca and Goa, they possessed a distinct advantage over their Spanish rivals. Nevertheless, through pacts and alliances with the natives, the Spanish garrisons continued to hold out into 1528. In January, the Portuguese managed to burn a Spanish vessel that was under construction on Tidore. Shortly thereafter, Urdaneta led an attack on the town of Tuguabe near the Portuguese stronghold of Ternate. Despite the latter's superior numbers, Urdaneta seized and held his target.[27]

On March 27, 1528, the Spaniards at Tuguabe were astonished to see a ship flying Spain's colors approaching. Any hope of significant reinforcement was soon dashed, however. After hearing Areyzaga's account, on October 31, 1527, Cortés had dispatched from Nueva España three vessels to relieve any Loaísa survivors and thereby reinforce Spain's possible claim to the Moluccas. However, the fleet was scattered during a storm, and two of its ships were never heard from again. The *Florida*, under the command of Álvaro de Saavedra, completed the five-month crossing, with but forty mostly ill survivors.

Hernando de la Torre dispatched the *Florida* back to Nueva España with a letter to the emperor requesting immediate assistance for the desperate ninety Spaniards remaining in the Moluccas. The

---

26. Mitchell, *Friar Andrés*, 43–44.
27. Ibid., 44–45.

problem was that ignorance of prevailing Pacific winds and currents made the west-to-east crossing most difficult. A frustrated Saavedra ended up sailing along the coast of Papua New Guinea, thereby coming close to the Australian continent, before returning to Tidore on November 19, 1528. The *Florida* required serious repairs and was not able to set out again until May 3, 1529. Saavedra died at sea. Once again the attempt to make the eastward crossing failed, and the *Florida* returned to the Moluccas.[28]

By November 1529, the Spaniards' position had become all but untenable. When Torre vowed to hold out until the end at Tidore, Bustamante convinced a third of its garrison to surrender. Faced with harsh reality, the Spaniards capitulated. They were ordered by the Portuguese to relinquish Tidore and to remove themselves to the island of Zamafo.

After having led an expeditionary force against the Portuguese in some outer islands, Urdaneta returned to Gilolo, only to be confronted by the new reality. He then went under cover of darkness to Tidore to assess the situation. He found the Spanish fortifications in ashes. Urdaneta set about organizing resistance, centered in Gilolo among the remaining Spaniards and their native allies. He journeyed to Zamafo to convince Torre to join him. However, the commander had given his word to the Portuguese and urged Urdaneta to capitulate. He refused.[29]

On December 8, 1529, the *Florida* reached Zamafo, evidencing its failure to make the sea crossing. In light of this, some of the Spaniards at Gilolo went over to the Portuguese. Urdaneta and a few companions still refused to surrender. He then embarked on a personal odyssey over the next several months, during which he visited many islands. The young man (still only twenty-one years old) believed that as long as Spanish nationals remained at liberty in the Spice Islands, his emperor's claim to them retained credibility.

In May of 1530, while at Gilolo, Urdaneta learned of a widespread native conspiracy to massacre the Portuguese and Spaniards. He informed Torre at Zamafo and then made his way to Ternate as Torre's emissary to inform the Portuguese governor. The rebellion

28. Ibid., 48–50.
29. Ibid., 56–57.

was aborted. A grateful governor signed a friendship pact with the Spaniards, recognizing for the first time the mutual interests of all Europeans in the Moluccas faced with a common danger.

On November 3, 1530, a fleet arrived from Portugal with a new governor. It also brought the startling news that Emperor Charles V had betrothed his sister Catherine to the king of Portugal in 1529. Financially strapped by his war with France, Charles was unable to pay her dowry. The emperor had therefore relinquished his claim to the Moluccas for the sum of 350,000 ducats, as stipulated in the Treaty of Zaragoza (1529). The Spaniards' four years of resistance and persistence in the Spice Islands had been for naught.[30]

Since the Portuguese could not produce a copy of the new pact, there was incredulity among the Spaniards. Reduced to seventeen men in all, they continued to hold out at Gilolo. However, the Portuguese viceroy in Goa sent credible proof of the agreement. Torre then negotiated a lump-sum payment of two thousand ducats from the Portuguese for his men's expenses and assurance of their safe passage to Europe.

It was now 1534, and Urdaneta and a few companions resolved to stay behind to secure a cargo of cloves owed by the natives of Gilolo to the Spanish emperor. The Portuguese intervened and nullified the contract. It was not until February 15, 1535, that Urdaneta left the Moluccas. He visited Banda, Java, and Malacca, where he was reunited with Torre and the other Spaniards, who were still awaiting repatriation. As a security measure, the Portuguese limited the maximum number of Spaniards allowed to travel together to four; Urdaneta and three companions embarked on the *São Roque*, bound for Lisbon. Arriving there on June 26, 1536, Urdaneta was now the second man to have circumnavigated the globe. There, his precious diaries and charts were confiscated. The Spanish ambassador urged him to flee Portugal posthaste, because he was likely in personal danger. The Portuguese would surely try to prevent Urdaneta from sharing his extensive knowledge of the Moluccas with his emperor.

Urdaneta set out immediately on horseback for Valladolid. There, he constructed a report from memory, completing it on February 26, 1537. It extolled the wealth of the Spice Islands and urged the

---

30. Ibid., 58–62.

emperor to consider concluding a commercial treaty with their native rulers, obviously presupposing abrogation of the pledge to the Portuguese whereby Spain relinquished its claims in the area. Urdaneta also presented to the Council of the Indies a detailed report of the Loaísa expedition. He was awarded sixty ducats by the emperor for his eleven years of service and absence from Spain.[31]

Urdaneta's report highlighted the difficulties of utilizing the southern passage for maritime commerce. It was simply too distant and its climate too inclement, as underscored by the privations of both the Magellan and Loaísa expeditions. Indeed, the latter would be the last Spanish attempt to access the Orient through the southern passage. Henceforth, Spanish probes of the Pacific would originate in the Pacific ports of the Spanish colonial Americas. There was also interest in finding an even more elusive northern passage that, if discovered, would reduce the distances of a westerly sea route from Europe to the Orient by several thousand miles.

The Loaísa expedition left a legacy of litigation in Spain that lasted until 1550—one in which Cristóbal de Haro and the House of Fugger were both center stage. In essence, Cristóbal initiated the proceedings in 1538, claiming that he had been inadequately compensated for his investments in the Magellan and Loaísa ventures. Furthermore, King Carlos had promised both him and the House of Fugger participation in three future expeditions to the Moluccas that could never happen after the Treaty of Zaragoza. So both he and the Fuggers (subsequently in a separate lawsuit) were claiming part of the 350,000 ducats given to Carlos by the Portuguese. In the event, Cristóbal won some of his points, though not the one regarding the Portuguese payment.[32]

There was one other expedition sent directly from Iberia by the Spanish crown to explore the region around the Strait of Magellan. In 1529, King Charles conceded to a Portuguese, Simón de Alcazaba, the right to explore and claim much of the western South American coast south of Pizarro's concession in Peru. However, the Portuguese commander lacked funding, and so he negotiated for it with the House of

31. Ibid., 63–76.
32. Kellenbenz, *Los Fugger*, 540–46.

Fugger. It is likely (although not certain) that Cristóbal de Haro was involved.[33]

In 1534, two boats under Alcazaba's command set sail for the Strait of Magellan. Poor weather and other difficulties precluded the passage, and he decided to winter over at the site of present-day Chubut, in Argentina. There, two of his captains mutinied, killed Alcazaba, and proposed to the other crewmen that they become corsairs while working their way to safety in a French port. It was then that a Bizkaian, Charcoaga, master of the flagship, along with several other Bizkaians, seized control and stranded the mutineers on a desert island to await trial. They were subsequently condemned to death. The two ringleaders and another thirteen men in all were executed, causing the remaining mutineers to flee into the forest, never to be heard from again.

The fifty survivors, including twenty Bizkaians, made for Europe. Along the Brazilian coast, they lost one of their two vessels and were attacked by Indians before finally coming under the protection of a Portuguese settler. He provisioned them for their transatlantic voyage home.[34] This abortive expedition was yet another example of the fragility and futility of life in the southern passage. Alcazaba and his men would be the last Iberians to visit the Strait of Magellan for the next nearly half century.

Meanwhile, in Nueva España, shortly after Garay's death, there was a major rebellion of the Huasteca Indians in the Pánuco. The causes are unclear. Hernán blamed it on the continuing dissension against him fomented by a scattering of lingering Garay followers in the region. Donald Chipman concludes that the ongoing indeterminate status of the region's administrative structure since the ambiguous royal order of April 1523 was the major contributor. In any event, the rebellion resulted in several hundred Spanish deaths, making this one of the worst losses suffered by the Spaniards throughout their entire colonial history, and in a brutal punitive campaign

---

33. Ibid., 225.
34. Mitchell, *Friar Andrés*, 63–76.

by Cortés that culminated in the execution of the entire Huastecan leadership.[35]

Cortés now moved to both expand and to consolidate his authority and territory. Shortly after his military expedition to the Pánuco, Pedro de Alvarado was dispatched by Cortés to conquer Guatemala, a campaign that would last from 1523 to 1527. Between 1524 and 1526, Hernán himself led Spanish forces in the conquest of Honduras. On his return to Mexico City, Cortés was confronted with the factionalism and blatant rivalries that had developed among his subordinates during his absence.

But this was also a time of growing tension between Cortés and Nuño Beltrán de Guzmán, the man named (in 1525) to succeed Francisco de Garay as governor of the Pánuco. In 1526, Guzmán traveled from Spain to Nueva España in the company of the licentiate, or inspector general, Luis Ponce de León. They stopped in Cuba en route, where they met with Governor Velázquez. The governor and Bishop Fonseca were the two strongest anti-Cortés voices informing the Council of the Indies and the royal court. Guzmán and Ponce de León were clearly appointed to serve as the emperor's counterweight to Cortés. The licentiate was to investigate Hernán's past dealings and would even go so far as to have him arrested for a brief period.

Guzmán assumed his post in the Pánuco in May 1527. The following year, he was made the first president of a new audiencia of Nueva España, which had both administrative and quasi-legislative powers. Guzmán quickly developed the reputation of a cruel and ruthless ruler—given to enslaving Indians and castigating those Spaniards within his jurisdiction in the Pánuco who had received privileges and *encomiendas* (grants of rights to the labor and tribute of local Indians) for their loyalty and service to Hernán. Ironically, one of them was Miguel Díaz de Aux. After his earlier attempt to resupply Garay's colony, Díaz de Aux had joined Cortés and had served with distinction in the campaign against the Aztec Confederation. Cortés had rewarded him with an *encomienda* in the Pánuco and had

---

35. Donald E. Chipman, *Nuno de Guzman and the Province of Panuco in New Spain 1518–1533* (Glendale: Arthur H. Clark, 1967), 77–86.

appointed him mayor of the region's main settlement before departing for Honduras.[36]

In 1528, Hernán Cortés, fully aware that he had powerful enemies on both sides of the Atlantic, left for Spain to seek confirmation of his claims to northern Nueva España and beyond. He defended his record rather effectively at the royal court and was accorded several honors—these included the title of Marqués del Valle de Guajaca (Oaxaca). This included twenty-three *encomiendas* with twenty-three thousand Indian vassals. He was also inducted into the prestigious Order of Santiago. However, he was in essence relieved of his governorship of Nueva España.

In 1529, apparently convinced by rumors of fabled wealth to the north, Guzmán sent a land expedition that conquered the soon-to-be-created Nueva Galicia and established a fortified presence on the Pacific coast at Jalisco. His chief military officer was the Basque Cristóbal de Oñate. In 1531, Oñate would found a settlement that he named Guadalajara in honor of Guzmán's birthplace in Spain. Juan de Oñate, Cristóbal's brother, was subsequently its mayor.

Cortés returned to Nueva España in 1530. That year, Guzmán was removed as head of the audiencia and appointed governor of the newly created (out of his northwestern conquests) province of Nueva Galicia while retaining his post as that of the Pánuco, as well. This meant that Cortés's chief rival now controlled both the Gulf and Pacific coastlines of northern Nueva España. Nevertheless, that same year, Cortés founded Acapulco with a shipyard to produce vessels for Pacific exploration and commerce.

In 1532, Cortés outfitted two ships under the command of Diego Hurtado de Mendoza. The goals were to discover the fabled Strait of Anián, the northern passage from somewhere in the North Pacific to the Gulf of Saint Lawrence that would provide the shortest critical route from Europe to the Orient, on the one hand, and assert Cortés's claim to any newly discovered northern lands, on the other. Hurtado sailed from Acapulco, and when he sought permission to land at Jalisco for supplies, it was denied by Nuño de Guzmán. The explorers sailed onward and soon faced a serious water shortage. Some of the men mutinied and insisted on heading back southward on one

---

36. Ibid., 92–95.

of the vessels. At one point, they landed in search of water and were attacked by Indians that were hostile to Spaniards due to Guzmán's regular incursions and slave raids. All but two of the Europeans were killed, the survivors making it to a Guzmán outpost. Hurtado himself continued northward, probably to about the Río del Fuerte in present-day Sinaloa, and then disappeared—also probably killed by Indians.[37]

Cortés dispatched two more vessels from Acapulco to avenge the Hurtado expedition's deaths and to search for any survivors. The two captains were his cousin, Diego de Becerra, and Hernando de Grijalva, a relative of Garay's Juan de Grijalva. They quickly separated, Becerra heading north as ordered and Grijalva turning back south. Becerra was said to be too haughty and temperamental for Grijalva's tastes. Becerra's pilot was the Basque Fortun (Ortuña) Ximénez de Bertadona, from Bizkaia. According to Bernal Díaz de Castillo, he was "a good navigator and mapmaker."[38] He was clearly experienced, having been one of several of the early Basque explorers of Chile.[39]

On December 10, 1533, shortly after Grijalva's departure, Ximénez, in league with "other Bizkaian mariners," led a successful mutiny—killing Becerra and some of his supporters in their sleep. Two Franciscan friars stopped the slaughter, and after assuming command, Ximénez put them ashore, along with the wounded. He proceeded to the present-day port of La Paz, thereby becoming the discoverer of Baja California, unaware that he had landed upon the southeastern tip of a peninsula, rather than a large island. It was there then that Ximénez and twenty of his men were killed by Indians. The survivors sailed south, and when they made port at Jalisco, their boat was commandeered by Guzmán. They recounted having seen vast oyster-shell beds that nourished the belief that the waters to the

---

37. James R. Moriarty, "The Discovery and Earliest Exploration of Baja California," *San Diego Historical Quarterly* 11, no. 1 (January 1965): 3–4. Also Asun Garikano, *Kaliforniakoak (1533–1848): Euskaldunen lanak Kaliforniaren esplorazio eta kolonizazio garaian* (Iruñea/Pamplona: Pamiela, 2013), 17–22.

38. Quoted in Ibid., 18.

39. José Manuel Azcona Pastor, *Possible Paradises: Basque Emigration in Latin America* (Reno: University of Nevada Press, 2004), 40.

north of Acapulco harbored abundant pearl fisheries.[40] By this time, Guzmán was probing with land parties the region well to the north of Sinaloa.

In 1535, Cortez himself headed up a combined land and maritime expedition to the north, in part designed to punish Nuño de Guzmán for his treatment of Hernán's earlier explorers. In the event, the two men's forces failed to meet. Cortés now established a colony at La Paz, in Baja's Santa Cruz Bay, from which he sent land expeditions to probe the unknown. They found little, and many of the colonists perished.[41] Cortés was at La Paz when Antonio de Mendoza, the Marqués de Cañete, arrived in Nueva España to assume his duties as its first viceroy. He sent a boat under the command of Francisco de Ulloa to inform the marqués that he was being ordered back to Mexico City. At this point, both Cortés and Nuño de Guzmán were told to desist from launching their own explorations of the north—future ones were to be exclusively crown initiatives.

Guzmán was clearly in trouble by this time. He had several acerbic critics, including Mexico City's (and the New World's) first archbishop—the Basque Juan de Zumárraga. The archbishop reported that during Guzmán's tenancy as governor of Nueva España, he was afraid to send letters to Spain through regular channels and resorted to smuggling them out via the Basque ethnic seafaring network. Chipman cites several Guzmán detractors, including his biographer José Santana, who wrote of Nuño's "cruelty of the highest order, ambition without limit, a refined hypocrisy, great immorality, ingratitude without equal, and a fierce hatred of Cortés."[42] In 1537, Guzmán was arrested, tried, and sent back to Spain. His New World career was now over.

In 1537, there was another Spanish crossing of the Pacific that began in Nueva España. That year, Francisco Pizarro, besieged in Peru, sent an urgent request for assistance to Cortés. Two vessels were dispatched under the command of Hernando de Grijalva, but by the time they reached Peru, the situation there was under control. Gri-

40. Bernal Díaz de Castillo, *Historia verdadera de la conquista de la Nueva España*, 2 vols. (1632; Madrid: Historia 16, 1984), 2:392–94.

41. Moriarty, "The Discovery," 4–6.

42. Quoted in Chipman, *Nuno de Guzman*, 142.

jalva decided to explore California coastal waters instead, but on his way there, he was blown off course and far out to sea. He therefore resolved to make for the Moluccas. In 1538, his flagship, the *Santiago*, arrived in the Spice Islands with but twelve bedraggled survivors, who were promptly arrested by the Portuguese.[43]

In 1539, in defiance of Mendoza, Cortés dispatched Francisco de Ulloa northward with three boats—probably with orders to continue the search for the northwest passage. He first anchored at La Paz, just off Cortés's abandoned settlement (now in ruins after having been destroyed by the Indians). Ulloa next sailed northeastward to the coast of Nueva España and probed the entire length of the Gulf of California to its terminus at the delta of the Colorado River.

It was then that Ulloa decided to bear southward along the coast-line of Baja California. This was a puzzling decision; rather, he might have been expected to probe the mighty Colorado. Marco Polo's jour-nal was well known at this time, and it spoke of the great Coromara River in China, which passed through some of its wealthiest and most populated areas. Could the mighty Colorado's delta actually be the terminus of Coromara? Nearly two centuries later, in 1692, the geog-rapher and mapmaker Planicus was still designating the Colorado the "Rio Coromara."

In any event, Ulloa returned to La Paz and then rounded the southern tip of Baja—having completed the first circumnavigation of the Gulf of California, now known also as the Gulf of Cortés. He proceeded up Baja's west coast until he discovered Cedros Island. From there, he dispatched one vessel back to Nueva España with news of his discoveries to that point. He undoubtedly continued his north-ward probe, and there is controversy concerning his ultimate fate. For some historians, he simply disappears at this time. However, James Moriarty and others believe that there is sufficient documentary evi-dence of his subsequent presence in Nueva España to argue that he survived the expedition.[44]

By now there were other developments to inflame the Spanish imagination. In 1536, Álvar Núñez Cabeza de Vaca, one of the few survivors of the ill-fated Pedro de Narváez expedition to the west

---

43. Mitchell, *Friar Andrés*, 78.
44. Moriarty, "The Discovery," 17.

coast of Florida, turned up in Nueva Galicia, near Culiacán, with three companions after having wandered for eight years across the American Southwest. Cabeza de Vaca claimed to have heard of (but not seen) fabulous cities of gold. In 1539, Francisco Vásquez de Coronado, governor of Nueva Galicia, ordered a new probe into the region. The expedition's most notable members were the Moroccan named Estevanico, one of Cabeza de Vaca's companions, and a Franciscan friar, Marcos de Niza. Estevanico died along the way, and Fray Marcos returned to Nueva España claiming to have seen from a distance a fabulous golden city called Cíbola that was larger than Mexico City.

A formal investigation and another expedition both failed to verify the friar's account. There were even questions about the friar's credibility. Some skeptics believed Cíbola to be pure invention. Nevertheless, Viceroy Mendoza remained intrigued, and in 1540, he decided to launch a combined land and sea expedition. Coronado was charged with commanding the large land force, accompanied by Fray Marcos de Niza. In August of 1540, Hernando de Alarcón sailed from Acapulco with two ships to the head of the Gulf of California. He was to rendezvous with and resupply Coronado. After anchoring in the Colorado River delta, Alarcón proceeded in longboats as far upriver as the Colorado's confluence with the Gila River—but without encountering Coronado. He left a note and buried supplies for the land expeditionaries.

Coronado's large force proceeded slowly and cautiously. Fray Marcos's Cíbola turned out to be a disappointing complex of Zuni Indian pueblos. Coronado banished the friar back to Nueva España in disgrace. Coronado lingered in the Southwest and did battle with hostile Indians on more than one occasion. He was wounded in a battle with the Zunis. He dispatched one group to search for the Colorado River and Alarcón's supplies. They actually retrieved them and managed to discover the Grand Canyon along the way. Coronado, told by an Indian that there was a fabulously wealthy city to the northeast, pushed into the present-day state of Kansas in a fruitless search for Quivira. In 1542, and now in present-day New Mexico, Coronado was injured seriously in a fall from his horse. It was decided to return to Nueva España. Two Franciscan friars were left behind to evangelize the Indians. On balance, Coronado's mission had been a failure.

Meanwhile, in 1540, Andrés de Urdaneta and a fellow Basque from the Loaísa expedition, Martín de Islares, were recruited by Pedro de Alvarado, the governor of Guatemala, to accompany him from Spain back to the New World. Urdaneta brought with him his nephew, Ochoa de Zabala. Alvarado, by now Cortés's keen competitor, was particularly interested in furthering exploration of the Pacific. He and Viceroy Antonio de Mendoza commissioned a Portuguese shipbuilder and captain, João Rodrigues Cabrilho (Juan Rodríguez Cabrillo, in Spanish), to construct and command a fleet that would search for the Strait of Anián and possibly a new maritime route to the Spice Islands and China. But while preparations were underway, Alvarado received a desperate request for assistance from Cristóbal de Oñate, the beleaguered acting governor of Nueva Galicia in Coronado's absence, who faced a major Indian rebellion. In June of 1540, Cabrillo and Alvarado embarked with three vessels from Acajutlán on the Pacific coast of El Salvador, intending to assist Oñate before making the Pacific crossing. Urdaneta was the expedition's pilot. They first sailed north to the port of Jalisco, where Urdaneta was put in command of 150 infantrymen and some cavalry that were combined with the forces of his fellow Basque, Oñate.[45] The vastly outnumbered Urdaneta/Oñate contingent prevailed in the decisive battle, killing and capturing eight thousand of the Indians.

---

45. There would be a pivotal Basque contribution to the exploration and development of northern Nueva España. In 1546, Cristóbal (born in either Vitoria, Araba, or Oñate, Gipuzkoa) and his fellow Basques Diego de Ibarra (born in Eibar, Gipuzkoa) and Juan de Tolosa (likely from Tolosa, Gipuzkoa) were discoverers of the fabulous silver mines at Zacatecas. Diego de Ibarra founded the city of Zacatecas and became its first mayor. He later married (in 1556) the daughter of the viceroy of Nueva España, Luis de Velasco y Ruiz de Alarcón. Diego's nephew, Francisco de Ibarra (born in Eibar, Gipuzkoa), came to Zacatecas. In 1562, Francisco headed an expedition to the northwest in search of the fabled city of Cíbola. In the process, he founded the province of Nueva Vizcaya and its capitol, Durango—named after the town of origin of Archbishop Zumárraga. Francisco became the new province's first governor. Juan de Tolosa married Leonor Cortés Moctezuma, Hernán's daughter, and then prospected for new silver deposits north of Zacatecas with Luis Cortés, son of the Marqués de Oaxaca. Then, in 1598, Domingo's son, Juan de Oñate, husband of Juan de Tolosa's daughter (Isabel de Tolosa Cortés de Moctezuma), led an expedition to the American Southwest and established a colony at the site of present-day Albuquerque. He and his brother, Cristobal, both subsequently served as governors of Nuevo México.

Nevertheless, the intended voyage to the Orient was aborted when Alvarado perished in the fighting.

Antonio de Mendoza, viceroy of Nueva España and one of the financial backers of the Alvarado expedition, retained his strong interest in Pacific exploration. In 1542, he backed two fleets from the port of La Navidad, Jalisco. On June 27, Cabrillo set out from there, heading north with three ships. Cedros Island was his first stop, and by the end of August, he was sailing in uncharted waters. On September 28, he entered present-day San Diego Bay, becoming the first European to set foot in Alta California. He continued up the California coast, visiting Santa Catalina and San Clemente Islands and naming other coastal features along the way. In mid-November, he reached the Russian River, whence he turned back south. Cabrillo missed the entrance to present-day San Francisco Bay, but did enter and chart Monterey Bay—naming it Bahía de los Pinos. He decided to winter over in the Santa Barbara Islands, and it was there that he died, on January 3, 1543, from a gangrenous wound, having shattered his shin earlier while defending some of his men during an Indian attack.

Before his death, Cabrillo entreated his second in command, Bartolomé Ferrelo, to continue with the exploration. Ferrelo sailed north to southern Oregon, to 43 degrees latitude, before heading south to escape inclement weather. He visited and named Cape Mendocino in honor of his viceroy. The survivors of the Cabrillo expedition arrived back in La Navidad on April 14, 1543.[46]

Viceroy Mendoza was particularly fixated upon the Philippines, and he offered Urdaneta command of a new probe in their direction. However, the Basque was more interested in exploring both northern Asian waters and the South Pacific. He had learned of Papua New Guinea from Saavedra and may well have wished to search for the rumored southern continent of Terra Australis, as well.[47]

When Urdaneta demurred, Mendoza appointed Ruy López de Villalobos commander of a six-vessel expedition, including intending settlers. It left La Navidad in November of 1542 with explicit orders to take possession of the Philippines. Four Augustinian friars

46. Theodore H. Hittell, *History of California*, 4 vols. (San Francisco: N. J. Stone, 1898), 1:73–78.

47. Mitchell, *Friar Andrés*, 80.

formed part of the contingent, including Gerónimo de Sanesteban. On January 19, 1543, Villalobos reached Mindanao and claimed it for Spain. Dwindling stores and the unremitting hostility of the natives ruled out permanent settlement, so Villalobos was forced to sail on to Tidore, arriving on April 4. Potential disaster was averted when Gerónimo de Sanesteban managed to convince the governor that the Spaniards were not challenging Portuguese hegemony, but were only seeking assistance in their hour of misfortune.[48]

Sailing westward from Nueva España to the Philippines was relatively simple. Villalobos traversed the Pacific to Mindanao in three months, having paused at some islands along the way. The real navigational challenge was to discover an easterly route for the return voyage. Before quitting the Philippines, Villalobos dispatched the *San Juan de Letrán* in search of easterly prevailing winds. Like most of their predecessors, these explorers failed to do so and eventually had to make their way to Tidore.

On May 16, 1545, the *San Juan de Letrán* left Tidore again in search of the sea route back to Nueva España, captained by Iñigo Ortiz de Retes.[49] He attempted the crossing by sailing south to the coast of New Guinea, which he claimed for Spain and named Nueva Guinea, since its black natives reminded him of those of Guinea in Africa. Utterly frustrated in his attempt to effect an easterly crossing, in early October, Ortiz de Retes was back in Tidore. It was then that the Portuguese dispatched the Villalobos crewmen to Europe via their well-established route to Lisbon. Villalobos himself became ill and died in Amboina. The last rites were administered to him by the future Saint Francis Xavier, the Basque missionary who would proselytize India and China.[50]

Meanwhile, Urdaneta had been appointed by Mendoza to the important posts of *corregidor* and *visitador*—royal inspector of government administration—in Michoacán. When, in 1547, word reached the viceroy of the excesses in Peru of Gonzalo Pizarro (Fran-

48. Ibid., 82.

49. Juan Génova Sotíl, after underscoring that we lack specific biographical information regarding this figure, notes that he was likely descended from Araba. We are told, "His name and his second surname seem to point clearly to his condition as Basque." Juan Génova Sotíl, "Ortiz de Retes, por aguas australes," in *Descubrimientos*, Landín Carrasco et. al., 2:379.

50. Mitchell, *Friar Andrés*, 84.

cisco's brother and self-proclaimed successor), Mendoza assembled an armada of six hundred men to remove the usurper. He named Urdaneta commander of the military expedition. However, just before the fleet set sail, word arrived that Gonzalo had been defeated, and so the mission was aborted.

In 1552, Urdaneta effected a major change in his personal life. He professed religious vows and entered the Augustinian convent where Gerónimo de Sanesteban was the prior. Mairin Mitchell speculates that the decision was likely influenced by a tight web of religious Basques prominent in Mexico City at the time, notably archbishop Juan de Zumárraga, chronicler Fray Gerónimo de Mendieta, and Diego de Olarte, a soldier under Cortés who became a missionary after the conquest of Mexico.[51] Significantly, the Augustinians were Spain's preeminent missionary order in the mid-sixteenth century, as evidenced by the participation of its four friars in the Villalobos expedition. Urdaneta obviously had much in common with them.

For twelve years after professing his religious vows, Urdaneta led the life of a cenobite. However, he had not completed his destiny as explorer. Mendoza's successor, Viceroy Luis de Velasco,[52] interested in extending Spanish imperial sway, consulted Urdaneta regarding the Moluccas and Philippines. In 1558, Velasco wrote King Philip II urging that new westward sea voyages be undertaken from Nueva España. He further recommended that Urdaneta be designated the first expedition's guide because of his lengthy experience in the Moluccas, his navigational and cosmographic skills, and his knowledge of the native languages.[53]

On September 24, 1559, King Philip II, desirous of bringing the Philippines within Spain's orbit, ordered Velasco to mount an expedition. Given Urdaneta's experience, the king requested his involvement. In light of such official pressure, the friar's superior not only

---

51. Ibid., 86.

52. Like the surname Mendoza, Velasco has Basque (Arabese) etymological roots.

53. Mitchell, *Friar Andrés*, 98. Furthermore, "Urdaneta's aptitude for languages is marked throughout his career; not only did he master those commonly used in the Moluccas, but also those—and in a very short time—in some of the Philippine Islands, and later in life more than one of the Mexican languages. There is no doubt that his native Euskera equipped him to learn, more quickly than non-Basque speakers, languages totally unrelated to those of the Indo-European groups." Ibid., 59–60.

gave permission, he ordered Urdaneta to accede. So on September 24, 1559, the somewhat reticent monk wrote the king accepting the charge.

Velasco asked Urdaneta to nominate the expedition's captain general. The friar's choice was fellow Gipuzkoan, Miguel López de Legazpi, a man that Velasco described to the king as Urdaneta's relative and friend. Legazpi was not a mariner. Rather, for twenty-nine years, he had resided in Nueva España, working as a legal scribe and holding posts such as secretary of Mexico City's municipal council. He was also a member of the Confraternity of the Name of Jesus of the Friary of Saint Augustine, providing him with a direct spiritual link to Urdaneta, as well.[54]

Actual construction of the fleet, which was under Urdaneta's supervision, lasted for five years. In 1561, the friar wrote a long memorial to the king, a kind of progress report. In it, he expressed his doubts about targeting the Philippines, since, in his view, they were largely devoid of spices and were probably legally within the Portuguese sphere. Rather, he urged that New Guinea be the destination and that Spain establish her Asian base of operations there. According to Mitchell, "had Urdaneta's advice that New Guinea be the objective of the expedition prevailed, it is not improbable that the discovery of Australia would have been a Spanish one."[55]

Urdaneta's proposal was opposed by the admiral of the fleet, Juan Pablo de Carrión, a veteran of the Villalobos expedition. He had visited New Guinea, and in August of 1564, depicted it as barren in a letter to the king. He supported the monarch's original intent of making the Philippines the sole destination of the expedition. There was obvious malice or simple envy in play, as well. Carrión states:

> Nevertheless Fray Andrés de Urdaneta has said definitely that he will not sail with the fleet if it goes where I have said. As the Captain-General, Miguel López de Legazpi, is of his [Basque] nation and country and is his close friend, his desire is to please the friar in everything. And as the said General knows nothing of those regions or of matters of navigation, he goes by what the friar says in all things.[56]

---

54. Ibid., 105.
55. Ibid., 116.
56. Quoted in ibid., 111–12.

Viceroy Velasco died before the fleet set sail and the audiencia, the high court of justice in Mexico, prepared instructions ordering Legazpi to sail directly to the Philippines following the Villalobos route. They were not to be opened until the expedition was at sea, thereby preventing Urdaneta from defecting. He had been named by his order's superior as prior of the contingent of six Augustinian missionaries, vastly empowered to bring the light of Christianity to "certain islands that lie between the Equator and the Arctic and Antarctic poles, and below the torrid zone itself,"[57] possible additional evidence of Urdaneta's desire to find Terra Australis.[58]

The expedition set sail on November 20, 1564, from La Navidad. The fleet's four vessels carried a total of 350 men. Again, the Basque ethnic web, solidified even further by kinship and other ties, was evident. Legazpi's grandson and Urdaneta's nephew were along, and of the six Augustinians, Pedro de Gamboa, Martín de Rada, and Andrés de Aguirre were Urdaneta's fellow Basques.

On the fourth day, Legazpi opened his instructions. Urdaneta and the other Augustinians were chagrined by the news that they were des-

---

57. Ibid., 110–11.

58. It is worth considering an extensive quote from Urdaneta's *Memorial*, since it underscores his exploratory predilection, his belief that a southern continent might indeed exist, and his navigational acumen: "If we cannot leave New Spain before November 10th we should commence the voyage between that date and January 20th, or a few days later, sailing southwest, making for New Guinea, until we reach Latitude 25° or 30° S, unless we should discover the coast before that. If that coast of New Guinea continues down to the Antarctic Pole or toward the Strait of Magellan, as is hoped to be the case, we should find it before we reach 30°, even though it does not bear east a quarter south-east as does the part discovered, but may turn from there to the south-east. In my opinion, in the new charts which have come to New Spain that coast is drawn more than a hundred leagues longer than actual discovery shows it to be. But taking all this into consideration, if it runs in a direction south-east from the farthest cape found to the east, we should meet it before reaching 30°. If, however, we sail to 30° and do not find the coast of New Guinea we should navigate from this point to 30° directly west for a distance of two hundred leagues, given fair weather. Then we should set our course west, northwest, and west, to fall in with the last cape that has been discovered, and which is shown in 5° S in the account and the map which I have of that coast. The part of the coast of New Guinea which we strike, the time at which we do so, and the winds which then prevail, will determine how we sail along that coast, making what discoveries we may, bearing in mind that we must reach the Philippines at the latest by the beginning of November 1562. If we leave Acapulco on January 20th at the latest, or earlier as recommended, with fresh winds in our favour, we should cross the Line in a few days, and this we should aim at, so as to avoid crossing at the time of the Equinox, the season when calms generally occur below the Line. Continuing in the Latitude South at the time just mentioned, this would give us ample time to explore the coast of New Guinea and other islands if such exist there." Quoted in ibid., 108–9.

tined for the Philippines; however, their vow of obedience triumphed over personal ire. On February 13, 1565, the expedition reached Samar in the Philippines, whereupon Legazpi claimed the archipelago in the king's name. Urdaneta eventually advised Legazpi to establish a permanent settlement on Cebu, the initial outpost of Spanish hegemony in the islands and one that would endure for more than three and a half centuries.

From the outset, Urdaneta and Legazpi set a moderate tone there, usually refusing to resort to particularly punitive retaliation when spurned or even attacked. Mitchell notes,

> Much has been written about the cruelty of the conquistadores, and if the leyenda negra is particularly true in the New World it is not so of the Philippines, where Legazpi and the friars maintained an exemplary standard of conduct towards the natives, and dealt severely with those Spanish soldiers whose rapacity brought discredit at times to the new colonial venture. In the history of colonization that of the Philippines is almost unique, in that it involved no slavery.[59]

A key, if not the prime charge to Legazpi was discovery of the elusive easterly return route from the Philippines to Nueva España. Given the Portuguese monopoly over the westward sea lane between Asia and Europe, without the capacity to complete the round-trip between Asia and Spain's New World colonies, it was simply impossible to establish trade with the Philippines, let alone a settled Spanish colonial presence there, without violating the Treaty of Zaragoza.

Urdaneta's previous experience in the Moluccas had sensitized him to the seasonal shift in the region's prevailing winds. Furthermore, his relationship with Gerónimo de Sanesteban in Mexico City doubtless gave Urdaneta detailed knowledge of the Villalobos expedition's two failed attempts to return to Nueva España from the Moluccas via a southern route.[60] On June 1, 1565, Urdaneta left the Philippines in the *San Pedro*, which was under the command of Legazpi's young (sixteen-year-old) grandson, Felipe de Salcedo. It seems likely that Urdaneta was the actual commander. Other Basques on the vessel included Friar Andrés de Aguirre; the boatswain, Francisco de

---

59. Ibid., 124.
60. Ibid., 140.

Astigarribia; the ship's mate, Martín de Ibarra (all Bizkaians); and the scribe, Asensio de Aguirre.[61] About one-third of the crew were Gipuzkoans.[62]

According to Mitchell,

> Urdaneta, by starting early in June, just before the strong north-east winds commenced, and when he had behind him the south-west monsoon blowing to the west to carry him, at that season, up to the latitude of the Ladrones showed a better sense of timing than did his predecessors and by leaving when he did he minimized the risk of meeting with typhoons, which originate as a rule east or south-east of the Philippines, that is, in the seas near the Moluccas, a region well known to Urdaneta.[63]

Once in the northern latitudes, the *San Pedro* picked up the summer months' prevailing northeasterlies. On September 26, the ship reached the American mainland in the vicinity of California's Cape Mendocino after having sailed 11,160 miles without a landfall—the longest continuous oceanic voyage to that date in the age of European exploration. Despite Urdaneta's care in provisioning the vessel well, the length of the crossing meant that most of the crew was scorbutic. Nevertheless, the riddle was solved, and the route of the Manila galleon was now established.

Among the ranks of the intrepid sixteenth-century explorers of Pacific waters there are two controversial Basque commanders—Alonso de Arellano, of Navarrese descent, and the Gipuzkoan Pedro de Unamuno. Arellano's fame regards his captaining of the *San Lucas*, a vessel in the López de Legazpi expedition that was separated from the rest after but two days at sea. Most historians believe that Arellano and his first mate conspired to reach the Philippines and then return to Nueva España before the main fleet, thereby claiming the honors and spoils of any discoveries. In fact, the *San Lucas* did reach Mindanao ahead of its admiral, avoided linking up with the other vessels while in the Philippines, and then departed on April 22, 1565, for

---

61. Amancio Landín Carrasco and Luis Sánchez Masiá, "Urdaneta y la vuelta de poniente," in *Descubrimientos*, Landín Carrasco et. al., 2:496.

62. Garikano, *Kaliforniakoak*, 25.

63. Mitchell, *Friar Andrés*, 134.

Nueva España, arriving there on August 9 after following the northerly route espoused by Urdaneta.[64]

Arellano then made his way to the Spanish court to claim his prize. He was still there when Urdaneta arrived on the scene and immediately denounced the deserter. The captain of the *San Lucas* was summarily detained and remanded to Nueva España. There, he was tried by Miguel López de Legazpi himself and imprisoned.[65]

While Arellano would continue to be regarded for the remainder of his life as an importunate opportunist and social outcast in Spanish colonial society, his monumental achievement remains. To traverse the Pacific in both directions in such a small craft, devoid of any support from the larger fleet, was virtually unthinkable. Along the way, he made several new discoveries that filled in critical parts of the map of Central Pacific geography.[66]

Although Arellano and Urdaneta had demonstrated the feasibility of crossing the Pacific from west to east via a northern route, the journey remained risky and extremely arduous. Clearly, it would be less so if there was the possibility of provisioning a vessel along the way. From the outset, then, the viceroys of Nueva España had an intrinsic interest in exploration of both the Pacific north of the Marianas and the coast of Alta California—the likely first continental landfall of a ship coming from the Orient.

This agenda was informed by the observations of Fray Andrés de Aguirre. In 1584, back in the Philippines, he wrote a letter to the archbishop of Mexico City, who was also serving as viceroy of Nueva España, in which he described the visit that he and Urdaneta made to King Philip II in Spain shortly after their epochal Pacific crossing. Urdaneta told the monarch on that occasion about his conversation with a Portuguese ship's captain who claimed to have been blown off course by a severe storm in northern climes while on a journey from Malacca to Japan. On the ninth day, he came upon two islands that

---

64. Urdaneta remained the likely source of such knowledge, since, at Viceroy Velasco's behest, he had addressed the expedition's officers in this regard while the preparations were still underway in Nueva España. Landín Carrasco and Sánchez Masiá, "Urdaneta," 2:491–92.

65. Amancio Landín Carrasco and Luis Sánchez Masiá, "El viaje Redondo de Alonso de Arellano," in *Descubrimientos*, Landín Carrasco et. al., 2:473.

66. Ibid., 2:491.

he called the Isles of the Armenian, after a merchant traveling aboard the ship. He named one island Rica de Oro (Rich in Gold) and the other Rica de Plata (Rich in Silver) since the inhabitants—who were white, well dressed in silk and cotton clothing, and speaking a language that was neither Chinese nor Japanese—were in possession of a large quantity of the precious metals. Fray Aguirre was vague about their location, but placed them to the east of Japan at the latitude of between 35 and 40 degrees north.

About this same time, in December 1584, Francisco Gali, captain of the galleon *San Juan*, reached Acapulco with a report of having visited the Isles of the Armenian and confirmed the mineral wealth of their inhabitants. The new viceroy ordered him to return to the Philippines to prepare an expedition to explore the North Pacific as far as the Straits of Anián (the present-day Bering Straits), mapping the various islands along the way, as well as suitable possible ports in Alta California. Meanwhile, the archbishop of Mexico City wrote the king urging that an expedition be launched to contact the Isles of the Armenian, because they might serve as an ideal place to resupply vessels on the Manila run. After his east-to-west Pacific crossing, Gali's two vessels were deemed to be unfit for the challenge, and while in the Philippines awaiting construction in Nueva España of replacements, Gali died suddenly in January 1586.[67]

Little is known about Gali's successor—the Basque Pedro de Unamuno. He may have been Gali's pilot during his last voyage across the Pacific. In any event, Unamuno departed Manila with two vessels in the latter half of 1586. Ostensibly, he had set out to explore the North Pacific, but turned up in Macao, instead. He and his men were detained by the military governor, suspected of seeking to trade for valuable Oriental goods in clear violation of the Spanish King Philip's assurance to the Portuguese (and by then he was king of Portugal, as well) that they would continue to enjoy a monopoly on commerce in their colonial ports. Unamuno was tried, but acquitted and released after claiming to have sought refuge in Macao after being blown off course. Nevertheless, the military governor had filed a complaint with the Spanish governor in the Philippines, and before Unamuno could

67. Fernando Guillén Salvetti and Amancio Landín Carrasco, "Miscelánea," in *Descubrimientos*, Landín Carrasco et. al., 3:864–68.

reclaim his vessels, Manila officials arrived in Macao to escort them back to that city. Unamuno expected the worst and refused to accompany them. Instead, he purchased a small frigate in Macao and set sail to carry out the viceroy of Nueva España's mandate to explore the North Pacific. His contingent included several Basques, most notably a Franciscan friar, Martín Ignacio de Loyola, nephew of the Gipuzkoan Saint Ignatius.[68]

Unamuno first concentrated upon a search for the Isles of the Armenian. Despite considerable thoroughness, he was unsuccessful and concluded (rightly, as it turned out) that the fabled islands were an illusion. Unamuno then tried to explore farther north, reaching the latitude of 39 degrees before turning back due to the cold and adverse seas. He failed to find a single speck of land. Finally, he sailed on to Alta California, likely landing first at Morro Bay. He claimed it in the name of King Philip and then proceeded to map the area, thereby providing the authorities in Mexico City with their most comprehensive description of Alta California to date.[69]

68. Ibid., 3:868–71.
69. Ibid., 3:873.

5

Dubious Fame and Elusive Fortune

The Spanish explorations in the Pacific Ocean that we have considered to this point were inspired by the search for a westerly sea route for trade with the Orient, particularly in spices. The quest for precious metals was concentrated upon the New World. Even there, it was informed largely by the premise that if there were gold, silver, and precious stones to be had in a particular area, its indigenous population was already engaged in mining and utilizing them. It was not until the eighteenth century that Spaniards began to prospect systematically for undiscovered deposits, and even then, the search was uneven. For example, despite their presence in Alta California throughout the first half of the nineteenth century, the Spaniards overlooked the abundant and quite accessible placer gold on the western slopes of the Sierra Nevada range that would later drive what came to be known as the California Gold Rush.[1] The precious metals' trail was even cooler in Pacific waters. Indeed, as a part of Spain's Manila trade, beginning in the late sixteenth-century, Asia would emerge as a major consumer of New World silver production, rather than as a supplier of precious metals.

Nevertheless, the last significant paroxysm of Spanish exploration of the South Pacific was inspired by the search for mineral wealth—in the guise of King Solomon's lost mines in the mysterious land of Ophir. The search for them had fired the imaginations of the earliest Iberian explorers. The Portuguese believed them to be in East Africa, while Magellan placed them in the Lequeos and Columbus in Hispaniola. O. H. K. Spate, (citing Jack Hinton) notes that "as geographical knowledge extended eastwards and westwards without Ophir being

---

1. Maurice G. Holmes, *From New Spain by Sea to the Californias 1519–1668* (Glendale: Arthur H. Clark, 1963), 216.

recognized, its supposed position moved with that knowledge, always a little ahead of the latest discovery."[2] A targeted attempt to discover Ophir somewhere in the South Pacific informed three linked voyages over the last third of the sixteenth century and the first decade of the seventeenth: the expeditions of Álvaro de Mendaña (1567–1569), of Mendaña and Pedro Fernández de Quirós (1595–1596), and of Quirós and Luis Váez de Torres (1605–1606), which Spate labels "among the most remarkable in the whole history of maritime discovery, alike in their geographical results (long misunderstood as these were) and as a story of high ideals, bitter disillusions and sufferings, baseness and grandeur."[3]

This search for wealth, whether imagined or real, resulted in efforts at colonization, themselves amalgams of baseness and grandeur, combining visions of riches and power beyond the dreams of those who were content to remain in the Old World with pious efforts to bring true religion to the inhabitants of the new one. And because the monarchs and subjects of the Hispanic nations were not alone in harboring such visions, the Spanish and Portuguese soon found it necessary to establish outposts to defend their claimed hegemony over their new discoveries and to serve as bases for further explorations. As carried out in expeditions led by Álvaro de Mendaña and the Basque soldier of fortune Sebastián de Vizcaíno, these efforts brought their own bitter disillusions and sufferings as Old World colonists frequently encountered both unwelcoming environments and hostile inhabitants unwilling to cede their own world to the claims of another.

Mendaña—and Sarmiento

The story of the South Pacific expeditions in search of wealth begins with the extraordinary figure of Pedro Sarmiento de Gamboa, son of a Galician father and Basque mother. His early years are largely undocumented, although it is known that he arrived in Lima after a sojourn in Mexico. By 1565, Sarmiento had fallen afoul of the Inquisition in Peru, charged with necromancy. He was found to have had

---

2. O. H. K. Spate, *The Spanish Lake.* (Canberra: Australian National University Press, 1979), 121.

3. Ibid.

made two rings for which he claimed supernormal properties. They were embellished with Chaldean letters, inscriptions, names, and astronomical characters and were to be used in rituals designed to obtain for their bearers good fortune in life, love, and war. To the archbishop of Lima, it all smacked of witchcraft.

Sarmiento put up a spirited defense, but the fact that he had previously run afoul of the Inquisition in Mexico over an ill-advised practical joke scarcely helped his case. On May 8, 1565, he was found guilty and ordered to attend a penitential mass in order to make public abjuration for his sins. He was then to be banished from the New World. He was also detained in a monastery until such time that his transfer to Spain could be arranged. Sarmiento declared his intention to appeal the sentence to the pope. But at that point, Lope García de Castro, licentiate governor of Peru, intervened. The banishment was rescinded, and Sarmiento was released from custody. Nevertheless, with the Inquisition as an adversary, his standing in both Mexico and Peru seemed quite shaky.

By this time, his knowledge of Inca legends had convinced Sarmiento of the existence of fabled lands both to the east of the Andes—the elusive El Dorado—and across the Pacific to the west. Given his difficulties in Lima, he was not only inspired to explore the unknown, but was positively motivated to do so.[4]

Sarmiento's personal predicament coincided with active interest in Peru regarding the possibility of discovering the Isle of Solomon—the fabled location of King Solomon's gold mines—somewhere off the coast of Chile. In 1565, there had even been an abortive private initiative, and in 1567, Governor García de Castro appointed his twenty-five-year-old inexperienced nephew, Álvaro de Mendaña, to head an expedition to search for rich islands "between New Guinea and this coast."[5]

Sarmiento not only joined the expedition, but in his chronicle of it, he claims to have been its inspiration. Through his previous study of Inca legends, he had learned of the mythical voyage to the west of Túpac Yupanqui and twenty thousand sailors that discovered

---

4. Stephen Clissold, *Conquistador: The Life of Don Pedro de Sarmiento* (London: Derek Verschoyle, 1954), 22–24.

5. Spate, *The Spanish Lake*, 121.

rich islands and whence they returned with slaves, gold, and silver. Sarmiento was convinced that they were the outposts of a southern continent that stretched from Tierra del Fuego to within 15 degrees of the equator, beginning approximately six hundred leagues west of Peru. He claims that he was initially offered command of the two-vessel expedition by the governor, but refused when he was denied full authority over its every aspect. Mendaña was then appointed commander and named Hernán Gallego as his chief pilot. Sarmiento agreed to captain the flagship *Los Reyes*. According to J. C. Beaglehole, Sarmiento's "capacity was great, and his deeds made him famous in later years; but his character was not an attractive one. He was a remorseless enemy, cruel in revenge, a bad subordinate and a difficult commander, and he brooded furiously over the elevation of Mendaña."[6]

The tension was exacerbated when Mendaña followed Gallego's advice (rather than Sarmiento's) regarding the route. As for the expedition's purpose, the idealistic young commander was also generally out of step with most of the participants. Mendaña had greater zeal for the colonization and evangelization of pagan lands than for the search for material wealth.[7]

The two ships were at sea for eighty days before sighting land with a coastal range that was so lofty as to appear continental. After initial friendly overtures, the natives withdrew. Mendaña sent a party ashore, under Sarmiento's command, charged simply with making contact. Sarmiento overstepped his orders, kidnapping the chief and his uncle while dispatching one native with his sword. This was but the first in a series of such misunderstandings. As a consequence, the Europeans were unsuccessful in establishing working relations with the natives—let alone converting them to Christianity.

At one point, a landing party successfully scaled the coastal mountains in the expectation of sighting a vast continent, but instead verified that they were on a large island. They named it Santa Ysabel. Mendaña ordered construction of a small brigantine capable of exploration of the reef-infested waters in further pursuit of Sarmien-

---

6. J. C. Beaglehole, *The Exploration of the Pacific* (1934; London: Adam and Charles Black, 1966), 42.

7. Spate, *The Spanish Lake*, 121.

to's continent. They came upon another substantial island—Guadalcanal—to which Mendaña moved his larger ships. Its natives proved to be even more hostile than those of Santa Ysabel.

Extremely short of food, once again, Mendaña sent Sarmiento ashore to make contacts. When he failed to do so, he emptied a village of its stores and retreated with hostages just in time to avoid attack. Soon thereafter, nine members of a landing party in search of water were slain, and Sarmiento became the agent of Spanish revenge. Unable to engage the elusive natives in open combat, he torched their villages. When a possible peace mission of several men in a canoe approached, all were killed and their quartered bodies placed at the scene of the watering party's massacre.[8]

During a stop at Malaita, the Spaniards mistook for gold the glitter of iron pyrite in the stone of a native's war club. After visiting several more islands, despite native hostility, on the island that they named San Cristóbal the explorers were finally able to recondition and provision their ships.

The expedition had clearly failed in its purpose of finding the southern continent, and Mendaña decided to hold a general meeting to deliberate their next move. The friars and some officers wished to make for New Guinea and Manila. However, some soldiers believed that gold might yet be discovered and wanted to continue exploring the island chain. Sarmiento "who had no fear of 'Indians'. . . was generally opposed to counsels of prudence." Nevertheless, Mendaña decided to attempt a return to South America by sailing southeast toward the coast of Chile, still in search of Sarmiento's southern continent.[9]

As yet, the impracticality (given the prevailing winds) of a west-to-east southern crossing of the Pacific was imperfectly understood. After weeks of futile sailing, Mendaña faced growing opposition among the crew. By then, he was north of the equator, and he ordered his two ships to make for California. They were separated and then buffeted by a hurricane that nearly sank them both. It took more than three months to make the ill-advised but eventually successful crossing. The two vessels were reunited and repaired in Colima. It was

---

8. Beaglehole, *The Exploration*, 45–50.
9. Ibid., 52.

there that long-standing disagreements between Mendaña and Sarmiento became a feud. Sarmiento filed a sworn statement accusing his adversary of dereliction of duty. Mendaña seized and destroyed Sarmiento's papers and charts.

When the two vessels reached Nicaragua, Sarmiento again filed accusations against his commander, but was arrested instead. He managed to escape, but was wary of proceeding to Peru as long as Mendaña's uncle was its governor. Mendaña arrived at Callao in September of 1569, nearly two years after his departure from there.

While Sarmiento languished in Nicaragua, contemplating pressing his charges against Mendaña in Spain, fortune was to favor him. Francisco de Toledo was appointed viceroy of Peru, and while in transit to assume his new post, was likely intercepted by Sarmiento in Panama. The details of what transpired are unclear, although the outcome is not. According to Stephen Clissold, "Don Francisco de Toledo, the newly appointed Viceroy, Governor, Captain-General and President of the Royal Audiencias, was at this time a grizzled soldier and administrator of fifty-four years of age, small and wiry of stature, bigoted, autocratic, and painstakingly conscientious, of unimpeachable integrity and inexhaustible energy. Between Sarmiento and such a man there must have existed an immediate affinity."[10]

Toledo remained in Panama for three months. When he entered Lima, on November 30, Sarmiento was a trusted member of his entourage, and the new viceroy was already displeased with Mendaña. Indeed, the latter's career was at this point severely damaged, and it would be more than a quarter of a century before he was able to realize his obsession with returning to colonize his Pacific discoveries.[11]

Shortly after assuming his post in Peru, Viceroy Toledo decided to conduct a survey or "visitation" of his realm—one that would last for five years. He asked Sarmiento to accompany him as his chief cosmographer and chronicler. In Toledo's opinion, as a historian, Sarmiento was "the most able man in this subject that I have found in these lands."[12]

---

10. Clissold, *Conquistador*, 47.

11. Ibid., 45–47.

12. Rosa Arciniega, *Pedro Sarmiento de Gamboa: El Ulises de América* (Buenos Aires: Editorial Sudamericana, 1956), 24.

Despite a keen desire to resume his own explorations of the Pacific, Sarmiento accepted the assignment. During it, he authored a book on Inca history largely based upon interviews conducted with Incan elders who antedated the Spanish presence in Peru. In part, the purpose was to demonstrate that the Incas had been conquerors of other peoples and therefore had no more "original" claim to political hegemony over their empire than did the Spaniards, as the latest in the line of usurpers.[13]

Easily given to grandiose speculations, in his *Historia*, Sarmiento posited that the Americas were the western (and unsubmerged) part of the vast lost continent of Atlantis. Finding reference to a great flood in Inca legends, he believed that this biblical event had destroyed the eastern part of Atlantis. Most of the Native Americans were descendants of the Mesopotamians and Chaldeans about whom Plato had written. During his initial travels in Mexico, Sarmiento had noted the resemblance of the aborigines to the Greeks in their dress and bearing, as well as in certain words and letters of their language. He posited that they might well be descended from the weary mariners who accompanied an aged Ulysses on his last voyage into the setting sun toward an unknown land.[14]

Sarmiento also participated in the siege of Vilcamba, last redoubt of the Incas, and claimed to have captured their leader, Túpac Amaru, himself. He then engaged in the unsuccessful military campaign against the ferocious Chiriguanos.[15]

Despite such service, in November of 1575, Sarmiento was charged with necromancy and imprisoned in Lima by the Inquisition. Once again, the irascible defendant found himself at cross purposes with authority, though as usual, he was undaunted:

> He was accused of having read the lines of a lady's hand and predicted that two men would lose their lives on her account. Moreover, he had dared to assert that the Gospel was not sufficiently preached in Spain. Two witnesses had heard him make this remark; and when one of them

---

13. Clissold, *Conquistador*, 68–70.

14. Ibid., 72; Arciniega, *Pedro de Sarmiento*, 25–26.

15. Amancio Landín Carrasco and Luis Sánchez Masiá, "El descubrimiento de las Islas Solomón," in *Descubrimientos españoles en el Mar del Sur*, 3 vols., Amancio Landín Carrasco et al. (Madrid: Editorial Naval, 1992) 2:546–48.

attempted to expostulate with him and declared that such an opinion was disrespectful to the Church, he had retorted arrogantly that "he knew very well what he was saying, better indeed than men like the person who was now rebuking him, whose thick skulls stood in need of a good schoolmaster, whereas he, with his superior intelligence and exceptional memory, had studied the matter and knew all about it, and much else besides.[16]

In 1578, Sarmiento was found guilty, but was released with the stipulation that he recant and attend mass on feast days, standing in shirtsleeves and holding the candle of the penitent. He was spared greater public humiliation or banishment from Peru only through the viceroy's intervention.[17]

Sarmiento's public persona would not be fully rehabilitated until the next year, when Peru was faced with external threat from the English corsair captain of the *Golden Hinde*. Sir Francis Drake stunned the unfortified Pacific Spanish colonies out of their complacency by becoming the first European to enter the Pacific from the Atlantic in nearly half a century. Indeed, Drake's accomplishment was even more ominous than imagined, since, rather than traversing the Strait of Magellan, he had actually rounded Cape Horn, a possibility that was as yet unbeknownst to the Spaniards.[18] They persisted in the belief that Tierra del Fuego was the northern tip of a vast southern continent. The corsair then proceeded up the Pacific coast of the Americas, attacking ships at sea and at anchor, as well as several ports.

Drake's first hostile act against the Spaniards was at Valparaiso, where he commandeered the *Los Reyes*, the very vessel that Pedro Sarmiento de Gamboa had captained during the Medaña expedition and that was now engaged in coastal trading. It was carrying three hundred pounds of gold.[19] Drake then proceeded to Peru, where he narrowly missed seizing a treasure ship at Arica. At Callao, the *Golden Hinde* made a daring entry into the harbor, where it became becalmed. When news reached Lima, the viceroy mobilized all able

---

16. Clissold, *Conquistador*, 105.

17. Landín Carrasco and Sánchez Masiá, "El descubrimiento," 548.

18. Spate, *The Spanish Lake*, 249.

19. Samuel Bawlf, *The Secret Voyage of Sir Francis Drake, 1577–1580* (Vancouver: Douglas and McIntyre, 2003), 128.

bodies—including Pedro Sarmiento de Gamboa, who was then aboard one of the two pursuit vessels that narrowly failed to engage the Englishman during his escape.

Viceroy Toledo convinced the audiencia to implement emergency measures. A ship was sent to alert all Spanish coastal settlements between Callao and Panama, and a war galley was dispatched to probe the intervening coastal bays and inlets to ferret out the corsair. A third vessel was ordered to Nicaragua and on to Mexico to apprise the viceroy of Nueva España of the danger.

At the time, the English corsair John Oxenham and several of his crew were imprisoned in Lima. Oxenham had attacked Panama but, after some initial success, was captured. The prisoners were interrogated and stated that their queen must have authorized Drake's voyage and that it was probably his intention to found an English settlement somewhere in the Pacific. Furthermore, if Drake were triumphant, there doubtless would follow many other English expeditions intent on establishing a foothold. Asked how Drake planned to return to England, Oxenham replied that he might go back through the Strait of Magellan, but that he could also be headed for the elusive northern passage. In short, Drake's presence, and his fellow Englishmen's speculations about it, exacerbated fundamental Spanish concerns—the possibility of a European foe challenging their Pacific colonial monopoly while controlling a convenient northern access to it.[20] Toledo dispatched two ships with reinforced artillery under the command of his son, Luis, to pursue Drake on the high seas. General Diego de Frias Trejo was named admiral, and the consummate navigator Pedro Sarmiento de Gamboa was made his chief advisor and sergeant major.

Meanwhile, Drake pursued and overtook the treasure galleon *Nuestra Señora de la Concepción*, which was bound for Panama. The booty was so great that it required three days to replace the *Golden Hinde*'s ballast with Spanish silver. Drake then set sail for Nicaragua to careen his vessel in order to make needed repairs. His pursuers, under the command of Luis de Toledo, probed the northern South American coastline. Sarmiento concluded that Drake must have captured the treasure ship and therefore had no reason to remain in South

---

20. Ibid., 140–41.

American waters. He advised Toledo to bypass Panama and press the search for the English interloper in the direction of Nueva España. Toledo refused, anxious as he was to embark in Panama for Spain to deliver his father's report to the king. Drake was thereby afforded valuable breathing room.[21]

The English corsair was keenly aware that he needed a second vessel, so, while repairing the *Golden Hinde* in Nicaragua, he kept an armed pinnacle in readiness should one appear on the horizon. He managed to intercept a forty-ton bark in the Gulf of Nicoya that happened to be carrying two pilots charged by the viceroy of Nueva España with transporting the new governor of the Philippines to Manila. They had with them all of the relevant navigational charts for the Pacific crossing. Drake pressed the senior pilot into his service and put the rest of the sequestered vessel's contingent ashore.

Drake then proceeded up the coast of Nueva España and captured and briefly held one ship bound southward from Acapulco laden with Chinese cloth, silks, and porcelains. Its principal passenger was a Basque nobleman, Don Francisco de Zarate. Drake treated him well before putting him ashore along with his fellow passengers. Drake then put into the southern Mexican port of Guatulco to make preparations for an ocean voyage. The local magistrate dispatched mounted messengers to Mexico City to warn the viceroy of corsair's presence. On April 16, 1579, Drake left Guatulco, never to be sighted again by the Spaniards.

Meanwhile, in Panama, Pedro Sarmiento de Gamboa was compiling the details of Drake's South American depredations. In addition to sowing fear and panic along the entire littoral, Drake had seized 447,000 pesos, as well as unknown quantities of porcelain, jewels, and precious stones. Sarmiento calculated the remaining damages to ships and settlements to be 100,000 pesos, and he was as yet unaware of the details of the corsair's impact in Nueva España.[22]

The key question was Drake's intended homeward route. Sarmiento rejected the possibility of a return via the Strait of Magellan, given the high state of alert in Peru and Chile. He also discounted a transpacific crossing, which would eventually subject the English-

21. Ibid., 146.
22. Ibid., 154.

man to the gauntlet of Portuguese control of Asian waters. Rather, Sarmiento was convinced that Drake would seek the elusive northern passage. According to Sarmiento's report:

> From the present month of March onwards, until September, summer and the hot season prevail as far north as the cape of Mendocino in forty-three degrees. That would be the shortest and quickest route for getting from this sea to his country, and while this route is not familiar to the pilots here, because they do not normally navigate in that region, it is not unknown to the cosmographers and particularly to the English who navigate to Iceland, Bacallaos [Newfoundland], Labrador, Totilan and Norway. For them it is familiar and they are not afraid of navigating very far north. As this corsair has, moreover, navigated in the aforementioned parts and is so well versed in all modes of navigation, it may be inferred and believed that he must know about all this. A man who has the spirit to do what he has done will not be lacking in courage to persevere in his attempt, especially as he can take advantage, at present, of its being summer in the polar region.[23]

Unbeknownst to Sarmiento, Drake's crew was quite international in makeup and included a contingent of Bizkaians—certainly another of the corsair's septentrional strengths, since by then, Basques had been the dominant European seafarers in the North Atlantic for more than half a century.

Drake, in fact, explored Canadian Pacific waters in search of the northern passage before finally relenting and striking out for the Moluccas and an eventual return to Europe via the Cape of Good Hope, thereby entering the select ranks of the world's few sixteenth-century circumnavigators. Arriving back at Plymouth on September 26, 1580, Drake's status in England, and particularly that of his considerable booty, remained in doubt for awhile. Indeed, there even existed the remote possibility that it might be restored to Spain, and in December of 1581, Philip II appointed Pedro de Zubiaure, a Basque residing in London, where he was an agent for Sevilla's merchants'

---

23. Zelia Nuttall, ed., *New Light on Drake: A Collection of Documents Relating to his Voyage of Circumnavigation 1577–1580*, trans. Zelia Nuttall (London: Hakluyt Society, 1914), 75.

guild, as his personal representative in the ultimately futile negotiations to recover the treasure.[24]

Meanwhile, in October of 1579, Pedro Sarmiento de Gamboa had been ordered by Viceroy Toledo to secure the Strait of Magellan. His mission was to traverse it from west to east (an as yet unaccomplished navigational feat) to ascertain the feasibility of fortifying the southern passage, as well as to engage Drake in combat, should he be found lingering there. Toledo also believed that if the strait could be secured and settled, it would open a sea route between Peru and Spain that would obviate the existing costly transporting of cargo by land across the Isthmus of Panama.

Sarmiento was given supreme command of two vessels, of which the *Nuestra Señora de la Esperanza* was his flagship. Admiral Juan de Villalobos captained the *San Francisco de Asís*, and it was now Sarmiento's turn to have to deal with insubordination. Villalobos was recalcitrant to enter the formidable passage and used the first excuse to abandon the mission and return to Callao. Sarmiento pressed on alone, spending two months in the strait, mapping the many channels, determining possible settlement sites, and describing the flora and fauna. At one point, he was wounded in the forehead by a hostile arrow. Sarmiento then proceeded on to Europe to report his findings to his monarch.[25]

In September of 1580, a few days before Drake reappeared in Plymouth, Sarmiento met in Lisbon with Spanish King Philip II, the newly installed ruler of Portugal. Shortly thereafter, the Spanish ambassador to London, Bernardino de Mendoza, reported Drake's triumphant homecoming and warned his king of the possibility that the dreaded English corsair, and others, as well, would likely embark soon for South America.

In Peru, the response was to constitute a naval force, the so-called Armada of the South Seas, to patrol the coast and protect the silver galleons.[26] In Europe, there were lengthy deliberations and differences of opinion among Philip's royal advisors. Eventually, he decided to

---

24. Bawlf, *The Secret Voyage*, 185–92.

25. Clissold, *Conquisador*, 117–30.

26. Hugo O'Donnell, *España en el descubrimiento, conquista, y defensa del Mar del Sur* (Madrid: Mapre, Editorial, 1992), 151–54.

adopt a multifaceted strategy that included Sarmiento's recommendation of fortifying the Strait of Magellan while establishing a permanent settlement there.

During the summer of 1581, an expedition of twenty-three ships and approximately three thousand participants, including about three hundred intending settlers and their families, was assembled. While Pedro Sarmiento de Gamboa was the logical choice for commander, court politics and social-class considerations dictated otherwise. Over Sarmiento's protests to the king, the quarrelsome and indecisive Diego Flores de Valdés was chosen instead, a man whose experience had been limited to the relatively routine assignment of escorting fleets from Sevilla across the Atlantic to the Americas. However, Sarmiento was appointed governor and captain general of the colony. Command was further fragmented by inclusion of Alonso de Sotomayor, the governor of Chile, and his six hundred troops.[27]

The initiative, of course, failed to account for the fact that, unbeknownst to the Spaniards, Drake had discovered Tierra del Fuego to be a large island that could be rounded, rather than the northeastern tip of an austral continental barrier. The Spaniards also were misinformed by Sarmiento's glowing report of the region's agricultural potential and abundant wildlife, written after his earlier west-to-east traverse of the passage.

The ill-fated adventurers surely contained in their ranks a disproportionate number of Basques. Sarmiento de Gamboa was empowered to recruit them, and in one of his reports,[28] he gives the surnames of most individuals. The captain of the almiranta—the second-in-command's ship—was the Basque-surnamed Juan de Garibay. His

---

27. Spate, *The Spanish Lake*, 268–70.

28. Pedro Sarmiento de Gamboa, "Touching the Captains and Ships, Masters and Pilots, that his Majesty appointed for the fleet sent for the enterprise of the Strait of the Mother of God, previously called of Fernando de Magallanes, and a list of the settlers in the Strait," in *Narratives of the Voyages of Pedro Sarmiento de Gamboa to the Straits of Magellan*, ed. and trans. Clements R. Markham (London: The Haklyut Society, 1895), 219–25. The Markham translation of Sarmiento's report omits the names of the colonists. From Pastells's full reproduction of the entire document, it is clear that they were in the vast majority Andalusians: P. Pablo Pastells, *El descubrimiento del Estrecho de Magallanes en conmemoración del iv centenario*, 2 vols. (Madrid: Sucesores de Rivadeneyra, 1920), 2:138–53. There is no listing of the ordinary mariners manning the boats, but, given the pointed efforts to recruit them in the Basque Country, we might assume that many were Basques.

ship's master was "a Biscayan named Juan de Arancibia."[29] The master of the flagship was "a Biscayan named Martin de Guirieta."[30] No fewer than three of the other ships' captains and ten of the ships' masters were Basque surnamed. Two of the vessels—the *Santa María de Begoña* and *San Estevan de Arriola*—carried Basque names. We are told:

> Besides the above-named Captains there were others, namely, Domingo Martinez de Avendaño, who went to Biscay for sailors, and did not return before the ships left Lucar, so when he came to Cadiz, Diego Flores gave him command of the frigate *Magdalena* . . . and Rodrigo de Rada, who also went to Biscay for sailors at the same time as Avendaño, and went without a ship as far as the Cape Verdes, when he was given command of the *Begoña*.[31]

As the preparations fell behind schedule, the fleet missed the proper sailing season (not later than August). Over the objections of both Flores and Sarmiento, Spain's supreme naval commander ordered the expedition to depart on September 25. Within a week, the expedition was buffeted by a storm, losing six ships and eight hundred men before limping back to Cádiz to regroup.

It sailed again on December 9 under orders to winter in Brazil. While there, to Sarmiento's chagrin, the crew sold many of the supplies needed by the colonists and wasted considerable invaluable gunpowder in idle salutes and fireworks. Sarmiento quarreled frequently with Flores, but his only real authority was over his colonists, whom he now engaged in the construction of prefabricated housing. Meanwhile, word spread throughout the expedition that they were on a fool's mission. Not even the devil would attempt to enter the strait, even to seduce a soul. It was said that only a madman like Pedro Sarmiento would try.

---

29. Markham, *Narratives*, 219.

30. Ibid.

31. Ibid., 221. Sarmiento's familiarity with Bizkaia and interest in it is further underscored by his authorship of an unpublished treatise entitled "Parecer dirigido al rey sobre el modelo y traza de los galeones que se mandaron construir en Vizcaya para servicio de la Armada Real" (Opinion directed to the king regarding the model and design of the galleons that were ordered to be constructed in Bizkaia to serve in the Royal Fleet).

When they finally left Brazil, Sarmiento was no longer on the flagship with Flores, consigned instead to the worm-eaten *Begoña*. It promptly foundered and sank, with considerable loss of lives and stores. The fleet regrouped at Santa Catarina. Flores sent three ships back to Río for repairs and proceeded southward with the remainder. At the Rio de la Plata, Alonso de Sotomayor, who had tried unsuccessfully to mediate the many disputes between Sarmiento and Flores, abandoned the expedition by taking his three ships upriver and then marching his six hundred men across the Andes to Chile.

In February, the remainder of the expedition reached the strait. Flores made two unsuccessful attempts to enter it against the strong tidal currents. Ignoring Sarmiento's pleas to persist, Flores ordered the fleet to Brazil, followed by a furious Sarmiento. The armada reassembled in May of 1583 in Rio, and Flores announced his intention to return to Spain. Again ignoring Sarmiento's objections, Flores departed with six vessels. The colonial enterprise had been reduced to five ships under the command of Diego de Ribera and 548 intending colonists under Sarmiento's authority. They left on December 8, 1583, and on February 1, they were again off the Strait of Magellan.

After three unsuccessful attempts to penetrate the channel, only to be expelled by the tidal currents, Sarmiento decided to erect a settlement near the mouth, on the barren and windswept Cabo Vírgenes. There were fewer than 350 persons, including 177 soldiers, in the new installation, which was christened Nombre de Jesús (Name of Jesus). Many stores were lost during a botched attempt to beach a ship that was to be used for building materials. Sarmiento and Diego de Ribera quarreled, and the latter set sail, leaving the colony with but one small and damaged ship, the *Santa María de Castro*.

Nombre de Jesús was to be but the forward post, and not the permanent settlement. Instead, in his earlier exploratory voyage, Sarmiento had selected the better-protected Cabo Santa Ana as the more suitable site for the colony. He sent the *Santa María de Castro* ahead to begin cutting timber for construction. Sarmiento then set out on foot with a hundred soldiers. The many indentations of the coastline meant that with but eight days' rations, they would have to cover more than fifty kilometers a day. The inadequately clothed and shod men endured cold, famine, and an Indian attack, reaching the limits of their endurance on the nineteenth day. It was then that Sarmiento sighted a longboat, and his men came down to the beach for the joyful reunion, some crawling on their hands and knees.

On March 25, 1584, Sarmiento founded his second settlement, Ciudad de Don Felipe (Town of Don Philip), named after his monarch. It included a wooden church and magazine. The site was palisaded, and six cannon were mounted on a seaward bastion. A few crops were planted, and foraging provided meager results—rations were now in extremely short supply. Sarmiento had to put down a conspiracy to seize the lone ship for an escape from the colony. He executed the ringleader.

On May 25, Sarmiento sailed for Nombre de Jesús to fortify it further. There he found that there had been another mutiny, an execution, a fight with hostile Indians, and a persisting shortage of rations. A furious gale broke his anchor cable, and the *Santa María de Castro* was swept to sea with Sarmiento and his crew aboard. Thirty-four days later, after having experienced extreme cold and hunger that was so great the crew survived by gnawing on leather, Sarmiento arrived in Brazil.[32]

Diego de Ribera had left some stores at Rio de Janeiro that Sarmiento now dispatched to the strait in a small supply ship. In Pernambuco, he secured his own vessel and more adequate provisions. He headed south with them, but was shipwrecked off Bahia. All was lost, and Sarmiento, bruised and bleeding, made it to shore on two boards nailed together. He then reassembled more stores and a vessel, departing for Rio on January 13, 1585. From there, he headed to the strait, but encountered a terrible storm. Seven weeks later, he was back in Rio after having had to jettison most of his supplies, only to find in its port the rescue ship that he had dispatched the previous December. It also had failed to reach the desperate colonists. Sarmiento set about repairing his damaged ship, cannibalizing an old wreck for nails and fittings. Tar was obtained from Bahia and grease by capturing two whales in the harbor. But the months dragged by, and he had to face down yet another mutiny.

Sarmiento decided to seek more efficacious assistance in Spain. On June 22, 1586, more than two years after the *Santa María de Castro* had been blown out of the Strait of Magellan, a frustrated Sar-

---

32. Spate, *The Spanish Lake*, 271–74.

miento departed Bahia on a Portuguese caravel to plead before King Philip himself for aid for the now abandoned colonists. It was at this point that his life (or is it his saga?) took a truly bizarre turn.

The caravel was seized near the Azores by English privateers in the service of Sir Walter Raleigh. Sarmiento arrived in Plymouth as a prisoner on the last day of August. He met with his captor in Windsor, where they conversed in Latin. Clearly, the two men were more than simply compatible. Raleigh listened to Sarmiento's observations about the Indies with rapt attention, referring, in his book *History of the World*, to his prisoner as a "worthy gentleman." Of particular interest to Raleigh were the tales about El Dorado, the lost city of the Incas, in far-off Guyana. Raleigh would risk his reputation and life in the quest for it. Sarmiento thereby handed his English benefactor a truly poisoned chalice. In this regard, Clissold observes: "Even in captivity, Sarmiento was not one to cease from pursuing his own will-o'-the-wisp. His was a nature which imparts to others the fervor of its own delusions and lures them on to the quest, which can only end in tragedy."[33]

Raleigh was so impressed with Sarmiento that he arranged for both of them a private audience with Queen Elizabeth, also conducted in Latin. The substance of their exchange is unknown, but it seems likely that Sarmiento was charged with some sort of diplomatic mission to King Philip—one of a series of abortive English peace overtures to Spain designed to head off impending hostilities between the two countries. In any event, Sarmiento was released from custody and given the resources with which to travel to Spain. He first went to Paris, where he met with Bernardino de Mendoza, the former Spanish ambassador in London and now King Philip's representative in France. He then headed south, but was intercepted and incarcerated by the Huguenot Count of Bearn, the future King Henry IV of France.

A desperate Sarmiento would languish in the prison of Mont de Marsan for three years, writing pleas for assistance to both the English queen, Elizabeth, and the Spanish king, Philip II. While his own monarch tarried, Queen Elizabeth and Sir Walter Raleigh dispatched the latter's nephew to France to plead (albeit unsuccessfully) for the

---

33. Clissold, *Conquistador*, 189.

prisoner's release.[34] Sarmiento's imprisonment transpired while the two European powers squared off in military confrontation, spear-headed by the ill-fated Spanish Armada (1588). It was not until 1590 that King Philip finally decided to ransom his incarcerated subject for the amount of six thousand ducats and four select horses.

A white-haired and toothless Sarmiento appeared before Philip in El Escorial, offering to organize a relief mission to the Strait of Magellan, totally unaware that the colony had long since perished. Indeed, more than three years earlier, in February of 1587, the English corsair Thomas Cavendish, commissioned by the English crown in 1586, at twenty-six years of age, to emulate Drake's predations in the Americas, entered the strait with three ships and found but fifteen men and three women surviving at Nombre de Jesús. As an act of mercy, he volunteered them passage, but while they dithered over whether to accept the offer of a heretical enemy, a favorable wind for traversing the strait began to blow, and Cavendish opted to take advantage of it. He did board one Spaniard at Nombre de Jesús and then sailed on to Rey Don Felipe. There he found a city of the near dead, inhabited by a few emaciated and prostrate settlers. Cavendish stopped only long enough to seize the cannons that Sarmiento had mounted to inter-dict the passage of interlopers through the strait. The English corsair rechristened the place Port Famine. When, at the beginning of 1590, the Englishman Andrew Merick visited Port Famine, he removed its sole survivor.[35]

After exiting the Strait of Magellan, Thomas Cavendish pro-ceeded up the Pacific coast of the Americas, raiding towns and plun-dering nine Spanish ships along the way. From a captured ship's pilot, he learned that a Manila galleon was scheduled to arrive in Nueva España soon and that it would likely make its first New World land-fall at Cabo San Lucas, on the tip of Baja California. It was there that Cavendish careened his two remaining ships, the *Desire* and the *Con-tent*, in October of 1587, and sent out patrols to await the galleon.

The ship that Cavendish awaited, *Santa Ana*, under the command of the Basque Tomás de Alzola, had left the Philippines along with a

---

34. Adolfo Lafarga Lozano, *Los vascos en el descubrimiento y colonización de América* (Bilbao : Editorial La Gran Enciclopedia Vasca, 1973), 175.

35. Clissold, *Conquistador*, 193–94, 97.

sister ship, the *San Francisco*, and both were wrecked by a typhoon off Japan. The *San Francisco* was a total loss, and the repaired *Santa Ana* continued its Pacific crossing, arriving at Cabo San Lucas on November 4, 1587, heavily laden with treasure, two hundred men—and no cannons.[36]

The *Desire* and *Content* thus were able to leave Baja California loaded with plunder, bent upon completing a circumnavigation back to England. They were separated, and the *Desire* put into Guam for supplies. The *Content* was never heard from again. Cavendish reached England by way of the Cape Good Hope on September 9, 1588, just a few months after the defeat of the Spanish Armada. While not even twenty-eight years old as yet, he was now both triumphant and quite wealthy. He was celebrated and knighted by Queen Elizabeth. By 1591, Cavendish had another commission as a corsair for a repeat performance and launched his second expedition to the Strait of Magellan. However, this time, he was unable to reach the Pacific and retreated to Brazil, where he lost most of his men in a battle with the Portuguese. Cavendish died of unknown causes at age thirty-one on the return trip across the Atlantic.

After returning to Spain, Sarmiento was appointed as a *censor*, public accountant, by the Council of the Indies. He continued to urge dispatch of a relief expedition to the colony that he had founded, seemingly still ignorant that it had perished. Clissold gives us a last glimpse of Sarmiento serving as admiral in charge of a squadron of galleons assigned to escort a fleet to the New World. Neither his nor its fate have been recorded.[37] Rosa Arciniega maintains that Sarmiento was given command of a vessel in the summer of 1592 and that he died while sailing it to Lisbon from Sanlúcar de Barrameda.[38] Clements Markham presents evidence that Sarmiento may have gone to the Philippines, whence a Pedro Sarmiento commanded an unsuccessful expedition designed to conquer Tidore. If that man was the same protagonist of the above account, then he probably died soon thereafter in Manila, since by then, he was quite elderly. But precise

---

36. Despite the predations of Drake nine years earlier, the colonial authorities still remained complacent regarding the security afforded by their monopoly of the "Spanish Lake."

37. Clissold, *Conquistador*, 200.

38. Arciniega, *Pedro Sarmiento*, 229.

information regarding Sarmiento's demise is as lacking as that for his early years.

The words of Samuel Eliot Morison perhaps best summarize the career of this extraordinary man:

> Pedro Sarmiento de Gamboa, in addition to his literary gifts, proved to be an expert and courageous soldier, mariner, and navigator. He knew the secret of command, humoring his men as far as the state of things allowed, winning their confidence; and he was notably equipped with that indomitable perseverance which deserves, though it does not always win, success. The one thing that he could not cope with was being placed under the orders of a tricky, incompetent courtier who was also a ruffian and a coward [Flores]; as if Magellan had been made subordinate to Cartagena. Under this impossible handicap he did all that he could to fortify the Strait, and it was not his fault that the garrisons were left to perish. A sincere Christian, he attributed all his escapes from marine disaster to the Heavenly Host, and his loyalty to the king never wavered. No more truehearted, loyal, and brave man ever sailed the far-off seas.[39]

Failed Colonies

Álvaro de Mendaña may have been an ineffectual leader, but he could never be faulted for lack of persistence. Outmaneuvered and discredited by Pedro Sarmiento de Gamboa in the aftermath of their failed Isle of Solomon venture, Mendaña never relinquished his dream of returning to the South Pacific. Indeed, at times, he was overzealous in pursuing it. On two occasions, he was actually imprisoned by Viceroy Toledo, likely for his impatience and impertinence.[40] In 1574, at age thirty-four, Mendaña obtained royal approval from Madrid for a new expedition and was even named *adelantado* (governor) of the Solomons. However, Toledo remained at his post in Peru until 1581 and continued throughout his term to frustrate the efforts of the would-be explorer. Toledo's successor as viceroy, García Hurtado de Mendoza, was more favorably disposed to Medaña's project. Nevertheless, the

---

39. Samuel Eliot Morison, *The European Discovery of America*, vol. 2, *The Southern Voyages*, A.D. 1492–1616 (New York: Oxford University Press, 1974), 706–7.

40. Amancio Landín Carrasco and Luis Sánchez Masiá, "Archipiélagos de Marquesas y Santa Cruz," in *Descubrimientos*, Landín Carrasco et al., 2:583.

preparations for it seemed interminable. It was not until 1595, nearly three decades after the first exploration of the Solomons (1567), that the new expedition was launched.

By then, Mendaña, while himself a Leonese, had married the redoubtable Galician Isabel Barreto, who, along with her three brothers and a sister, joined the expedition. Many of the expedition's members, including Pedro Fernández de Quirós (Queiróz), the subsequent commander of his own probe of South Pacific waters, were Portuguese. Such a Hispano-Luso partnership was furthered by the uniting of the two countries in 1580, albeit in a troubled union, not to mention by the considerable degree of linguistic and cultural affinity between Galicia and Portugal.

It was Mendaña's plan to return to the Solomons to assume his post as *adelantado* and resume the search for the southern continent. The ranks of the participants included about one hundred intending settlers and two Franciscans. However, while it seems clear that the "civilizing" mission remained paramount in the commander's mind, it was shared fully only by the friars and probably by Quirós. A large majority of the contingent, including many of the supposed settlers, was more influenced by the irresistible quest for fortune. Instead of abating after the disastrous expedition of 1567, rumors of the fabulous wealth of the Solomons had actually persisted.[41]

In sum, Mendaña now commanded an initiative that was rife with cross-purposes. In the event, as Spate would note, "In all 'the tragical history of the Sea' there can scarcely be a more moving and terrible story than that of Mendaña's second, and last, voyage, unless it be Sarmiento's lingering disaster in the Straits."[42]

The expedition, consisting of two galleons and two smaller vessels, left Callao on April 9, 1595. It sailed northward toward the port of Paita, requisitioning provisions along the way. The camp master, a man named Manrique, proved to be particularly quarrelsome and sowed dissension. At Paita, Quirós, the chief pilot, almost abandoned his post. On June 16, the four vessels set sail from South America and made good progress, coming upon a group of islands that Mendaña declared to be his Solomons—thereby displaying his questionable

---

41. Spate, *The Spanish Lake*, 126.
42. Ibid., 127.

navigational skills. While they were in the right latitude, they were still 50 degrees longitude from his earlier discovery.[43]

The initial exchange between the Europeans and natives followed the established pattern of previous experience. Mutual curiosity soon gave way to the indigenes' overly enthusiastic and easily misinterpreted advances. These, in turn, triggered a violent response. The expedition moved from island to island over the next two weeks, by which time (as Quirós would recount in his subsequent written report) the toll of slain natives stood at about two hundred. There was the particularly infamous case of a Spaniard, simply intent upon demonstrating his marksmanship, killing with a single shot both a native and the child he was holding.[44]

Mendaña realized his navigational error and named the island group of his latest discovery the Marquesas de Mendoza (after Peru's viceroy). In summing up the expedition to this point, Ernest S. Dodge observes, "Mendaña's discovery of the Marquesas Islands was even more disastrous for the Polynesians than his discovery of the Solomons had been for their Melanesian brothers."[45]

He set sail and yet again grossly underestimated the remaining distance to the Solomons. On August 8 or 9, he promised landfall by nightfall. Yet it would be another month, not until September 8, that the expedition reached another significant island group. To complicate matters, the Santa Cruz Islands (as they would become known), were covered with smoke caused by a volcanic eruption. In the midst of this, the almiranta *Santa Isabel*, with its contingent of 182 persons, became separated from the flagship and was never seen again.

Mendaña claimed to recognize the first island (Ndeni) and called it Santa Cruz. After a series of tense encounters with the curious natives that resulted in the death of several, the Europeans went ashore at a place they called Graciosa Bay. Mendaña ordered the founding of a permanent settlement and then remained aboard his flagship while the colony was under construction. By then, there was palpable dissension in the ranks. Few were content with the mundane

---

43. Ibid., 128.

44. Ernest S. Dodge, *Islands and Empires: Western Impact on the Pacific and East Asia* (Minneapolis: University of Minnesota Press, 1976), 18.

45. Ibid., 18.

task of building an agricultural colony. Indeed, Quirós would accuse some of them of deliberately slaughtering natives in order to provoke attacks that would destroy the fledgling initiative. Camp master Manrique proved to be the prominent malcontent, whose insubordination bordered upon mutiny. He ordered punitive raids against the natives on his own authority. One of his aides ignored Mendaña's specific instruction not to harm Malope, the friendly local chief. That same day, probably in retaliation and at the insistence of Doña Isabel and the Barretos brothers, Mendaña had Manrique and a fellow instigator killed and beheaded.

Disheartened by the ruinous outcome of his failed dream, on October 18, Mendaña died. His will and testament named his brother-in-law, Lorenzo Barreto, as captain general of the expedition and his wife, Doña Isabel, heiress of the title *adelantado* of the Solomons. Lorenzo, however, soon succumbed to a wound received in combat with the islanders, and Quirós assumed effective command. Morale was further undermined when the expedition's Franciscan vicar died shortly after confessing Lorenzo.

Illness then broke out among the Europeans, and by November 7, when they abandoned the settlement to move on board their ships, there were but fifteen healthy men in all. On November 18, a scant two months after their arrival at the inaptly named Graciosa Bay, the survivor's of Mendaña's disastrous second voyage set sail for Manila under Quirós's command. That voyage would take them nearly two months and would produce an additional fifty deaths in the ranks. Consequently, by this time, of the nearly four hundred persons who left Paita the previous June, all but one hundred had either perished or disappeared.[46]

None of the key figures in the accounts of Mendaña's second expedition were Basque. However, we might note that the surname evidence suggests that as much as 10 percent of the expedition was of possible or probable Basque descent.[47]

---

46. Spate, *The Spanish Lake*, 128.

47. Celsus Kelly, *Calendar of Documents: Spanish Voyages in the South Pacific from Alvaro de Mendaña to Alejandro Malaspina 1567–1794 and the Franciscan Missionary Plans for the Peoples of the Austral Lands 1617–1634* (Madrid: Franciscan Historical Studies [Australia] in association with Archive Ibero-Americano, 1965), 399–409.

Vizcaíno

Meanwhile, in the North Pacific, having been burned twice by English corsairs, Spanish officialdom was now quite sensitive to the need for better security along the Manila run. There was a keen interest in establishing a fortified presence somewhere along the California coast, both to resupply and to protect from corsairs the crews of the Manila galleons, weakened as they were by their Pacific crossing.[48] So careful exploration and mapping of Alta California became a priority.

Consequently, in 1594, one of the pilots on the *Santa Ana*, the Portuguese Sebastião Rodrigues Soromenho (Sebastián Rodríguez Cermeño), in command of the Manila galleon *San Agustín*, was ordered to explore the California coast along his way to Nueva España. He arrived at Drakes Bay to the south of Point Reyes in Alta California on November 4, 1595. He then constructed a smaller craft to explore the coast with his exhausted and emaciated crew. They were at the mercy of hostile Indians. While the details remain unclear, the *San Agustín* was lost somehow, along with its treasure. Cermeño and a few battered survivors arrived in Nueva España in January of 1596—having demonstrated the futility of "exploring" with a large treasure ship.[49]

Sebastián de Vizcaíno, "a Basque soldier of unusual talent," according to Richard F. Pourade,[50] had remained in Nueva España after the *Santa Ana* debacle. For his former losses and service, he petitioned the government to be put in command of a Manila galleon, but was given the lesser reward of appointment as mayor of Tehuantepec. He then formed a commercial company for exploration and colonization of the Gulf of California. He planned to target

---

48. W. Michael Mathes, *Vizcaíno and Spanish Expansion in the Pacific Ocean, 1580–1630* (San Francisco: California Historical Society, 1968), 11.

49. Asun Garikano, *Kaliforniakoak (1533–1848): Euskaldunen lanak Kaliforniaren esplorazio eta kolonizazio garaian* (Iruñea/Pamplona: Pamiela, 2013), 54.

50. Richard F. Pourade, *The Explorers, 1492–1774* (San Diego: Union-Tribune Publishing, Copley Press, 1962), 62. W. Michael Mathes believes that Vizcaíno, despite his surname, was actually a native of Exremadura. Mathes, *Vizcaíno and Spanish Expansion*, 28. While that may be possible, it raises, rather than obviates, the question of Sebastián's Basque ethnic awareness.

its reputed pearl-rich oyster beds while mining for salt, gold, and silver, as well.

On November 16, 1593, Viceroy Velasco issued Vizcaíno an exclusive contract (good for four years) to exploit the ten leagues of coastal area from La Navidad to California. At the end of that term, a report was to be filed, and, if satisfactory, the license could be extended for an additional sixteen years. The crown was to receive one-fifth of all gains. Anyone who violated Vizcaíno's concession would have his vessels and cargo seized (to be divided between the crown and license holders) before being banished from New Spain.[51]

The departure of an expedition was delayed for two years while Vizcaíno and his partners coped with a series of legal altercations and financial difficulties. It was in the summer of 1596 that the three vessels left Acapulco, northward bound. There were 230 men in all, many intending colonists accompanied by spouses and children. There were five Franciscan friars, as well, to minister to the spiritual needs of the Europeans while evangelizing the Indians.[52]

After landing near the tip of Baja and being well received initially by the Indians, Vizcaíno established his new colony at La Paz on about the site of Cortés's ill-fated 1535 settlement. Almost immediately, he faced dissension in his ranks as many of the settlers despaired that the place was suitable for agriculture. Some wanted to return immediately for Nueva España. Vizcaíno proclaimed that any deserters would be executed and ordered construction of houses in his absence. On October 3, he took two vessels, the *San Joseph* and the *Tres Reyes*, and proceeded northward to explore the coast in search of pearls and precious metals. They became separated in a storm and, on October 13, he and the crew of the *San Joseph* were enticed ashore by some welcoming Indians. Initial peaceful trade quickly evolved into a confrontation. Vizcaíno and about twenty-five men made it back to the ship, leaving a like number on shore to await the return of the sole longboat. Rather than retreat immediately, the master sergeant decided to do battle. For the next hour, he ignored Vizcaíno's shouted order to come aboard. Then, when the Spaniards were attacked by five hundred Indians, it was too late. The longboat was lost, and nineteen

---

51. Mathes, *Vizcaíno and Spanish Expansion*, 27–28.
52. Ibid., 30–34.

of Vizcaíno's men drowned in their heavy armor. Six wounded ones managed to swim to the *San Joseph*. He named the place Puerto de la Muerte (Port of Death). Lacking a landing boat, Vizcaíno now had no choice but to return to the colony—arriving there on October 18.

Meanwhile, construction had proceeded apace. But then, on October 21, a strong wind blew sparks from a cook fire into a thatched roof, and half of the new structures were burned to the ground—along with a substantial amount of the expedition's supplies. So on October 28, Vizcaíno abandoned the colony and sent two vessels back to Nueva España. He then headed north again with the *San Joseph* to continue his explorations. This new initiative proved to be as star-crossed as all of his others. It barely survived a severe storm, and then someone sabotaged the vessel by boring a hole in its hull—an attempt to force the commander to abandon further probing of the unknown. Vizcaíno was unable to identify the culprit(s). After he repaired that damage to the *San Joseph*, the vessel developed serious rudder issues. It was therefore decided to head southeast, and on November 17, the coast of Nueva España was sighted. On December 7, the *San Joseph* limped into to the port of Salagua, and the abortive mission was over.[53]

Back in Nueva España, Vizcaíno filed his report with the new viceroy, Gaspar de Zuñiga y Acevedo (the fifth Count of Monterey). He blamed his failure upon bad weather and reiterated his belief that there were vast riches to be had in the north. He asked that his mandate be expanded:

> Vizcaíno then asked for thirty-five thousand pesos for supplies, ships, and fittings to be obtained under supervision of a royal official, an encomienda of Indians for five generations for each settler, the title and privileges of an hidalgo of Castilla and León for each settler, exemption from cargo or sales taxes for thirty years, placement of the area conquered under direct viceregal jurisdiction, and the supplying of goods at prices paid by Manila ships. In return, Vizcaíno agreed to take five ships with artillery, one hundred and fifty armed men, divers and pearl fishing equipment, a year's rations, religious ornaments, and gifts for the Indians, as well as to pay to the Crown one-fifth of the value of pearls and minerals, one-tenth of the fish taken, barreled, salted, and delivered in Acapulco, and one- twentieth of the value of salt recov-

---

53. Ibid., 35–39.

ered from the deposits. The expedition was to explore the Gulf of California, take possession, found settlements, and map the region up to one hundred leagues inland, for which Vizcaíno requested the title of general and adelantado, the powers of a governor to appoint officials, the sole jurisdiction of viceroy over the area, and the tribute of twenty thousand Indians in entailed perpetuity.[54]

Amazingly, Viceroy Zuñiga approved the petition and forwarded it to the king on July 6, 1598. While the first expedition had certainly failed, the viceroy believed that Vizcaíno was simply the most experienced and competent man to continue the undertaking. The king and the Council of the Indies both approved the proposal, as well, with few caveats. The duration of the *encomienda* given to each settler was reduced somewhat, and Vizcaíno was to avoid further violent confrontations with the Indians. In the event, however, all proved stillborn when Philip II died a few months later and state priorities shifted from exploration of the Gulf of California to improving security along the Manila run.[55]

In 1600, there was a rumor in Peru that the Dutch corsair, Oliver van Noort, had entered the Pacific through the Strait of Magellan. The viceroy of Peru dispatched Hernando de Lugones to search for him. Lugones left Acapulco on August 13, 1600, bound for Cabo San Lucas. He did not find any sign of the Dutchman and declared the Manila run to be safe.

Viceroy Zuñiga now made plans to explore and chart the west coast of Baja California and that of Alta California. Three vessels were eventually outfitted and placed under the command of Sebastián Vizcaíno. The viceroy was obviously concerned that his commander would be tempted to reenter the Gulf of California—an initiative that he specifically forbade under pain of death. However, Vizcaíno was assured that once he had completed his mission of charting the California coastline, he would be allowed to pursue his own interests in the Gulf of California. Meanwhile, he was to prepare detailed maps of the Pacific coastline of California from Cabo San Lucas to Cape Mendocino, including islands, reefs, bars, and the entrances to bays.

---

54. Ibid., 41–42.
55. Ibid., 41–43.

He was to give saints' names to those places lacking one. Vizcaíno was not to go inland and was to avoid conflict with the natives.[56]

Vizcaíno left Acapulco with his three ships, the *San Diego*, the *Santo Tomás*, and the *Tres Reyes*, on May 5, 1602. They sailed north along the coast to La Navidad and then to Mazatlán Islands before making the crossing to Cabo San Lucas, arriving on June 8. For the next six months, the expedition carried out the detailed mapping of the coastline, and on December 4 were anchored in Monterey Bay, naming it after his viceroy. He spent considerable time searching the area for the lost *San Agustín*, but without success. By now, more than forty of his men were gravely ill, and a council of officials decided that the *Santo Tomás* should be sent with them back to Nueva España. It departed on December 29, carrying Vizcaíno's endorsement of Monterey Bay as the ideal harbor for resupplying Manila ships—not altogether an accurate assessment, given its open exposure to Pacific winds—along with his request that a ship be sent to La Paz with the supplies that he would need to explore the Gulf of California. He was clearly confident that Cape Mendocino was now within his easy reach. At this point, the *Tres Reyes* raced ahead far to the north and reported finding what appeared to be a vast river—they named it the Río Santa Inés—that might well be the Strait of Anián itself.

On January 12, 1593, Vizcaíno's flagship, the *San Diego*, reached Cape Mendocino. By now, the weather was stormy and bitterly cold, so it was decided to head south. On January 25, they were off Santa Catalina Island, but the crew was too weakened by scurvy to attempt an anchorage. Arriving at Cedros Island on February 11, it was now necessary to go ashore in search of water. Vizcaíno anchored the ship with a light anchor, fearing that his men might be too weak to pull up a regular one. He went ashore with six men, and they had an altercation with hostile Indians—they fired their harquebuses at them. To this point, the entire expedition had been remarkably free of such incidents. They had to cut the anchor cable, and then on February 18, the *San Diego* was off Cabo San Lucas. Given their sad condition, it was decided not to go to La Paz for the hypothetical rendezvous with the requested supply ship. Rather, they sailed straight for the coast of Nueva España, arriving at the Mazatlán Islands on February 18.

---

56. Ibid., 54–59.

Leaving his spent crew behind, Vizcaíno and five men took the long-boat to the main coast to seek assistance in the nearby town of San Sebastián. They missed the road and were wandering about lost, but fortunately ran into a muleteer from Culiacán who directed them to the town. Vizcaíno purchased supplies and was pleased to find that his crewmen were over their scurvy, having discovered a cactus fruit that cured it. On March 21, 1603, Vizcaíno anchored at Acapulco—his third visit to California now over.[57]

According to W. Michael Mathes,

> Vizcaíno had succeeded in charting the California coast and in crystal-izing its geographical nomenclature. The voyage, however, was far from an absolute success for while Vizcaíno had discovered Monterey Bay, he had overlooked the greater possibilities presented at San Diego, he had failed to recover the lost cargo of the *San Agustín*, and he had failed to discover the great bay later to be known as San Francisco. Further-more, the exploration carried out by the crew of the *Tres Reyes* and the resulting report of the Río Santa Inés revived the interest in a passage from the Pacific to the Atlantic. This concept of a passage was to con-fuse cartography of northwest America for almost two centuries, since, while Vizcaíno's charting from Cabo San Lucas to Cape Mendocino was generally accurate, from the latter point northward it was based upon the inaccurate reporting of impressionable seamen and clouded by myth. Nevertheless, by completing the task which so many naviga-tors had failed, Vizcaíno had stimulated new interest, and the way was open for potential settlement and development of California as the east-ern terminus of trans-Pacific navigation as well as the further extension of New Spain northward.[58]

Vizcaíno went to Mexico City to present his findings to Viceroy Zuñiga in person and to request just recompense. The viceroy, already informed by the crewmen of the *Santo Tomás* and *Tres Reyes* (both of which reached New Spain well before the *San Diego*), had already written the king proclaiming the expedition to be a great success. On May 23, it was now Vizcaíno's turn to write his monarch, urging settle-ment of Monterey Bay and requesting compensation for his services. Viceroy Zuñiga quickly wrote his own letter in support of Vizcaíno,

---

57. Ibid., 60–103.
58. Ibid., 107.

urging that he be appointed general on the Manila run and that his voyage from the Philippines should include the plan and provisions to establish a permanent Spanish presence in Monterey Bay. Through the summer and into the autumn, matters proceeded apace in Madrid, including positive testimony from many of Vizcaíno's companions regarding his competence as a commander. By November, Zuñiga was actually proceeding with the planning for the Manila-to-California voyage as if royal approval of it was foreordained.[59]

Before any of this could be implemented formally, however, Zuñiga was transferred to Lima (1604), where he became the viceroy of Peru. His successor in New Spain, Juan de Mendoza y Luna, proved to be jealous of the accomplishments of both his predecessor and his predecessor's protégé, Sebastián Vizcaíno. Mendoza soon appointed his wife's uncle, Diego de Mendoza, in Vizcaíno's stead as general of the next Manila galleon. By the spring of 1604, the two viceroys were engaged in a struggle for the monarch's attention and approval, Mendoza arguing that Zuñiga's appointments and plans were no longer valid once he left his post in Nueva España. The new viceroy praised Diego de Mendoza as his choice of general and reappointed Vizcaíno as mayor of Tehuantepec, instead. Mendoza was now arguing against the worth of the California settlement, since by that point in their journey, the Manila mariners were within relatively easy reach of Acapulco and had no need to lay over. Currently, the Manila galleon would put into port in Japan before crossing the Pacific. However, that was an extremely dicey arrangement, because diplomatic relations with the Japanese were mercurial. What was really needed was a Spanish North Pacific possession such as afforded by the as yet undiscovered Rica de Oro and Rica de Plata Islands.[60]

In the event, in August of 1606, Mendoza was sent a royal order to revive development of the California settlement at Monterey Bay under Vizcaíno's aegis. He should be appointed general of the Manila ships for the years 1607 and 1608, would be allowed to select settlers for the new colony, and would be awarded twenty thousand pesos for its provisioning. In April of 1607, the Council of the Indies rewarded Vizcaíno's previous service with a four-thousand-peso lump-sum

59. Ibid., 105–10.
60. Ibid., 111–12.

payment, an *encomienda* of Indians "for two lifetimes," and a ten-thousand-peso annual pension for life.[61]

Mendoza was now winding down his tenure as viceroy and claimed not to have received the royal order in time to implement it. Besides, Vizcaíno had departed for Spain before receiving his good news and was therefore no longer available in Nueva España. Mendoza reiterated his opposition to the Monterey Bay settlement, adding that it would be vulnerable to attack by corsairs. He communicated his thoughts to his successor, Luis de Velasco. Meanwhile, in Spain, Vizcaíno learned of his good fortune and appointment as general of the Philippine ships. He departed for Nueva España on December 21, 1607, to begin his new duties, but a series of storms and the capture of a French corsair off Guadeloupe delayed the arrival of his ship at Veracruz until March 21, 1608.

It was now too late for him to leave on the Manila ship from Acapulco, so Vizcaíno argued that he should send the settlers of Monterey Bay directly from New Spain. This triggered a debate over whether that was the ideal site for the California settlement. San Bernabé or Cabo San Lucas, both on the tip of Baja, might actually be better. From them, the galleon could proceed directly to Europe through the soon-to-be-discovered Strait of Anián. (At this time, it was still thought that it might be reached by sailing up the Gulf of California.)

There was now a surprise. On September 27, a royal order reassigned Vizcaíno to the task of finding Rica de Oro and Rica de Plata—sailing as soon as possible from Manila with two ships. He would be given twenty thousand pesos pesos for provisioning the settlers of the new discoveries. In the event that the islands could not be found, he was authorized to proceed to California to establish the Monterey settlement. Viceroy Velasco remained skeptical of the existence of Rica de Oro and Rica de Plata, and there ensued considerable deliberation (and delay) in Mexico City over the plan. The strategy then shifted to the possibility of searching for the fabled islands directly from Nueva España.

Meanwhile, in Spain, there was renewed interest in the Strait of Anián after Commander Lorenzo Ferrer Maldonado sent the king a report in the summer of 1609 claiming to have sailed from Europe

---

61. Ibid., 112.

most of the way through it at about 60 degrees latitude before turning back. He claimed to have met some Hanseatic Lutherans who were using the passage to trade directly with China. He requested royal financing for a new expedition that would explore, map, and fortify the strait at its western terminus to keep other Europeans out of the Pacific. By 1610, the various possibilities were still under discussion in both Madrid and Mexico City, and Vizcaíno remained in Nueva España, immersed in his administrative duties and personal affairs.[62]

By the end of the first decade of the seventeenth century, Spain had negotiated with Japan the right to explore and chart part of its coast, given the need of Manila galleons to put in there. After sending their own diplomatic mission to the Spanish court, the Japanese agreed to receive both a Spanish ambassador and Christian missionaries. A Franciscan, Fray Luis Sotelo, became the key figure in the organization of the latter. It was now decided to incorporate the search for Rica de Oro and Rica de Plata into the Japanese initiative. Sebastián Vizcaíno was appointed both as Spain's new ambassador and as head of the combined explorations. On March 22, 1611, Vizcaíno departed Acapulco for Japan and landed there on June 10 after a harrowing crossing. He decreed that any Spaniard causing conflict with the Japanese would be subject to the death penalty. There then ensued a disagreement over protocol. Vizcaíno insisted that European custom be observed (he refused to remove his shoes and relinquish his arms) during the ceremony at which he was to present his diplomatic credentials to Hidetada, son of Emperor Iyeyasu. When told that this was unacceptable, Sebastián threatened to leave immediately for Nueva España, and the Japanese relented. Gifts were exchanged, and the Japanese acceded to many requests, except one: that Japan renounce the agreements that it had made with the Dutch. Vizcaíno had argued that they were rebellious subjects of Spain and therefore not legitimate parties to international agreements, but to no avail.

On October 23, Sebastián launched his voyage to chart the northern Japanese coast. Over the next month and a half, he gave Spanish names to many of its features, before abandoning the project in early December due to increasingly bad weather. During much of the following year, Vizcaíno made preparations for exploration of the

---

62. Ibid., 113–20.

North Pacific in quest of Rica de Oro and Rica de Plata. After hearing rumors from the English and Dutch that the Spaniards planned to use those islands as a base from which to invade Japan, Japanese officials insisted that Japanese accompany the Spaniards during the expedition. On July 9, 1612, Vizcaíno had a chilly meeting with Hidetada and was informed that while Japan still desired good relations with Spain, Christianity was now to be banned and its churches demolished. He was given permission to leave, gifts for the viceroy of Nueva España, and a loan of two thousand taels (the Japanese currency). On September 16, Vizcaíno departed Japan, planning to search for the fabled islands Rica de Oro and Rica de Plata, but without success. Then, on October 14, a major storm began that lasted for four days. On October 29, given that the *San Francisco* was no longer seaworthy, it was decided to return immediately to Japan, where they arrived on November 7. For the next several months, Vizcaíno was frustrated in his attempts to secure support for his return voyage to Nueva España. His embassy was now deemed unworthy of credit by Japanese officialdom and by Japan's Spanish merchant community alike. The highly stressed Sebastián fell seriously ill.

This allowed Fray Sotelo to take the initiative. By now, he had the full support of the powerful daimyo, or lord, of Sendai, Date Masamune. Fray Sotelo opposed the new anti-Christian policy and refused to dismantle his churches. He was imprisoned briefly, and after proving still adamant upon his release, was again detained and this time sentenced to be burned at the stake. Date Masamune intervened and saved Sotelo on condition that he leave Japan.

The daimyo wanted Franciscan missionaries in his territory. He was also disposed toward receiving and resupplying the Manila galleon, trading with the Spaniards, even allowing them to settle permanently in Sendai while retaining their own courts of law. He also promised to execute English, Dutch, and any other enemies of Spain found in his domain. Sotelo convinced Date Masamune to organize his own mission to the Spanish court for further negotiations. The daimyo agreed and appointed the friar as his personal ambassador.

Meanwhile, Date Masamune had contracted with Vizcaíno to support construction of the *San Juan Bautista* for the Europeans' return voyage to Nueva España. It departed under Vizcaíno's command on October 27, 1613, with Fray Sotelo and 180 Japanese (bound for Europe) on board. Once at sea, Sotelo and the Japanese effectively commandeered the vessel, and the still-ailing Vizcaíno was now a passenger on his own ship. The *San Juan Bautista* reached Acapulco on January 25, 1614, and Sotelo and his Japanese contingent shipped out for Spain on June 10. In the event, despite being received in Madrid and later at the Vatican, Sotelo's entourage was treated gingerly in Europe. There was the clear risk of antagonizing irrevocably the increasingly anti-Christian and anti-European shogun and his advisors, should the idiosyncratic proposals of a regional lord be implemented.[63]

On balance, Fray Sotelo's mission was a failure:

> As Vizcaíno, unhampered by religious zeal, had observed, Japanese policies were too variable to permit secure Spanish establishments in Japan, and within ten years after his return to New Spain, Vizcaíno's predictions were borne out by the closing of Japan to Spain, and an intense persecution of Christians. Furthermore, the loss of the Moluccas and other Dutch and English gains in the Pacific had left Spain little more than a few small islands and the Philippines as bases in the Far East.[64]

The Quirós and Torres Expeditions

Even while in Manila, after Mendaña's discovery of the Marquesas, Quirós seemed determined to return to them, as well as to explore beyond. Fearing that the English might colonize the islands and thereby challenge Spanish hegemony in the South Pacific, Quirós implored the Philippines' governor, Morga, to keep Mendaña's findings a secret. In 1597, Quirós was in Peru, pleading with Viceroy Velasco for support of a new expedition. He was urged instead to travel to Spain to make his case for royal approval and financing.

In 1600, Quirós was in Rome, where he secured the endorsement of the Spanish ambassador to the Vatican, various mathematicians and cosmographers, and eventually the pope, after a personal audience. In 1603, Quirós received royal approval of a modest expedition to the South Pacific, but only over the objections of Doña Isabel's new husband, who regarded himself to be the successor *adelantado* of the Solomons. That objection was disarmed by Quirós's pledge to restrict

---

63. Ibid., 135–53.
64. Ibid., 153.

his initiative to the Marquesas and any new discoveries. Clearly, his main goal was to find the elusive continental Terra Australis. Were he to fail in that effort, he would attempt to circumnavigate New Guinea to chart its coastline in order to determine definitively its island status. Having done this, he would sail on to Europe via the Cape of Good Hope, that being possible given the extant unification of Spain and Portugal.[65]

Quirós returned to Lima with a strongly worded letter from the king ordering Peru's new viceroy (none other than Gaspar de Zuñiga— just transferred from Nueva España) to prepare the expedition. Quirós was provided two vessels—the flagship *San Pedro y San Pablo* and the *almiranta San Pedro*—as well as a smaller launch for inshore work. Given his demanding character, undoubtedly, Peruvian officials felt relieved when he set sail from Callao on December 21, 1605.

Like his predecessor Mendaña, Quirós was a borderline religious fanatic, an obsession that placed his evangelical priorities squarely at odds with the more secular goals of most members of the expedition. We have noted the considerable Basque presence among Mendaña's crew and colonists, as well as its absence in the ranks of the leadership. We know less about the ethnic makeup of the Quirós expedition, but of the ninety-two members (out of the total of two hundred and fifty to three hundred persons) identified in the various accounts, approximately 10 percent had Basque surnames.[66]

The commander would have to endure the self-serving machinations of the most prominent man in the expedition, Don Diego de Prado y Tovar, and enjoyed the loyalty of his almirante, Luis Váez de Torres—both non-Basques. But there was also the acerbic criticism of Quirós's navigational skills (shades of Mendaña) by his chief pilot, the Basque Juan Ochoa de Bilbao.[67] Juan de Iturbe, the Basque-

---

65. Spate, *The Spanish Lake*, 133–34.

66. Celsus Kelly, *La Austrialia del Espíritu Santo: The Journal of Fray Martín De Munilla O.F.M. and Other Documents Relating to the Voyage of Pedro Fernández de Quirós to the South Seas (1605–1606) and the Franciscan Missionary Plan (1617–1627)*, 2 vols. (Cambridge: Cambridge University Press and Hakluyt Society, 1966), 2:373–76.

67. According to Prado's account of the expedition, Ochoa was born in Sevilla. Henry N. Stevens, ed., *New Light on the Discovery of Australia as Revealed by the Journal of Captain Don Diego de Prado y Tovar* (London: Hakluyt Society, 1930), 89. If so, he was likely descended from the extensive Basque colony established in the fifteenth century in that key Andalusian arterial in the American run.

surnamed accountant of the expedition, penned a comprehensive and not particularly flattering (of Quirós) account of the voyage.[68]

The seasonal winds of the South Seas were but poorly understood, and as it turned out, the expedition was tardy in departing. (In retrospect, Quirós would blame the delay on the viceroy's insistence upon a last-minute progress report.) In any event, the expedition failed to take advantage of the favorable southeast trade winds. While Mendaña had averaged twenty-seven leagues a day (and required but sixty-nine days to sail from Lima to Santa Cruz), Quirós's progress was more on the order of ten. On March 25, after ninety-four days of sailing without making a consequential landfall, a council was convened on board. There was considerable disagreement regarding the distance sailed thus far and as to the expedition's current location.

Ochoa de Bilbao's criticism of his commander's judgment resulted in his being reassigned from the flagship to the almiranta. In many regards, Ochoa was cut out of the same whole cloth as Pedro Sarmiento de Gamboa. Prado notes that

> the Chief Pilot, Juan Ochoa de Bilbao, for his good deeds had been sentenced to the galleys for six years in Cartagena, and the Viceroy commuted this sentence on condition that he should serve his Majesty in that voyage without pay, and on arriving at Manila, the chief and capital city of the Philippine Islands, he should then have completed his liability in regard to the galleys; but as this pilot had many debts to merchants in Lima he was seized for 16,000 ducats which they had entrusted to him and which he had gambled away; and so that his Majesty's service should not be hindered the said Viceroy agreed with the merchants that the said Quiros should be security and should undertake not to release him in Manila, but to deliver him up in Seville, when please God the President and Auditors of the Contratación would ship and forward him to Lima and deliver him to his creditors, which obligation the said Quirós undertook.[69]

At one point in the expedition, Prado was approached to lead a mutiny against Quirós, but refused to join in. He clearly informed his commander, and Quirós ordered "the Chief Pilot Juan Ochoa de

---

68. Spate, *The Spanish Lake*, 133. To my knowledge, there is no published record of Iturbe's birthplace and family background.

69. Don Diego de Prado y Tovar, in Stevens, *New Light*, 97.

Vilbao to be seized and taken to the Almiranta with verbal orders that he should be garroted at once and cast into the sea after confession." Prado advised Luis Vaez de Torres not to carry out the execution without written orders, reasoning that Ochoa was charged with delivering the pilot to his creditors at the end of the day. Down the road, Quirós might deny having even issued the death sentence, should the merchants of Lima protest over having lost their debtor. Thus was Ochoa saved from death.[70] Nor was he chastened or timid after this close call. At one point, the Spaniards were besieging some natives who had taken refuge in a mountaintop fortress. Ochoa and a Galician volunteered to scale the cliff together to attack the defenders. Halfway up the cliff face, they were pelted with stones and came tumbling down, losing their weapons and even the better part of their clothing along the way.[71]

Morale and water were both running dangerously low when, on April 7, the island of Tamauko, about 150 kilometers northwest of Santa Cruz, was sighted. The natives proved friendly and their chief helpful. He informed Quirós of the directions and names of many islands, including reference to the great land of "Manicolo" to the southeast. The Spaniards kidnapped four of the local islanders to serve as possible interpreters and set sail for the fabled continent. While rounding Tikopia, three of the captives escaped by swimming to shore. A week later, on May 1, the expedition arrived at a great mountainous land that Quirós pronounced to be "La Austrialia del Espíritu Santo."[72] As it turned out, Quirós had mistaken the largest island (3,885 square kilometers) of the New Hebrides for the southern continent, a land mass that to this day retains the name of Espíritu Santo. It was there that he declared the foundation of a phantasma-

---

70. Ibid., 113. It would seem that the foregoing is correct, since Ochoa de Bilbao was one of five signatories who confirmed the accuracy and authenticity of Prado's account. Ibid., 203–5.

71. Ibid., 153.

72. There is a degree of speculation regarding the intended semantics of the early denominations of the southern continent. "Terra Australis" seemingly refers to "Southern Land," whereas "Austrialia del Espíritu Santo" may well be a paean to both the royal house of Quirós's monarch (the Austrian Habsburgs) and his religious devotion. Landín Carrasco and Sánchez Masiá regard the latter term to be a double entendre that incorporates all of the above. Landín Carrasco and Sánchez Masiá, "Archipiélagos," 594.

goric city to be called nothing less than New Jerusalem, its port Vera Cruz, and its nearby river the Jordan.

Hostilities with the numerous natives broke out almost immediately, and a disconsolate Quirós soon had to accept that his hope of converting them to the faith was impractical. He further demonstrated his tenuous grasp on reality by ordering establishment of a Spanish municipality, replete with offices and magistrates. According to Spate, "On Pentecost Day, 14 May, he [Quirós] took possession of the lands, as far as the Pole, in the names of the Trinity, Jesus, St. Francis, John of God, and King Philip III."[73]

Quirós then instituted an Order of the Holy Ghost that blended secular chivalry with religion. The Franciscan friars in the expedition refused to wear the blue cross of the new order, arguing, much to Quirós's chagrin, it was against their vows. At this point, the commander suffered a nervous breakdown. Then, abruptly, on Corpus Christi Day, May 25, he announced that they would abandon the settlement and set off to explore new areas.

The expedition's three ships put out to sea, but a serious (if nonfatal) fish poisoning of the crew and adverse weather forced them back toward Vera Cruz. Quirós planned to fortify it. The almiranta and the launch managed the return, but the commander's ship, the capitana, was unable to reach shore. There is a degree of confusion in the accounts regarding the reason for their separation on the night of June 11, including the possibility of a mutiny aboard the commander's vessel. Opinion as to what to do next varied. On the flagship, some of the crew argued for sailing to Santa Cruz, others for attempting crossings to either Manila or Acapulco. Juan de Iturbe objected and argued in written protest that they should continue with exploration of the unknown.[74] In the event, the safer alternative of making for New Spain prevailed.

Quirós eventually returned to Spain, where he began years of writing requests for royal support of a new expedition. He also crafted several rather vainglorious and pathetic defenses of his lega-

---

73. Spate, *The Spanish Lake*, 136.
74. Kelly, *La Austrialia*, 356–58.

cy.[75] Quirós was given to claiming to be the second Columbus and also to comparing himself to Caesar, Hannibal, Alexander, Pyrrhus, da Gama, Magellan, Pizarro, and Cortés.[76] Iturbe weighed in with the opinion that a new expedition was indeed in order, but that it should not be under the command of Quirós, given his prior performance, which had disqualified his leadership.[77]

During Quirós's lengthy stay in Europe, in 1609, the Dutch East India Company contracted with an Englishman, Henry Hudson, to explore the North American Atlantic coast in search of the northern passage. While he mistook for it the river that bears his name, this commercial partnership by two of Spain's key rivals underscored the vulnerability of Spanish hegemony in Pacific waters. It would also initiate the North American colonization schemes of first the Dutch (the founding of New Amsterdam in 1624) and then the British (conversion of New Amsterdam to New York in 1664), developments that would ultimately threaten Spain's control of the Caribbean and Atlantic areas that had come to be known as the Spanish Main.

In 1614, Quirós, while still in Madrid, received a royal mandate to launch a new South Pacific exploration from Peru. It seems that the Spanish authorities feared both the telescoped intrusion into the Pacific by the English or other European powers and the possibility that a definitively spurned Quirós might offer his services and knowledge to one of the aspiring usurpers among the foreign monarchs. In the event, it proved academic when Quirós died in Mexico en route to Peru to take up his charge.[78]

While the 1605–1606 Quirós expedition had proven, on balance, to be a failure, it did leave one impressive legacy. After the separation of the capitana and almiranta at Vera Cruz, Luis Vaez de Torres, in command of the latter, resolved to continue exploring the South Seas. He skirted the coast of Espíritu Santo sufficiently to determine that it was an island, rather than the southern continent. He then sailed to the southwest without making land. So he altered his course to the

75. Spate, *The Spanish Lake*, 137–38; Landín Carrasco and Sánchez Masiá, "Archipiélagos," 595–97.

76. Spate, *The Spanish Lake*, 141, 323.

77. Kelly, *La Austrialia*, 356–65.

78. Landín Carrasco and Sánchez Masiá, "Archipiélagos," 596–97.

northwest and navigated accurately to the southeastern extremity of New Guinea. It was there that he decided to enter the treacherous strait that to this day bears his name, likely sighting Australia's Cape York Peninsula in the bargain.

Torres then made his way up the west coast of New Guinea, taking possession of parts of it for Spain. Eventually, he arrived in Manila, whence he sent details of his discoveries to Quirós, who then incorporated them into his incessant stream of memorials. Indeed, despite the efforts of the Spanish crown to suppress such information, some of it found its way into print and was then translated into foreign languages. In this fashion, Europe's awareness and knowledge of the South Pacific was expanding, auguring future challenges to its status as the "Spanish Lake."[79]

Decline of the Luso-Hispanic World Empire

For more than a century and a half after the Quirós/Torres expedition (1605–1606), there were scarcely any new Spanish initiatives in the South Pacific. It would seem that the combined failures of Medaña and Quirós to find the fabulous treasure portended in the Solomon and Ophir fables had finally dissuaded the dreamers. Save for a few exploratory thrusts of little consequence, from a European standpoint, the South Pacific entered a deep slumber. So although the Pacific region remained under nominal Spanish hegemony, it was so remote as to be beyond the pale of contemporary concern as Spain entered into a period of profound economic and political crisis at home and with respect to other ascendant European powers.

This is not to say that there were not those who advocated Pacific exploration. Of particular note were the attempts of the Franciscans to secure support from the Spanish monarch for further probes of the South Pacific in search of the Austral continent that was surely located there. Their primary concern was the spiritual fate of its inhabitants. The Franciscans enlisted the assistance of one of the most renowned cosmographers and mathematicians of the day, the Basque-surnamed

---

79. Spate, *The Spanish Lake*, 138–43.

secular priest Juan Luis Arias de Loyola.[80] In his capacity as the former chronicler of the Indies in the Royal History Academy, he had written regarding the transpacific voyage of Juan Fernández that discovered a southern landmass between Tierra del Fuego and New Guinea, possibly New Zealand.[81]

In about 1621, Arias de Loyola wrote his *Memorial presentado por el Doctor Don Juan Luis Arias al Infante Don Fernando [de Austria] dándole cuenta de los descubrimientos verificados en el Hemisferio Austral y entre ellos él de Juan Fernández, a fin de que se interesase la conquista espiritual de sus habitadores* (Memorial presented by Doctor Don Juan Luis Arias to the Infante Don Fernando [of Austria] informing him of the verified discoveries in the Southern Hemisphere and among them that of Juan Fernández, for the purpose of arousing interest in the spiritual conquest of their inhabitants). The document cited the voyages of Mendaña, Quirós, and Vaez de Torres, as well.[82] Arias de Loyola argued that the Spanish crown had contracted with the Vatican to propagate the faith everywhere and was therefore under obligation to do so in the South Pacific. Furthermore, the astronomical and geographical evidence from the region suggested the existence there of a vast fertile land. Invoking an analogy with China, he suggested that the presence of vast archipelagos such as those encountered by Mendaña and Quirós portended the nearby presence of a large land mass.[83] The initiative was stillborn when the

---

80. Between 1591 and 1595, Arias de Loyola was the lecturer regarding geography and navigation in the Royal Mathematical Academy. Manuel Esteban Piñeiro, "Las academias técnicas en la España del siglo xvi," *Quaderns d'Historia de l'Enginyeria* 5 (2003–2004): 12. In 1603, Arias de Loyola, along with Luis de Fonseca Coutiño, was reputed to have discovered the famed "fixed point" determination of the compass that was so critical to calculating longitude. In 1611 and 1612, he was at court seeking to claim a monetary prize and lifelong pension from the king should his calculations regarding fixation of the compass and the determination of longitude prove verifiable, see Kelly, *Calendar of Documents*, 69. Ten years later, he was still at it while complaining that were he to reveal his secret calculations, he should be compensated with considerably more than was being considered. Ibid., 317, 325. Indeed, the Arias de Loyola initiative was so well known that the famed poet Francisco de Quevedo made reference to it in his work *Los sueños* (1627).

81. Kelly, *Calendar of Documents*, 122.

82. Indeed, in one of his many petitions (1610) to the king for support of a new expedition, Quirós proposed taking Arias de Loyola along. Ibid., 270.

83. Ibid., 329–30.

government agreed to authorize further expeditions—but only with private financing and/or that of the Franciscans themselves.

The situation regarding the Californias was somewhat different. By this time, as we have seen, there had been several expeditions to both Baja and Alta California, and both were well situated strategically along the Manila run. Then, too, reports (and a little bit of evidence) of their wealthy pearl fisheries had persisted for nearly a century, since the Cortés-sponsored explorations during the 1520s and 1530s. Similarly enduring were the rumors of fabled mineral wealth to be found in the interior of the vast North American continent. The prospects of pearls, gold, and with the ultimate prize of possibly finding the Strait of Anián thrown in for good measure all underpinned one proposal after another to probe further Nueva España's northern hinterland.

Of particular relevance to this account was the approval in 1611 by King Philip III of a partnership headed by a court favorite, Tomás de Cardona, for a ten-year exclusive license to exploit the pearl fisheries of Spain's maritime possessions.[84] At the same time, its vessels were to be at the disposition of the royal authorities whenever it was deemed necessary. The crown was to receive one-fifth of the profits.

In July of 1613, six boats departed Spain for the New World under the command of Francisco Basilio, with Nicolás Cardona, nephew of the founding partner, Tomás, second in command. The fleet engaged in pearling off several islands in the Caribbean, acquiring twenty-eight black slaves who were to be the divers. (Ever since 1585, it was prohibited to use Indians for this purpose, since blacks were seen as much better suited for the task.)[85]

In 1614, the expedition reached Acapulco, where it began construction of three vessels. By this time, Basilio had died, and Nicolás Cardona was the nominal commander—sharing authority with Pedro Álvarez de Rosales and Juan de Iturbe. This was the same Iturbe who participated in the earlier Quirós exploration in the South Seas. The Cardona Company undertook construction of the *San Francisco*, *San Antonio*, and *San Diego* in Acapulco, intended for a pearling expedi-

---

84. Sanford A. Mosk, "The Cardona Company and the Pearl Fisheries of Lower California," *Pacific Historical Review* 3, no. 1 (March 1934): 50–51.

85. Ibid., 51–52.

tion in the Gulf of California. But in 1515, when the fleet was ready to leave for the north, it was learned that the feared Dutch pirate Joris van Speilbergen had passed through the Strait of Magellan with five or six boats. He had ravaged the South American coast and was now in the North Pacific. The mayor of Acapulco prohibited the departure of the three Cardona vessels in order to shore up his port's defenses. When, after two months, the pirate failed to appear, the little fleet was allowed to sail.

Their landfall was the site where Vizcaíno had been attacked by Indians in 1596, and the Cardona fleet received a hostile reception, as well. However, they unleashed two mastiffs upon the terrified Indians. The expedition engaged in pearl diving over the next several months. Iturbe then learned from the Indians that they had spotted a "house on the water," (likely a Speilbergen vessel), and the *San Francisco*, under command of Nicolás de Cardona, was seized by the Dutch off of La Navidad. They were lurking there, awaiting the arrival of the Manila galleon. Some of Cardona's crew escaped by swimming ashore, but many seamen, two friars, and eleven black divers were captured. The ship itself was renamed the *Perel* (Pearl in Dutch) and pressed into Speilbergen's service.[86]

The Dutch corsair now proceeded to Salagua and went ashore there in search of supplies, unaware that four hundred men under the command of none other than Sebastián Vizcaíno lay in ambush. There was a fierce fight. Speilbergen later wrote that the Dutch had killed many of the defenders while suffering minimal losses. Vizcaíno reported the opposite to his monarch, speaking of the enemies' "enormous losses" in his account. To underscore his point, Vizcaíno sent a pair of ears cut off the head of a Dutch corpse.

Iturbe, unaware of Cardona's fate, continued pearling for several more months. Then, at one point, he sighted a foreign ship and sent word to Acapulco. In November of 1616, Iturbe arrived back in Acapulco. He declared fourteen ounces of pearls to be his results, although it is clear that this was blatant underreporting.[87] Tomás de

---

86. Garikano, *Kaliforniakoak*, 70–71.
87. Mosk, "The Cardona Company," 59–60.

Cardona, in his memoirs, spoke ill of Iturbe, possibly out of envy of his captain's newfound personal wealth.[88]

There is another wrinkle to the story. It is part of the lore of contemporary treasure hunters that Iturbe dispatched a ship heavily laden with pearls to the north, believing that the Colorado River let into the Strait of Anián. The idea was to send to Europe by this route a smuggled cargo worth a vast fortune. It is believed that the ship ran aground in some small channel of the river's delta and periodically appears and disappears to this day according to the shifting of the sands.[89]

Over the next six decades, there were a series of contracts for pearling monopolies awarded by the crown in the Gulf of California, all of which attracted commercial sojourners, rather than serious explorers to the area, let alone intending settlers. Then, in 1678, there was a policy shift. There now would be an attempt actually to colonize California, financed by the crown itself. The following year, the Navarrese Isidro de y Antillón, governor of Sinaloa, was appointed to head the project. Within a five-year time frame, he was to establish a fortified colony in California. Since its long-term success depended upon evangelizing the Indians, three Jesuit priests were assigned to the expedition. These were the Italian Eusebio Francesco Chini (Eusebio Francisco Kino), Antonio Suaréz, and Matías Goñi. Not only were Goñi and Atondo from the same part of Navarra, they were also friends.

Preparations, including construction of the flagship *La Concepción* and the almirantas *San José* and *San Francisco Xavier* (named for the Navarrese Jesuit saint), took four long years. It was not until January 17, 1683, that the fleet, with more than a hundred persons on board, including some baptized Indian men and women for servants, departed Port Chacala for California. Everyone was under strict orders not to abuse the pagan Indians in any fashion and not to steal objects from them under pain of death. Given the sad history between Spaniards and California Indians, and particularly that with

88. Garikano, *Kaliforniakoak*, 73
89. Ibid., 73–74.

the European pearlers, extreme kindness and respect were likely the only means of winning them over.[90]

The fleet sailed to La Paz and disembarked. The intending colonists began constructing dwellings and other buildings and took possession of the site in the name of their monarch. At one point, it appeared that armed Indians were about to attack.

> As they approached, the Spanish soldiers ran to their defenses; but the intrepid Atondo, choosing different tactics, threw himself in front of their leaders and with terrific yells and assumed fierceness challenged the entire multitude. Such gallant bravery was too much for the Indian warriors. Such a voice as that of Atondo they had never before heard; such a fearful spectacle as he presented they had never before seen: for the moment they were paralyzed with astonishment; and, as Atondo advanced, they precipitately turned their backs and fled in disorder to their rancherias. Thus was the battle fought and won, like some of those depicted in Homer, by mere strength of lungs.[91]

But then relations deteriorated further. A few days later, an Indian wounded a Spaniard with an arrow, was caught, and then imprisoned. Meanwhile, one of the colonists disappeared, apparently killed by the Indians. (As it turned out, he had committed some sort of crime and voluntarily joined the Indians out of fear of punishment.) Then a group of warriors appeared in camp, demanding the release of their companion. Atondo convinced them to sit down to a meal, and when they were collected together at a table, on his order, a cannon was discharged, with the blast killing ten of them.

The Europeans were now clearly in a state of war with the tribe, and their food was running low. Two months earlier, a ship had been dispatched to Sinaloa for supplies, but it had not returned. So morale plummeted, and some of the colonists petitioned either to abandon the project or at least to move the colony to a more favorable location. A meeting was held that approved the latter move.

On October 6, 1683, the expedition sailed up the Gulf of California, stopping ten leagues north of Loreto. Again they began construction, which included a fort. On November 30, Atondo took formal

---

90. Ibid., 74–75.

91. Theodore H. Hittell, *History of California*, 4 vols. (San Francisco: N. J. Stone, 1898), 1:157.

possession of the new site, now named San Bruno. The Indians here proved to be much more peaceful than the ones at La Paz, and over the next few months, the Jesuits made inroads with their evangelization. By the end of a year, about four hundred Indians were desirous of baptism, but the friars were hesitant. The future of the colony was doubtful. Various expeditions had proven the surrounding areas to be arid and barren. The colony's crops failed, the local water supply was poor, and the climate was harsh.

Atondo sent two vessels north—one to explore further the coast in search of a better place for the colony and the other to engage in pearling. Both were failures. Then, too, there were new rumors of Dutch corsairs penetrating the area, and Atondo was now ordered to warn the Manila galleon. With his supplies and spirits dwindling, in May of 1685, he decided to abandon the colony and return to Nueva España.[92]

Back in Nueva España, Atondo petitioned for further official support and funding for a return expedition to San Bruno. However, his first expedition had been a major financial fiasco, and the crown now faced serious Indian rebellions in both Nueva Vizcaya and Nuevo México. His request was denied, and he slipped into obscurity. However, his expedition had not been a total failure. At one point, he had led the only land crossing to that date of the peninsula of Baja California.

Then, too, perhaps emboldened by their success at San Bruno, the Jesuits named Fray Juan María Salvatierra to head a California mission project. A Basque priest and professor of philosophy at the Jesuit College in Mexico City, Juan de Ugarte, was appointed fundraiser and treasurer for the future California missions. In 1697, the Jesuits returned to San Bruno and established the Loreto mission, which became the main base from which to evangelize Baja California over the next seven decades.[93] They founded seventeen missions in Baja. Out of the total of sixty-two Jesuit missionaries over that period, ten

92. Ibid., 1:158–60.

93. Garikano, *Kaliforniakoak*, 86–88. Less fortuitous were the missionary activities in Guam. In 1672, several missionaries were killed there by the natives, triggering thirty years of violence. In 1688, the Jesuits established the first permanent missions on the island. Dodge, *Islands and Empires*, 85. This persistence mirrored that of the civil authorities, since there was interest in establishing Guam as a mid-Pacific garrison and resupply port on the Manila run.

were of Basque descent. The Jesuits, desirous of erasing the unfortunate history of Indian-white relations, created their own fiefdom in the region, prohibiting both European settlement and pearling activities.[94]

94. William A. Douglass and Jon Bilbao, *Amerikanuak: Basques in the New World* (Reno: University of Nevada Press, 1975), 179–80.

6

Twilight of the Spanish Pacific

By now, Spain's real challenges were back in the Iberian homeland, with its frequently rocky and shifting alliances with its European neighbors. What follows[1] is a brief outline of the many salient factors that had arguably stretched Spain to the limit.

As we have noted, during the sixteenth century, under Charles V and then his son, Philip II, Spain became the preeminent military power in the Occident, the bulwark against Ottoman expansion in the Mediterranean, and the phalanx of the Counter-Reformation in Northern Europe, as well as increasingly the prime source of the supply of precious metals underpinning the continent's monetary system. Spanish military supremacy within Europe and Spain's expansion in both the Americas and the Orient placed heavy financial burdens upon the crown—translating into considerable dependence upon both domestic and foreign lenders, as well as periodic economic crises and collapses. Yet in 1600, Spain and Portugal combined had but slightly more population (between nine and nine and a half million inhabitants) than contiguous France alone.

Spain's European holdings (primarily the Low Countries, northern Italy, and the Kingdom of Naples) were far from ideally distributed with respect to their military defense. While Spain was nominally a part of the Habsburg dynasty, after the death of Charles V, the kinship ties underpinning such an alliance were more distant and less dependable. An obsession with controlling the political and religious destiny of the Low Countries embroiled Madrid in nearly a century of military engagements that excluded Spain from the benefits of the dramatic rise of the Dutch economy and that emboldened

---

1. For greater detail, see Stanley Payne, *A History of Spain and Portugal*, 2 vols. (Madison: University of Wisconsin Press, 1973), vol. 1, chapters 13–15.

an ascendant England to support its Protestant coreligionists. France, particularly under Louis XIV, viewed Spanish territories as targets of opportunity, prompting several wars between the two Southern European powers.

A self-centered Catholic hierarchy and aristocracy also challenged a weakened Spanish crown repeatedly throughout the mid-seventeenth century. Their combined gains undermined the state's income and its capacity to govern. Such problems were exacerbated by hyperinflation, scarcities of goods, the venality of bureaucrats, and periodic famine and plague.

Finally, with the passage of time, Spain's New World colonies matured into political and economic entities in their own right. Accordingly, New World–born *criollos* were increasingly less willing to follow blindly Madrid's lead, particularly with regard to Spanish mercantilism. Spain's American colonies were developing their own industries and markets. They were also becoming liabilities as both potential supporters of clandestine contraband commerce with foreign merchants (primarily Dutch) and possible targets of foreign aggression (primarily English).

These developments in Europe and Hispanic America placed Spain and Portugal on the defensive in both the Americas and in the Orient. While the unification of the Spanish and Portuguese thrones (1580–1640) ushered in a greater degree of Iberian collaboration, it also produced its own new challenges. In 1581 the Dutch rebelled against King Philip II's rule and thereby lost their access to trade with Lisbon—mainly in spices. In effect, that globalized the conflict, one that would endure for nearly three decades, until the independence of the Netherlands in 1607, since Dutch forces would test Portuguese/Spanish hegemony in both Latin America and Asia. In 1598, two Dutch freebooting expeditions passed through the Strait of Magellan into the Pacific. The one under the command of Oliver De Noort raided along the Spanish Pacific coast as far north as Panama. De Noort returned to Europe by crossing the Pacific and rounding Africa—thereby becoming the fourth man to circumnavigate the globe, after Magellan/Elkano, Drake, and Cavendish. Then, in 1609, Spain signed a treaty with the newly independent Netherlands that recognized and legitimated Dutch maritime penetration throughout the world.[2]

Nor were the Dutch alone in challenging Luso-Hispanic hegemony. In 1607, the English settled Jamestown, and the following year, the French founded New France in the future Quebec. As early as 1624, the British were ensconced on the island of St. Kitts, and that same year, a Dutch naval force, furthering the interests of the Dutch West Indies Company, attacked and occupied Brazil. Meanwhile, another Dutch naval incursion passed through the Strait of Magellan and provided the Chilean and Peruvian coasts with a reprise of De Noort's earlier predations, even triggering a serious naval encounter at Callao.[3] In 1634, the Dutch annexed Curaçao and two years later Aruba. In 1635, the French established a settlement at Martinique, and the English acquired Jamaica in 1655. These developments went largely unchallenged by the overextended and weakened Spain and Portugal. All were to become both centers from which to conduct contraband trade with Spanish and Portuguese colonies and launching pads for piracy against Spanish shipping in the Caribbean. In short, parts of northern South America and the Caribbean had become windows of vulnerability for the former Luso-Hispanic hegemony and of opportunity for the other European maritime powers.

There were also developments in Indonesia that portended ill for Spain's Pacific interests. Although by 1522 Portugal had established a presence in Jakarta, one that Spain would acquire (if but indirectly) when Philip II became king of Portugal in 1580, by century's end, such Luso-Hispanic influence was under serious challenge. In 1600, Queen Elizabeth chartered the British East India Company, and two years later, there was a Dutch East India Company, as well. In 1596, the Dutch constructed their own facilities in Jakarta and quickly emerged as its dominant European power. They also quickly captured Tidore and Ternate. In 1602, the British East India Company acquired a trading post nearby, and in 1615, the local sultan allied with a British force to attack the Dutch. The initiative failed, and by

2. Samuel Eliot Morison, *The European Discovery of America*, vol. 2, *The Southern Voyages*, A.D. 1492–1616 (New York: Oxford University Press, 1974), 729–31.

3. C. R. Boxer, *The Portuguese Seaborne Empire: 1415–1825* (New York: Alfred A. Knopf, 1969), 109; Malyn Newitt, *A History of Portuguese Overseas Expansion, 1400–1668* (London: Routledge, 2005), 223–26.

1619, the Dutch asserted colonial hegemony over Indonesia—renaming Jakarta as Batavia. Then, in 1664, King Henri IV launched the French East India Company and ordered that thirty vessels for it be constructed.[4]

In sum, by the early seventeenth century, non-Iberian European nations were acquiring both Southeast Asian and Caribbean strongholds and staging areas from which to probe the unknown Pacific world beyond.

Arguably, then, the Spanish neglect of the South Pacific at this time was due in large measure to the eclipsing of Spain's overly extended state and imperial power. It was a historical juncture at which all of the European powers were challenged by the extraordinarily sanguinary conflict that came to be known as the Thirty Years' War (1618–1648). The resulting Peace of Westphalia underscored that Spanish power had passed its zenith and was in decline. Spain was forced to give official recognition to Dutch independence. Also, partway through the conflict, in 1640, Portugal regained its sovereignty, allied with the anti-Habsburg side of the wider European conflagration, and then continued its belligerency with Spain for two decades after the Westphalia agreements. This, of course, interdicted Luso-Hispanic collaboration in voyages of discovery such as that reflected in the second Mendaña and Quirós expeditions.

The critical turning point occurred in 1700 with the death of the childless Spanish monarch Charles II. He had named his half sister's grandson, Philip, Duke of Anjou, as his heir. Philip was also the grandson of the French king, Louis XIV, prompting the Austrians, Portuguese, English, and Dutch to fear that Europe's balance of power was endangered by events in Spain. This triggered the Spanish War of Succession (1700–1713), which embroiled most European powers and led to British attacks upon Spanish (and French) colonial interests.

There would be no clear-cut resolution of the conflict, but the redefining Treaty of Utrecht obviously penalized the Spanish/French side the most. In return for recognition of Philip V as the successor of Charles II, it was agreed that he would renounce all claims to the French throne. Several key French princes were required to relinquish any possible birthright to the Spanish kingship. France conceded to

---

4. Morison, *The Southern Voyages*, 731.

Great Britain both territory and commercial rights in Canada. Spain lost most of her European holdings in the southern Low Countries, as well as in northern Italy to Austria. Portugal regained from Spain what is present-day Uruguay, and the contested boundaries of Brazil were recognized in favor of the Portuguese. Spain was forced to cede Gibraltar and Minorca to Great Britain. The British were also accorded the *asiento*, or right, to sell slaves within the Spanish colonies for the next thirty years.[5]

On balance, Spain had been pulled within the sphere of influence of an ascendant France, with considerable attendant restraints upon its independence of action and with its ties to the Habsburgs now severed after nearly two centuries. Spanish power and territory within Europe had both been diminished, and Spain's capacity to exercise a monopoly over the commerce with its own colonies had been compromised. In 1739, the so-called War of Jenkins' Ear with Great Britain broke out. Ostensibly, the issue was Spanish aggression in boarding British ships to countermand illicit smuggling, particularly that organized from British Jamaica. The bigger concern was Spain's desire to abrogate the *asiento* agreement prematurely. At the outset of the hostilities, the British sent one expeditionary force to assault the Spanish Main, while another, under command of Commodore George Anson, was dispatched to the South Pacific.

In many regards, the Anson initiative was so ill conceived and poorly planned that it cost the lives of nearly three-quarters of the nineteen hundred men aboard the eight vessels. (All but a few died of illness or starvation, rather than in combat.) The British fleet did manage, however, to intimidate the Spanish colonies of the southern South American coast. It almost intercepted (near Acapulco) a Manila galleon and in 1743 eventually captured the *Covadonga*, a heavily laden Acapulco treasure ship, in Asian waters. Components of the Anson force managed to occupy Juan Fernández Island off the Chilean coast. The fact that Anson managed to operate with relative impunity for more than two years in Pacific waters clearly underscored the tenuousness of Spain's hold on the region. This was reinforced in

---

5. Great Britain was also accorded sovereignty over Canada's Atlantic fishing grounds and promptly denied Spanish fishermen, in the main Basques, access to them.

1762, when, as a part of the Seven Years' War, English forces under William Draper and Samuel Cornish occupied Manila and plundered the city, holding it until 1764, when it was returned to Spain under a peace treaty between the belligerents.

In the immediate aftermath of the Seven Years' War, the uninhabited Falkland Islands became the object of a three-way power struggle. Arguably astride the gateway to the Strait of Magellan, the Falklands afforded strategic leverage over access to the South Pacific. The first move was the personal initiative of Louis Antoine de Bougainville, who, at his own expense, in 1763 established the French colony of Port Saint Louis there, on Berkeley Sound. Unaware of its existence, in 1765 the Englishman John Byron founded a Falklands settlement at Port Egmont. An alarmed Spain pressured the French government into forcing Bougainville to sell his claim, and he did so in 1766. Henceforth, Port Saint Louis was to be administered from Buenos Aires.[6]

In that same year, Great Britain dispatched the *Dolphin* to the South Seas, under the command of Samuel Wallis, accompanied by the *Swallow*, captained by Philip Carteret, to search for the rumored southern continent. They entered the Pacific through the Strait of Magellan, but then failed to find Australia. The expedition did, however, discover Tahiti and the island (Wallis) that would bear its commander's name. He completed his circumnavigation of the globe, arriving back in England in May of 1768, just in time to give James Cook navigational information before the latter's departure on his own first voyage of discovery.

Meanwhile, in 1768, as well, Bougainville outfitted the *Bourdeuse* at his own expense and was then formally authorized by the French government to explore the South Pacific. He, too, would round southern South America and complete another European circumnavigation

---

6. In 1770, an attack was launched from Argentina that extricated the British from Port Egmont, nearly precipitating war between Spain and Great Britain. The following year, it was returned to the British by virtue of a treaty. However, in 1774, in light of the impending American Revolution, the British began withdrawing from several New World footholds, including Port Egmont. From 1776 to 1811, it was administered by Spain as a Spanish possession until abandoned during the South American Wars of Liberation. Neither Great Britain nor Spain (and subsequently Argentina) ever formally renounced sovereignty over the Falklands— counterclaims that would culminate in their late-twentieth-century Falklands War.

of the globe. He failed to make any significant new discoveries, but managed to visit Tahiti a few months after Wallis's discovery of it. The following year, the French navigator Jean François de Surville visited unexplored (by Europeans) parts of Álvaro de Mendaña's Solomon Islands.

By this time, the European Enlightenment was in full swing, and the resulting privileging of scientific curiosity could scarcely fail to inform exploration of the South Pacific—the planet's least understood watery realm. Bougainville was an inveterate collector of specimens; the colorful bougainvillea plant remains his floral memorial. Perhaps the best example of this new spirit is evident in one of the missions of the first Cook voyage. Its chief botanist, Joseph Banks, whose very inclusion signals the shifting emphasis informing contemporary exploration, was charged with observing from Tahiti the transit of Venus across the Sun on June 3, 1769, in combination with similar observations to be made on that date by astronomers in Europe. By correlating the two perspectives, it was hoped that the distance between the Earth and the Sun could be calculated more accurately. The Cook expedition dallied for three months in Tahiti, and there was considerable fraternizing among the ships' crews and the indigenous population. Banks was fascinated by the Tahitians' language and customs and later wrote one of the pioneering anthropological texts, entitled *On the Manners and Customs of the South Sea Islands*.

The Belated Boenechea

Given all of the foregoing, in 1771, a clearly alarmed, though financially strapped, government in Madrid ordered Peru's viceroy, Manuel Amat y Junyent, to show the flag in the South Pacific. Amat resolved to sponsor an expedition that would target both Tahiti and Easter Island (the latter first "discovered" by the Dutch in 1722 and then visited briefly by Captain Felipe González in 1770, who claimed it for the king of Spain). It was an enterprise designed to explore two Pacific societies while determining the extent to which other European powers might already be engaged with them, thereby challenging Spain's longstanding claim to sovereignty throughout the region. Amat commissioned the veteran Gipuzkoan naval commander Domingo de Boenechea to organize the expedition.

Viceroy Amat personally supervised the preparations. Budgetary constraints limited the expedition to a single frigate—*El Águila*. On September 22, 1772, the viceroy gave the commander his sealed orders, not to be opened until he was ten leagues at sea. Amat (again as a cost-saving measure) had conflated the two objectives into a single voyage that was not to last more than six months. Upon opening his orders, Boenechea learned that it was left up to him and his officers to determine their itinerary and timetable. They decided to set out first for Tahiti and then to return to Valparaíso for supplies before continuing on to Easter Island. Regarding Tahiti, their mission included rectification of any errors or lacunae in Captain Cook's observations made there during his first voyage to the Pacific (1768–1771). Boenechea was to study the possibility of establishing a colony and Catholic mission while ascertaining whether the British had already colonized the island. Despite the limitations placed upon him by the tight six-month schedule, he was to avoid making sweeping, superficial, and largely useless observations such as those of Easter Island provided recently by Captains González and Ortiz. At both of its prescribed destinations, the present expedition was to identify specific sites for future construction of a fort and chapel. Boenechea was to treat the natives—their languages and cultures—with utmost respect. Hostilities were to be avoided, as was fraternizing with the women. He was to assign persons to learn the local languages and customs with an eye toward facilitating future good relations. Since it was "the purpose of the expedition to attract new souls to the Christian religion and new subjects to the king,"[7] the natives were to be cajoled, rather than coerced, into understanding and accepting Spanish spiritual guidance and political claims.

Having left Callao on September 26, 1772, and having visited several Pacific Islands along the way, on November 8, *El Águila* anchored off the coast of Tahiti. Boenechea immediately named the island "Amat." The natives welcomed the Europeans with enthusiasm, a carryover from their recent good experience with the English. The latter, however, had departed after leaving behind but a scattering of

---

7. Amancio Landín Carrasco and Luis Sánchez Masiá, "Los viajes promovidos por el virrey Amat," in *Descubrimientos españoles en el Mar del Sur*, 3 vols., Amancio Landín Carrasco et al. (Madrid: Editorial Naval, 1992), 3:729–31.

memories and a sprinkling of trade goods. To the Spaniards' relief, there would be no immediate competition over the European political hegemony of Tahiti.

During the next several weeks, the expedition carried out its orders scrupulously and without untoward incidents, befriending the locals and charting the entire coastline of their large island. The contrast with earlier bellicose encounters between Spanish expeditions and Pacific Islanders could not have been starker.[8] On December 21, Boenechea set sail for Valparaíso, arriving some sixty-one days and seventeen hundred leagues later off the Chilean coast on February 21, 1773. Since it had been nearly five months since his departure from Callao, it was simply impossible to include a meaningful visit to Easter Island within the time limits of the expedition's mandate. So he decided to return to the Peruvian port.

Boenechea had invited four young Tahitians to accompany him on his return voyage. One of them died in Valparaíso, a possible victim of scurvy. Before succumbing, he was baptized and given the Christian name of Francisco Boenechea. It seems likely that the commander was his godfather and that he conferred on the young man his own father's name.[9]

By now, the British were in control of the Falkland Islands, a critical entry point to the Strait of Magellan, and Cook's successes were inspiring preparations for further explorations of the Pacific, including Alta California. Encouraged by Boenechea's positive report concerning his stay in Tahiti, the Spanish naval minister and minister of the Council of the Indies, Julián de Arriaga,[10] urged Amat to found

---

8. Ibid., 3:747–55.

9. Ibid., 3:758.

10. Arriaga is clearly a Basque surname. Actually, he was most likely born in Segovia, and both of his parents were likewise of Castilian birth. Regarding his ancestry, it could be stated, "The paternal grandfather, Julián Manuel, following in the footsteps of his father and grandfather, had been a councilman and magistrate in several Castilian cities, like Ávila, Segovia or Burgos, land of his ancestors and of himself, these cities being not only the birthplace of his children but of several of his grandchildren as well." María Baudot Monroy, "Orígenes familiares y carrera profesional de Julián de Arriaga, Secretario de Estado de Marina de Indias (1700–1776)," *Espacio, Tiempo y Forma, Serie IV, Historia Moderna* 17 (2004): 166. Nor did the Julián of the naval ministry ever display throughout his career any particular tie to the Basque Country or penchant for a Basque identity. Such facts have not precluded Arriaga from being treated as a Basque—for example, see Juan Carlos Maestro Castaneda, "Orígenes y formación marinera de un gran hombre de estado: Julián de Arriaga (1700–1749)," in *Euskal*

a permanent colony on the island as Spain's bulwark in the South Pacific.

It was decided that the *El Águila*, commanded by Boenechea despite his by then frail health, and the smaller packet boat *Júpiter*, captained by (Basque-surnamed) José de Andía, would return as soon as possible to Tahiti. Pautú, a baptized Tahitian who had sailed to Peru with the commander after the first expedition, accompanied Boenechea as interpreter. The second voyage departed Callao on September 20, 1774. However, the *Júpiter* was hard-pressed to keep up with the faster flagship, and on October 5, the two vessels lost contact. They were not to be reunited until Andía reached Tahiti on November 15, a day later than Boenechea.[11]

After his two-year absence, the return of Pautú was greeted by the Tahitians with much jubilation.[12] Accompanying Boenechea were two Franciscan friars charged with establishing a church. One of the commander's first acts in Tahiti was to convene the local leaders to determine if they would accept a Christian mission in their midst. They agreed enthusiastically and promised assistance. Construction of a dwelling for the Franciscans began immediately, and on the first day of 1775, the completed mission house was consecrated during the first Christian mass on Tahitian soil. The local leaders committed to protect the missionaries and to feed them, if necessary. They also accepted Carlos III as their monarch. So Boenechea had realized both the religious and the secular goals of his mandate.

José de Andía wrote an extensive account of the expedition, laced with detailed natural-historical and ethnographic observations. Among the latter, he noted the presence among the native population of blond, blue-eyed individuals.[13]

Herria y el Nuevo Mundo: La contribución de los vascos a la formación de las Américas, ed. Ronald Escobedo Mansilla, Ana de Zaballa Beascoechea, and Óscar Álvarez Gila (Vitoria-Gasteiz: Servicio Editorial, Universidad del País Vasco, 1996), 285–91. It has even been claimed that he must be Bizkaian, but without specifying a birthplace—for example, by Eduardo de Urrutia, "Julián de Arriaga," in "Galería biográfica de vascos ilustres," *Euskalerriaren alde: Revista de cultura vasca* 4, nos. 76–77 (1914): 102.

11 Landín Carrasco and Sánchez Masiá, "Los viajes," 770.

12 Ibid., 771–72.

13 Ibid., 774.

In the first days of 1775, however, Boenechea became mortally ill. On January 26, he died and was buried next to the mission house. With the Spaniards having completed their exploration and documentation of Tahiti and nearby islands, Boenechea's successor, Tomás de Gayangos y de Morquecho, resolved to return to Peru. By then, the two Franciscan friars had lost their nerve and insisted upon leaving with him. When denied permission, as well as their request for bodyguards, should they stay, the friars reluctantly remained behind alone—but with the assurance that they would be repatriated later that same year, should they so desire. In September, a third expedition, again utilizing the *El Águila*, was sent from Callao to Tahiti under the command of (Basque-surnamed) Juan Cayetano de Lángara. The expedition was aborted on November 12, when the two friars insisted upon being repatriated to Peru. A few months later, a disgusted Viceroy Amat wrote Julián de Arriaga a bitter letter in which he accused the two Franciscans of being spineless failures.[14]

There was another naval episode during Amat's viceroyalty that is intertwined with the foregoing in the most bizarre of ways: the voyage of the star-crossed *Oriflama*, whose tale of woe is reminiscent of that of the fabled *Flying Dutchman*. The fifty-six-gun warship *Oriflama* was built in France in 1743 and was captured by the British in 1761. Later that same year, she was seized by the Spanish Navy and sold at auction as a merchant ship to the firm of Juan Bautista de Uztáriz (another Basque surname).

On February 18, 1770, the *Oriflama* left Cádiz, commanded by José Antonio de Alzaga, with José de Zavalsa serving as master and Manuel de Buenechea as pilot. (All three are Basque surnames.) More than five months later, on July 25, the *Oriflama* was spotted in the Pacific by the crew of the *Gallardo*. Its captain, Juan Esteban de Ezpeleta (another Basque surname), knew Alzaga and ordered that a friendly cannon shot be fired in greeting. When there was no reply, a boarding party was sent to investigate. It found that half of the *Oriflama*'s crew had died of a mysterious plague and the survivors were deathly ill.

Later that day, before the *Gallardo* could render assistance, the two vessels were separated by bad weather. It was said that as the

---

14 Ibid., 780–81.

distressed ship disappeared into the night, it was bathed in a ghostly light. On July 28, some objects from the *Oriflama*, as well as several bodies, washed ashore on the Chilean coastline. The following spring, Viceroy Amat sent Juan Antonio Bonachea in command of trained divers to search for the shipwreck. They were unsuccessful.

It might be noted that "Buenechea," "Bonachea," and "Boenechea" are interchangeable spellings in some of the Spanish records of the day. It is therefore quite possible that Manuel de Buenechea, Juan Antonio de Bonachea, and Domingo de Boenechea were all related.

Alta California and Beyond

The hegemony of the Spanish in the "Spanish Lake" was under pressure in the northeastern Pacific, as well. By the late eighteenth century, Great Britain was increasing its control of Canada and was clearly active in Pacific waters. By then, Captain James Cook had completed his first voyage (1768–1771). While concentrated in the South Pacific, it had already prompted Arriaga's reactions that resulted in the Bonaechea expedition.

In 1765, the Spanish *vistador* to Nueva España, José de Galvéz, ordered construction of an important naval facility on the Pacific coast of Nueva España. By 1767, San Blas de Nayarit had emerged as Spain's most important Pacific base for exploration of the Californias and the Pacific Northwest. Basques were particularly prominent in the ranks of the port's hierarchy:

> The first administrator of the region was the Basque Juan de Urrengoechea y Arrinda. Between 1767 and 1777 the head shipbuilder in San Blas was the Basque Pedro de Yzaguirre, who directed the construction of the schooner *Sonora* and the frigates Santiago and San José. When Yzaguirre retired to Spain in 1777, he was replaced by the Basque Francisco Segurola, whose previous post was in the shipyard of El Ferrol (Spain).[15]

That same year, 1767, the Jesuits were expelled by the Spanish monarch from Hispanic America for having accumulated too much power and influence. By then, there were twenty-one missions in Baja California where the Jesuits were to be replaced by Franciscans.

---

15 William A. Douglass and Jon Bilbao, *Amerikanuak: Basques in the New World* (Reno: University of Nevada Press, 1975), 182.

Galvéz then ordered that the Dominicans supplant the Franciscans in Baja to allow the latter, under the leadership of a Mallorcan friar, Junípero Serra, to serve as the phalanx for the evangelization of Alta California.

In 1769, Galvéz ordered a two-pronged expedition to establish a settlement and mission at San Diego. Fray Serra went there on the boat, while the land force was placed under the command of the governor of the Californias, Gaspar de Portolà y Rovira. The two contingents met at San Diego, and then Portolà marched northward for several months, eventually reaching the shores of San Francisco Bay. A year later, he returned and established a permanent settlement and mission at Monterey Bay.

In 1773, Minister Julián de Arriaga wrote to the new viceroy of Nueva España, Antonio María de Bucareli y Ursúa, a warning that the Russians were reputed to be exploring southward along North America's Pacific coastline. They might establish settlements that could controvert Spanish claims to hegemony in the North Pacific.

Upon receiving Arriaga's warning, Viceroy Bucareli resolved to launch serious explorations and defensive missions northward. He requested reinforcement of his naval personnel with accomplished commanders from Spain. This was approved, and six men were dispatched to San Blas—a contingent that contained three Basques: Bilbao-born Bruno de Hezeta y Dudagoitia, Juan Francisco de la Bodega y Quadra (a Lima-born Creole Basque),[16] and Sevillan Juan Manuel de Ayala y Aguirre, also of Basque descent.

Meanwhile, Bucareli ordered Juan Pérez, a senior naval commander at San Blas, to prepare for an expedition to explore the Pacific coast as far north as 60 degrees latitude. Juan Pérez left San Blas on January 24, 1774. Along his way, he left two Franciscan friars, Junípero Serra and the Basque Pablo José Mugártegui, at the San Diego mission, as well as the Basque Fray Amurrio at the Monterey mission. Pérez proved to be a timid explorer and turned back to Nueva España at Nootka Sound, well before completing his assign-

---

16 His father was born in Muzkiz, Bizkaia, and his mother, while born in Lima, was also descended from Basque parentage. Ibid., 239.

ment. He founded no colonies, nor did he take formal possession of any territory.[17]

At this time, there was another land expedition of some note. It originated at the Tubac presidio (just south of present-day Tucson, Arizona) and was the initiative of its commander, the Basque Juan Bautista de Anza Bezerra Nieto.[18] Anza proposed establishing an overland route from southern Arizona to stimulate colonization and missionizing of Alta California. He departed Tubac presidio on January 8, 1774, with a small military force, crossed the Colorado at its confluence with the Gila River, and arrived at the Mission San Gabriel Arcángel on March 22. He visited Monterey Bay to the north before returning to Tubac in May of 1744. He was rewarded by the viceroy and king with titles and given permission to organize a new expedition of colonists. This was to be a part of the heightened strategy to countermand possible Russian incursions into Alta California. The new expedition left southern Arizona in October 1775 and arrived in San Gabriel Arcángel in January. Anza left his colonists in Monterey and continued north to San Francisco Bay before returning to Arizona in the late spring of 1776.

Meanwhile, in 1775, three vessels, the *Sonora*, the *Santiago*, and the *San Carlos*, left San Blas for the north. The carried about one hundred and sixty men in all. The expedition was ordered to reach the latitude of 65 degrees north, claiming the territory along the way for Spain and reporting any signs of a Russian presence. It was led by Hezeta, with Bodega as his second in command. According to Michael E. Thurman, they were two of the port's "most outstanding men": "The elder officer, Bruno de Hezeta, was much more methodical and calculating than his junior officer, Bodega y Quadra, and therefore the consistent efforts of Hezeta, both as administrator and naval explorer in the department, account for a period of success in the 1770's."[19]

---

17 Michael E. Thurman, *The Naval Department of San Blas: New Spain's Bastion for Alta California and Nootka, 1767 to 1798* (Glendale: Arthur H. Clark, 1967), 125–40.

18 While born in Sonora, he was the son of Juan Bautista de Anza de Sassoeta of Hernani, Gipuzkoa—a prominent military commander and ranch owner in southern Arizona. Donald T. Garate, *Juan Bautista de Anza* (Reno: University of Nevada Press, 2003).

19 Thurman, *The Naval Department of San Blas*, 184.

Hezeta was the captain of the flagship *Santiago*, with Juan Pérez as his second in command. The *San Carlos* was commanded by Miguel Manrique, but almost immediately he showed signs of mental imbalance. He wept constantly and claimed that there was a plot to assassinate him. He kept six loaded pistols by his side. Manrique was replaced as the commander of the *San Carlos* by Ayala and taken back to San Blas, but not before the new captain was wounded in the leg when one of Manrique's pistols went off. Ayala's second pilot was the Basque Juan Bautista de Aguirre, and his chaplain was Vicente de Santa María, from Aras, Navarra, who would author one of the expedition's more informative diaries. It was now that Bodega y Quadra replaced Ayala as captain of the *Sonora*. So at this point, all three ships' captains were Basques.

The *San Carlos* quickly became separated from the other two and proceeded northward alone. Given bad weather, it took the *San Carlos* 101 days to sail from San Blas to Monterey. It was there that Ayala received the order to explore San Francisco Bay. While it had been overlooked by both Cabrillo and Vizcaíno, Portolà's expedition had sighted it. The previous year, in 1774, the land expedition of Juan Bautista de Anza from the Southwest had terminated at San Francisco Bay. He was now engaged in recruitment of colonists for a permanent settlement there. In anticipation of their arrival, the Spanish authorities were interested in exploring and charting San Francisco Bay thoroughly. In Monterey, Ayala received orders to carry out that task.

The *San Carlos* spent forty-four days in San Francisco Bay. Although his wound prevented Ayala from going ashore, his men carried out their assignments well. They had only a single longboat for the work, so their chaplain's desire to go ashore to evangelize the largely curious and peaceful Indians was frustrated. Supposedly a contingent of soldiers was on its way, and it was even possible that Anza's first colonist might show up, but no one appeared. On September 18, 1775, Ayala sailed out of San Francisco Bay, bound for Monterey. Fray Santa María left letters for future visitors at the foot of a cross. It was three days later that Hezeta sailed into San Francisco Bay, read the letters, and lit a bonfire (in vain) to see if anyone might respond.[20]

The *Santiago* and the *Sonora* had also been delayed unduly by winds and adverse currents. When they were finally off Monterey Bay (albeit far out to sea), Hezeta suggested that they put in to port for rest and supplies. Bodega objected, noting that they were already well behind schedule in carrying out the viceroy's orders. The days were passing, and they could spare no time if they were to reach 65 degrees north latitude.

Given Bodega's firm stance, Hezeta ordered the two ships to continue sailing northward. On June 9, 1775, they put into the future Trinidad Bay and proceeded to map the area. They then took formal possession of it before setting sail again. On July 13, they put into an inlet that they named the Rada de Bucareli. Thus far, they had experienced no trouble with the natives. But when Bodega sent a party ashore, it was ambushed, and seven Spaniards were killed while their powerless commander looked on. Before the *Sonora* could reach the *Santiago*, nine canoes of warriors surrounded it. Nevertheless, the Spaniards' first volley with firearms frightened off the hostile Indians.

Hezeta was now prepared to send the *Sonora* back to Monterey. However, Bodega and his first officer, Francisco Antonio Mourelle, talked him out of that decision. So the expedition proceeded northward to the present-day state of Washington, arriving near the approach to the Strait of Juan de Fuca.

Once again Hezeta proposed turning back south. Bodega's reply remained a firm no. He was determined to sail northward to 65 degrees latitude, as ordered by the viceroy. Hezeta continued on reluctantly, but over the next few days, the ships began sailing farther apart, until they were separated. It is thought that Bodega might have purposely effected the separation in order to hold to his northward course. By this time, there was scurvy aboard the *Santiago*, and its crew was agitating to abandon the mission. At the same time, the *Sonora* was tiny, frail, and barely seaworthy:

---

20 Asun Garikano, *Kaliforniakoak (1533–1848): Euskaldunen lanak Kaliforniaren esplorazio eta kolonizazio garaian* (Iruñea/Pamplona: Pamiela, 2013), 237–52.

The diminutive size of the "Sonora" scarcely qualified it for such a hazardous undertaking. Mounting two sails, the schooner measured thirty-six feet in length (at the keel) and twelve feet in beam, or about the equivalent of a warship's launch. For the expedition of 1775, the "Sonora" had been altered and fitted with a deckhouse, or covered cabin, for the protection of her crew. Inside the cabin, their accommodations included one small table, bunks for sleeping, and a large chest for clothing and personal effects. The cabin was so small that the men were obliged to stoop down upon entering, and all activities inside were hampered by the reduced height of the overhead.[21]

The *Sonora* lost sight of the *Santiago* permanently on July 31. Sailing ever northward, they braved cold climate and exposure, both of which were extremely severe for officers and crew alike during this portion of their voyage. Not daunted, however, both Bodega and Mourelle seemed determined to ascend to the limits prescribed by Viceroy Bucareli and to stake their own personal claim, as well as the sovereign claim for Spain, in several prominent bays and points.[22] Meanwhile, Hezeta had turned south and along the way encountered what he thought to be a vast bay that he was unable to enter due to the strong adverse current exiting it. He had discovered the Columbia River.[23]

Incredibly, the *Sonora* pressed on for the entire month of August. It went as far as 59 degrees north latitude, claimed several features along the way, and established a Spanish claim to the entire northwest Pacific coast from Monterey Bay to the Gulf of Alaska. They found no evidence of Russian activity, although there was indeed some by this time. Finally, on September 1, 1775, Bodega turned south. By now, almost all of his crew, including himself, were too weak to man their posts, sickened as they were with scurvy. Nevertheless, during the southward voyage, he continued to chart the coast between the Strait of Juan de Fuca and Monterey Bay, including his namesake, Puerto de la Capitán de Bodega, or Bodega Bay. On October 7, 1775, the *Sonora* anchored in Monterey Bay alongside Ayala's San *Carlos* and Hezeta's *Santiago*—the three Basque captains having achieved verita-

---

21 Thurman, *The Naval Department*, 149.

22 Ibid., 159.

23 Garikano, *Kaliforniakoak*, 258–60.

ble milestones in exploration.[24] Bucareli was particularly pleased and wrote as much to his commander at San Blas, Ignacio Arteaga (also of Basque descent).

In 1779, there would be one more significant exploration in Alta California and beyond. It was conceived almost immediately after the successful 1775 expedition, but there was now a shortage of ships and crewmen at San Blas. Existing resources there were stretched just supplying the expanding Spanish installations (presidios, missions, colonists) in Alta California. Bucareli ordered preparations for an exploration that would employ improved vessels. During 1777–1778, Bodega was dispatched to his native Peru, where he was able to purchase, outfit, and man a superb vessel, *La Princesa*. He then sailed it from Callao to San Blas, arriving on February 27, 1778. Meanwhile, a similar outstanding frigate, *La Favorita*, had been constructed at San Blas over a fifteen-month period.

A new expedition with ample supplies and personnel left San Blas on February 11, 1779. Arteaga, the commander in chief, captained *La Princesa*, and Bodega, his second in command, was in charge of *La Favorita*. Bodega's crew included Mourelle as the first mate and Ayala's former pilot, the Basque Juan Bautista Aguirre. They were to ascend to 70 degrees north latitude—exploring, charting, and claiming coastal features along the way. There was always the hope, of course, that they might find the Strait of Anián.[25]

In the event, they would reach Puerto de la Regla, or Spaniard's Isla, in Cook Inlet. They took possession of it and began exploring farther north from there. However, once again scurvy became a big factor, and on August 7, a seriously ill Arteaga ordered the ships to head south, overriding Bodega's objections. The two vessels became separated for five weeks, but later rendezvoused in early September in

---

24 Thurman, *The Naval Department*, 152–64; Garikano, *Kaliforniakoak*, 268–70.

25. Then, too, there was the ongoing concern over possible incursions of foreigners into the North Pacific. Indeed, the famous Captain James Cook had left England in 1776 on his final (and fatal) voyage. Clearly, the Spaniards were aware of this and issued a standing order to capture and execute Cook should he appear in North Pacific waters. In point of fact, Cook visited Nootka Sound in 1778. After enjoying good relations with the Indians there, he named a part of it Friendly Cove. He gathered a significant cargo of sea otter pelts. (They would make a big impression in Europe.) He sailed as far north as 70 degrees latitude to the Bering Strait in search of the Northwest Passage, but found icebergs, instead. He then turned south for his second visit to Hawaii and his appointment with death.

San Francisco Bay, where they received the welcome succor of the missionaries. The expedition lingered there for six weeks while the crews recovered. Word was received that war had been declared between Great Britain and Spain. So *La Favorita* and *La Princesa* headed for San Blas, arriving there in late November without incident. It was then that Arteaga and Bodega received news of Viceroy Bucareli's death. His replacement declared further explorations to be suspended because of the war.[26]

Nearly a decade later, after the war had ended, there was a reprise of Spanish interest in the Pacific Northwest. It was triggered in 1786 by word from the French explorer La Pérouse, given first to Spanish officials in Chile and then to Esteban José Martínez, commander of *La Princesa* and *La Favorita*, when the two men coincided after the French explorer put into Monterey Bay for repairs. La Perouse claimed that there was now considerable Russian activity along the northern Pacific coast of North America. Concerned officials in Nueva España began preparations for a new probe of the north.

On April 24, 1788, Martínez departed San Blas in command of two vessels. He found a Russian fur trading settlement on Isla de Trinidad that had been in existence for no fewer than nine years. It had many dwellings and warehouses. Many of the Indians had been baptized and were trapping fur-bearing animals for trade with the Europeans. Martínez then went farther north and found a Russian headquarters installation on Kodiak Island. He was told by its Russian commander that there were no fewer than seven Russian settlements flourishing along the coast of the Gulf of Alaska. The Spaniards were extremely well received. The Russians even disclosed their intention to establish a fortified position at Nootka Sound as a part of their strategy to contain British expansion into the area.[27]

Unsurprisingly, when Martínez arrived back in San Blas and filed his report, the viceroy ordered immediate preparations for a new expedition for the purpose of fortifying Nootka Sound. Martínez left San Blas on February 17, 1789, and headed straight to his final destination. It was a difficult journey, and he did not arrive there until May

---

26. Thurman, *The Naval Department*, 163–79.
27. Ibid., 267–73.

5. It was then, to his chagrin, that he found two American ships and a small British commercial fleet in the area.

Despite having been warned by the viceroy to be wary of American intentions, Martínez struck up a friendly relation with the Yanks. His ties with the Brits were chillier. It was then, through a series of machinations, that Martínez managed to impound two British ships and send them back to San Blas, along with their crews. Throughout the summer, he built shore facilities and fortifications, including artillery emplacements. But then a curious order arrived from Nueva España. He was instructed to abandon Nootka and return to San Blas for the winter. There is a scholarly controversy over the motives for the order, or even its validity. Nevertheless, Martínez dismantled his emplacements and prepared to head south. Just before departing Nootka, he captured an American vessel that, from a Spanish viewpoint, was engaged in illegal fur trade with the coastal Indians.[28]

The British now demanded release of the two vessels that Martínez had impounded and compensation—Spain refused. It appeared that the two countries were about to go to war again. In the event, that was avoided, but a difficult negotiation lay ahead. In 1790, the two countries signed the First Nootka Convention. It specified that British vessels could not trade or fish within ten leagues of the coast from Nootka south, whereas to the north of that point, they were free to operate onshore wherever there was no existing European settlement. It was agreed that both countries would send out an experienced navigator to effect their respective "Expedition of the Limits" to determine who was claiming what. Great Britain designated the task to George Vancouver.

After his earlier expeditions along the coastline of the Pacific Northwest, Juan Francisco Bodega y Quadra served for a few years with the navy in Spain. However, with the situation in the North Pacific heating up, it was clear that the naval base at San Blas needed reinforcement. Bodega was restless, and he petitioned for the opportunity to return to San Blas. He brought several officers with him, including Francisco de Eliza, of Basque descent.[29] Initially, Bodega dispatched three vessels under the command of Eliza with orders to

---

28. Ibid., 276–300.
29. Garikano, *Kaliforniakoak*, 284–87.

fortify Nootka Sound. They arrived there on April 3, 1790, and there were no other Europeans to be found. They set about their task at Friendly Cove, including installation of a shore battery of twenty new cannons, supplied from Havana and then transported by land across Nueva España.

Despite Bodega's order to avoid conflicts with the Indians, there were immediate hostilities. At one point, Eliza's men killed five natives who were trying to steal iron barrel hoops. Another fight erupted when the Spaniards tried to appropriate the lumber in the natives' dwellings for use in constructing their own facilities. By autumn, relations were so tense that the Spaniards were unable to go on hunting forays. There was much privation among the Europeans during that winter of 1790–1791. Nevertheless, little by little, Eliza was able to placate the natives, and the situation improved to the point that the Indians began providing the Spaniards with food. So now Spain had a fortified presence at Nootka.

During the summer of 1791, Eliza dispatched several exploratory expeditions to the north and the south, leading some himself. The Strait of Georgia was now discovered, as was the mouth of the Fraser River. There was even the thought that the latter might be the entry to the Strait of Anián. Unfortunately for the Spaniards, they did not follow up sufficiently, and it would be George Vancouver who, a year later, would explore and claim Puget Sound. Eliza was also interested in gaining better intelligence concerning the Strait of Juan de Fuca, since it seemed likely that it could become the demarcation point between the Spanish and British spheres of influence, necessitating relocation to there of Nootka Sound's Spanish settlement.

Then, in 1792, it was agreed that Vancouver and Bodega would meet in Nootka to negotiate the differences between the two countries over the future of the region. The Spanish plan was to send five vessels to the area in order to impress the English. The master shipbuilder at San Blas, the Basque Manuel Bastarrechea, had constructed the *Aránzazu*[30] and was ordered to now produce another schooner, the *Sútil*. About this time, the Italian explorer Alessandro Malaspina, in the service of Spain, visited San Blas. After meetings with members of Malaspina's crew who remained in San Blas, Bodega decided to add

---

30. The monastery of Aránzazu in Gipuzkoa is a major Basque Marian religious shrine.

a scientific dimension to the expedition. In addition to appointing a scientist and his aide, Bodega named a talented young Creole artist of Basque descent, Atanasio Echeverria, as illustrator.

Bodega, in command of the *Santa Gertrudis*, arrived at Friendly Cove on April 29, 1792. He was feted with a potlatch by the local chief. By May 13, all five Spanish vessels were in port after suffering weather damage. Over the next several weeks, Bodega repaired them and improved his shore facilities while awaiting Vancouver's arrival. Of considerable concern, however, was the appearance of no fewer than sixteen fur-trading English, French, American, and Portuguese vessels that summer. The "Spanish Lake" was obviously no longer exclusively Spanish.

Bodega also decided to dispatch the *Aránzazu* to the north. It was to search for the northwest passage and then, during its return, explore and chart all of the inlets between Bucareli Bay and Nootka Sound. Along the way, he named Aristazabal Island.[31] The journey lasted eighty-six days, and the *Aránzazu* arrived back at Friendly Cove on September 7.

Vancouver had arrived, finally, in late August, having engaged in his own charting of the northern coastline. Despite his irritation at having lost most of the summer (the season for serious exploration), Bodega received Vancouver with courtesy and hospitality. Actually, he was under orders to do so. His mission, after all, was defined as "diplomatic." Indeed, the two men hosted one another lavishly and struck up a genuine friendship. However, the negotiations were another matter. Bodega proposed that the boundary between the Spanish and British spheres of influence be fixed at the Strait of Juan de Fuca, and Vancouver proposed it be set at San Francisco Bay. They agreed to disagree. Meanwhile, Bodega proposed they name a large island Quadra and Vancouver in honor of their relationship. Once it became part of the English sphere of influence in the nineteenth century, that name eventually evolved into today's Vancouver Island. On their last night together in Nootka, Vancouver hosted Bodega at a sumptuous banquet aboard the *Discovery*, and the Spanish commander reciprocated

---

31. In honor of Gabriel de Aristazabal, a famed Spanish sea captain of Basque descent.

with an elaborate festival ashore. They agreed to meet again soon in Monterey.[32]

During his voyage south, Vancouver had a series of encounters with Basques. In San Francisco Bay, he was welcomed by the Franciscan friar Martín Ladaeta, who was from Kortezubi, Bizkaia. He invited the British commander to his mission. The Spanish governor gave Vancouver free reign of the area and even provided mounts for his reconnaissance.

Then, on November 27, Bodega and Vancouver rendezvoused in Monterey. Vancouver met with California governor, José Joaquín Arrillaga, a Basque from Aia, Gipuzkoa. He visited Mission Carmel in Bodega's company and met Fermín Lasuén, who was born in Vitoria, Araba, head of the Alta California missions. Bodega made repairs to Vancouver's vessel without charge.

The British left Monterey on January 15, 1793. In May of that year, Vancouver returned to California and again entered San Francisco Bay. However, this time, the reception was more formal. Arrillaga had been ordered by the viceroy to restrict Vancouver's movements so as to conceal from the British commander the many weaknesses of San Francisco's defenses. Vancouver departed immediately for the south, and Arrillaga dispatched a messenger to inform the presidios not to resupply the British. However, they arrived at Santa Barbara before the message, and Vancouver was well received by the commander of its presidio, Felipe Goicoechea, a Basque descendant.

The person at Santa Barbara who most impressed Vancouver was the Navarrese Fray Vicente de Santa María. The day before Vancouver's departure, Fray Santa María appeared with a small band of sheep and twenty mules loaded with supplies for the British. The friar and the commander of the presidio were then hosted at a dinner aboard the *Discovery*. When the British put the friar ashore, there was a great throng of Indians. At first, Vancouver thought they had come to see him off. In reality, they were worried about their friar, fearful that he had been harmed by the foreigners. Santa María reassured them, speaking their language with great fluency. As Vancouver then sailed north along the California coast, he named several features

---

32. Garikano, *Kaliforniakoak*, 290–302.

after his new friends—Point Fermín, Point Lasuén, Point Felipe, Point Vicente—but there would be no Point Arrillaga.

On January 11, 1794, Spain and Great Britain signed a final Nootka Convention. By then, Spain had agreed to compensate the British owners of the vessels seized by Martínez. The Spaniards also agreed to turn Friendly Cove over to the British. Instructions to that effect were sent from Spain to Bodega, but by then he was dead. He had died in San Blas from the health problems accumulated from his bouts with scurvy and years of residence in the unsalubrious naval port. The year 1793 had been particularly painful for Bodega. He had gone to Spain to petition for compensation from the government for his many years of service. By then, he was impecunious, having gone through his family inheritance by purchasing *La Favorita* in 1777 with his own funds and then by providing considerable financial assistance to the California missions. His petitions were in vain. Nevertheless, the impressive legacy of Juan Francisco Bodega y Quadra in the North Pacific is indisputable. He was clearly one of the greatest explorers to ever sail under the Spanish flag.

The Royal Philippine Company

For all practical purposes, Domingo de Boenechea's two rather attenuated voyages to Tahiti marked the end of Spanish exploration and political hegemony in the South Pacific. Indeed, those mantels would be wrested by the French and, particularly, the English. There remains one last Spanish/Basque legacy in the region worthy of consideration: the creation of the Royal Philippine Company (La Real Compañía de Filipinas) in the late eighteenth century. It was an outgrowth successor of the earlier (1728) Royal Gipuzkoan Company of Caracas (La Real Compañía Guipúzcoana de Caracas), which was itself modeled after such commercial behemoths as the British East Indies Company (founded in 1600) and the Dutch East Indies Company (1602).

At the time that the Royal Gipuzkoan Company received its charter from Philip V, the northern coast of South America was a semilawless appendage of empire. In return for a two-way trade monopoly between the region and Europe, the company agreed to provide a modicum of governance and coastal surveillance to control the contraband traffic between the locals and the Dutch. As might be imagined, such activities were thoroughly resented by Venezuela's creoles. Indeed, in 1749, there was a rebellion in the colony to the cry of "Long live the king, death to the Vizcayans!"[33]

The Royal Gipuzkoan Company of Caracas had been founded by Basques, and until 1750, the company's ships were allowed to dock in Bilbao and San Sebastián, whence the imports could enter the wider European markets without passing through Spanish customs. This created considerable prosperity for the shareholders, but also resentment in other commercial and governmental sectors that would eventually lead to restrictions being placed upon the company's privileges. By late century, on the one hand, its ownership was "diluted," in that Basques were no longer in control,[34] while, on the other, its fortunes were in serious decline.

Meanwhile, Asia and the South Pacific presented their own unique arrangements and challenges. As we have seen, there were feeble attempts to explore and control the latter from Nueva España and particularly from Peru,[35] but the resources were few and the distances vast. The other foothold of Spanish influence in the region was Manila. From the outset, it seemed ideally situated to facilitate trade with Asia, particularly with China, and the Philippines themselves were deemed to be a potential source of tropical products. Nevertheless, by the eighteenth century, the area had failed to realize its promise on either score.

Manila served as a pivotal point for a degree of commerce with the Asian mainland, funneling such luxury goods as silks and porcelains to Spain while transferring New World silver to the Orient. However, Portuguese control of the more direct and cost-effective route to Europe via the Cape of Good Hope proved restrictive, except during the sixty years when the two monarchies were combined. The

---

33. Douglass and Bilbao, *Amerikanuak*, 91.

34. Julio Caro Baroja, *Los vascos y el mar* (San Sebastián: Txertoa, 1981), 115–16.

35. Indeed, after Peru abolished slavery in 1854, it would seek laborers in the South Pacific for its plantations and guano-mining operations. During a seven-month period in 1862–1863, 3,634 people were "recruited" by means of fraudulent representations or outright kidnapping. About a third of the thirty-three ship captains engaged in the shameless business were Basque surnamed. See H. E. Maude, *Slavers in Paradise: The Peruvian Slave Trade in Polynesia, 1862–1864* (Palo Alto and Canberra: Stanford University Press and Australian National University Press, 1981), xix–xxi, 185, 188.

Manila run to Acapulco required crossing the Pacific Ocean, then unloading cargo, transporting it by land, and then reloading it for yet another sea voyage across the Atlantic to Europe. Furthermore, from the outset, the rather clumsy Manila run became a jealously guarded monopoly of certain Manila and Acapulco merchant clans. As for tropical agriculture, the Philippines had long lagged well behind the promise and expectations of its boosters. To add to the frustration, Manila had proven to be a security risk, evidenced by Anson's seizure of the treasure ship in Philippine waters in 1743 and English occupation of the city in 1762.

All of the foregoing constituted the backdrop prompting formulation of a proposal to found the Royal Philippine Company. Basques were clearly on all sides of the issue. Given that by the 1730s the Royal Gipuzkoan Company of Caracas was returning annual dividends to its shareholders on the order of 20 percent of their investment, it served as the inspiration for a similar Philippine initiative. In 1732, four Basque merchants based in Cádiz applied for a royal charter to traffic directly with Manila for ten years. While this was approved initially, before actual implementation, royal permission was withdrawn to favor a broader approach to Philippine trade.

Manila residents in control of the galleon traffic with Nueva España, including many Basques, regarded all such initiatives warily. In 1743, for example, Basque commercial interests represented 38 percent of the shares in the two vessels making the voyage to Acapulco.[36] But then there was the controversial role of Francisco Leandro de Viana— a Basque born in Araba who in 1748 was appointed the attorney general of the audiencia of Manila. Marciano de Borja tells us:

> Young, idealistic, and energetic, Viana immediately dedicated himself to his position. He took great interest in the study of the economic problems of the Philippines and proposed a number of plans to remedy them. His zeal in upholding the interest of the Spanish state and protecting the rights of the native Filipinos quickly earned him powerful enemies, including the Basque governor-general Pedro Manuel de Arandía and Arandía cohorts such as Francisco Zapata and Santiago de Orendain, a son of a Mexican Basque. His economic ideas, particularly his proposal

---

36. Marciano R. de Borja, *Basques in the Philippines* (Reno: University of Nevada Press, 2005), 62.

to open a direct trade route between Spain and the Philippines via the Cape of God Hope, clashed with the views of prominent members of the Consulado—the board of merchants created in 1769 to supervise the Acapulco galleon trade and adjudicate disputes among members of the business community—such as the Basque Pedro Lamberto de Asteguieta, Pedro Iriarte, Felipe Erquizia, and Pedro Echenique.[37]

In 1765, in the immediate aftermath of the English occupation of Manila, Viana wrote a treatise entitled "Demostración de el mísero deplorable estado de las Islas Filipinas" (Demonstration of the miserable deplorable state of the Philippines). He argued that proper policy could convert the Philippines from a net financial drain on Spain to a positive contributor to its national worth. He began his argument by noting that while the English were gone for the time being, they departed the Philippines with reluctance and would gladly return should the islands be abandoned by Spain. Viana argued that the English were enamored with the Philippines and fully conscious of their strategic value as a base from which to conduct both illicit commerce with Nueva España and attacks upon the entire American Pacific coast in wartime. He further argued neither papal bulls nor treaties any longer precluded Spain from sailing around the Cape of Good Hope. (In any event, by this time, the Portuguese historical monopoly of the route had been totally compromised by virtually every European naval power.) His key proposal regarded creation of a company that would carry Spanish goods from Cádiz to Manila for sale both in the Philippines and in China and that would then transport Philippine products to Europe on the return voyage. The latter would serve as the stimulus for the expansion of tropical agriculture in the islands. The benefits to both the Spanish and Philippine economies were evident.[38]

In 1773, the Royal Philippine Company was chartered to facilitate direct trade between Spain and Asia (primarily China and India), championed in Madrid by the French Basque economist François Cabarrús and other prominent Basques, such as Viana and Bernardo

37. Ibid., 63–64.

38. María Lourdes Diaz-Trechuelo Spínola, *La Real Compañía de Filipinas* (Sevilla: Escuela de Estudios Hispano-Americanos de Sevilla, Consejo Superior de Investigaciones Científicas, 1965), 12–14.

Iriarte, a member of Spain's Supreme Court. The concept was not implemented immediately; meanwhile, by the late 1770s, the Royal Gipuzkoan Company of Caracas was in financial difficulty. (It would be abolished in 1785.) This paved the way for creation of the new enterprise. According to Borja:

> In reality, the Royal Philippine Company was only a reincarnation of the Royal Gipuzkoan Company of Caracas. The transformation of the Caracas Company to the Philippine Company did not substantially change the Basque presence in and ownership of the new company. The former management team remained, as did many of the old shareholders, such as the province of Gipuzkoa, the *consulado* (board of merchants) of San Sebastián, the city government (*ayuntamiento*) of Donostia (San Sebastián), the University of Oñate, as well as individual investors such as Zuaznabar, Lopeola, Arbaiza, and Goicoa. The new list of shareholders also included the Spanish crown and the five major guilds in Madrid. Other aspects and properties of the Caracas Company, such as its shipyard in Bizkaia and its weapons factory in Placencia, were passed on to the Philippine Company.[39]

The Royal Philippine Company enjoyed some successes, particularly initially, but it also faced daunting challenges. While it secured the right to trade directly with Asian countries, its vessels were required to pass through Manila before returning to Spain, which often added an unnecessary expense. While it was also allowed to trade from Spain with the Latin American colonies, it was precluded from carrying cargoes from Manila to the New World, which, until 1815, remained the monopoly of the galleons involved in the Manila run. Four percent of the Royal Philippine Company's profits went to fund economic development in the Philippines, with spotty success. The European political climate also was unremittingly volatile throughout much of the company's history. It encompassed a war with Great Britain in 1796, the Napoleonic invasion and rule of Spain, Spanish insurrection against the French, and then the New World independence movements. Throughout, the Spanish crown was empowered to borrow money from the Royal Philippine Company, most of which was never

---

39. Borja, *Basques*, 71–72.

repaid. The Royal Philippine Company existed for nearly fifty years, until its charter was revoked by the Spanish monarchy in 1834.[40]

Basque Castaways: Evidence and Conjecture

In 1975, an Australian writer, Robert Langdon, published the first of two provocative works—*The Lost Caravel*—followed by the sequel *The Lost Caravel Re-explored* (1988).[41] His curiosity was piqued by certain anomalous accounts (such as that of José de Andía) of initial contacts between European explorers and natives from both eastern Polynesia and the Maori of New Zealand, describing natives who, in terms of their phenotype, were indistinguishable from Europeans— including some persons with blond or red hair and blue eyes.[42] There were certain other anomalies in the form of linguistic, mythological, and artifactual evidence that might be European in origin, as well. In Langdon's reading of the region's literature, such fragmentary evidence was too easily ignored, dismissed, or attributed to casual recent contacts.

Of particular interest were the four submerged iron cannons discovered on a coral reef off the island of Amanu in 1929 by a French sea captain, François Hervé, engaged in charting the Tuamotus. During his visit to the atoll, Hervé was shown the cannon site by the local chief, who recounted the oral tradition of a shipwreck eight generations earlier whose survivors had all been eaten by the natives.[43] Langdon speculated that there might indeed be underlying substance to the story, but that it was possible that the cannibalism was legendary. Rather, some European castaways might very well have intermarried with local women, and their descendants could have ventured afar in eastern Polynesia, thereby contributing the genes that accounted for the European appearance of some Polynesians.

After several years of research and by employing additional speculation, Langdon posited that while some of the original crew of castaways settled on Amanu, others might have salvaged and refitted the

---

40. Ibid., 72–74.

41. Robert Langdon, *The Lost Caravel* (Sydney: Pacific Publications, 1975); Langdon, *The Lost Caravel Re-explored* (Canberra: Brolga Press, 1978).

42. Langdon, *The Lost Caravel*, 113–19, 147.

43. Ibid., 13–14.

vessel and resumed their journey. Other than the cannons, there is no evidence at the Amanu site of a sunken ship, leading Langdon to speculate that the heavy cannons were jettisoned to float the damaged vessel. Eventually, those who were not too discouraged to continue the voyage made their way as far as New Zealand, where they were either shipwrecked anew or simply decided to settle. In either event, they were the source of the genetic underpinning of their Maori look-alikes.

Langdon concluded that the likely vessel of the European cast-aways was the *San Lesmes*, the caravel separated from the Loaísa expedition in 1526 as it exited the Strait of Magellan and entered the Pacific. All of the captains of the fleet were under orders to proceed to the Moluccas in the event they became separated from the others. The *San Lesmes* would have been following this order when shipwrecked off of Amanu. The cannons seemed to be from the late fifteenth or early sixteenth century, thereby lending plausibility to this conclusion.

And then there was the Basque paradox. The results of an international serological testing project of fifty relatively "isolated" populations by teams of geneticists (a precursor to the human genome project) discovered a high incidence of the A29, B12 haplotype of HLA (human leucocyte antigen) in a sample of eighteen Easter Islanders who had no known non–Easter Islander ancestry). The combination is found in no other non-Caucasian population, being unique to Europeans—Basques, in particular.[44] The Easter Islanders and a sample of Basques from the French Basque village of Macaye shared the distinction of having similar rates of the A29, B12 haplotype.[45] The Easter Islanders were closely related persons who counted among their ancestors an individual with distinctively European facial features.[46] Langdon believes that that person was a Basque mariner on

---

44. Langdon, *The Lost Caravel Re-explored*, 199–200.

45. Langdon summarizes the findings as follows, "The analyses revealed that 39 per cent of the unrelated Basques and 37 per cent of the Easter Islanders were carriers of the HLA gene B12. These were the highest and second highest proportions in the fifty-odd communities tested throughout the world. The figures for A29 were similar. The Easter Islanders, with 37 per cent, had the highest proportion in the world, while the Basques were second with 24 per cent." Ibid., 200.

46. Ibid., 213–21.

the *San Lesmes*, although it is unlikely that he actually reached Easter Island. Rather, a more likely candidate was his part-Basque descendant among the castaways from Amanu who, at some later date, were blown off course by a storm and ended up on Easter Island.[47]

The tantalizing Basque genetic evidence prompted Langdon to select the *San Lesmes* as the most likely source of European genes among a series of Spanish shipwrecks in Pacific waters during the sixteenth and seventeenth centuries. Initially, he tried to fix the ethnicity (Old World regional origins) of the 120 identified persons within the 450 or so members of the Loaísa expedition, employing the methodology of analyzing surnames plus ancillary evidence that I have used frequently in this book. Making the further assumption that Elkano, the officer charged with provisioning four of the expedition's seven vessels in the Basque port of Portugalete, likely recruited many fellow countrymen, particularly from his native province of Gipuzkoa and including five of his kinsmen, Langdon initially speculated that as many as a third of the crew were Basque.[48] He subsequently took the more conservative position that at least three, and possibly six, of the fifty to seventy crewmen of the *San Lesmes* at the time of its disappearance were Basques—therefore easily providing the Basque genes required for his arguments.[49]

It is perhaps appropriate, if not downright ironic, given the "mystery" surrounding the origins of the Basques in their European homeland that informed much late nineteenth-century and early to mid-twentieth-century anthropological pondering regarding the phenotypic and genetic makeup of the Basque population, that they are again the objects of similar speculation a century later and a world away.

47. Langdon, *The Lost Caravel*, 254.
48. Ibid., 32.
49. Langdon, *The Lost Caravel Re-explored*, 22.

Conclusion

There is a sense in which the conclusion to this book has been writing itself along the way. Although the Tordesillas Line divided the world in the late fifteenth century into two spheres of influence, the real contest between the Spanish and the Portuguese was an American one. By the end of the third decade of the sixteenth century, any competition over the Spice Islands was resolved by the Treaty of Zaragoza. They were Portuguese, period. Furthermore, Columbus's plan of sailing west in order to reach the Orient was prescient, but impractical. Rather than a new sea route to the Spice Islands and China, he "discovered" a vast continental barrier. The southern passage around it proved to be impractical from the standpoint of both distance and the physical challenge of making it through the Strait of Magellan. The northwest passage was simply illusory—at least until the present day, with our global warming. (And even now, it is seasonal and entails modern icebreakers.) It would not be until the first decade of the twentieth century that a canal across the Isthmus of Panama made sea traffic between the Atlantic and Pacific reasonable.

In short, by the end of the eighteenth century, for both Spain and Portugal, the Pacific game was all but over. Portugal maintained a tenuous foothold in Southeast Asia, but it was being challenged by the British and the Dutch. Portugal could no longer even pretend to police its former monopoly on the circum-African sea route to the Orient. There was still a Manila run between the Philippines and Nueva España, but in truth, it was of feeble real worth to either Spain or Latin America. The real death knell was tolled when Great Britain established a penal colony in 1788 on the shores of Botany Bay. Within a short time, both the entire Australian continent and New Zealand were divided into several British colonies. The nineteenth and early twentieth centuries would witness European imperialism throughout the South Pacific, spearheaded primarily by Great Britain and France. Spain and Portugal were not even minor players.

In the North Pacific, however, it was neither Great Britain nor Russia that ended first Spanish and then Mexican hegemony, but rather the westward expansion of the robust new nation called the United States. First, there was its Louisiana Purchase (1803), which removed France as a player in North America. Then, in 1818, the United States agreed to administer the Oregon Territory jointly with Great Britain. That lasted until the 1830s, when some inflamed Americans advocated going to war with Great Britain over demarcation of the boundary between British Canada and the United States at latitude 54 degrees 40 minutes. In the event, there was a compromise in the Treaty of Oregon (1846) at the forty-ninth parallel. It pretty much determined the border that obtains between Canada and the United States at present. Then, in 1867, the U. S. secretary of state, William H. Seward, negotiated purchase of any claims to Alaska from Russia for seven million dollars. Labeled "Seward's Folly" by its critics, the transaction effectively ended all Russian activity in North American Pacific waters.

Once Mexico gained its independence from Spain in 1821, it immediately confronted the insatiable territorial aspirations of its powerful northern neighbor. Creation of the Republic of Texas (1836), incorporation of it into the United States (1845), the Bear Flag Revolt in Alta California(1846), the Mexican-American War (1846–1848), the Treaty of Guadalupe Hidalgo (1848), and the Gadsden Purchase (1853–1854) all conspired to strip Mexico of the northern third of its national territory in little over three decades. In effect, Mexico had lost Texas, New Mexico, Arizona, parts of Colorado and Wyoming, Nevada, Utah, and Alta California. Then, at century's end, it would become Spain's fate to be all but wiped off the Pacific map. After losing most of Latin America in the independence movements of the beginning of the nineteenth century, the Spanish overseas empire was reduced to a few significant islands. In the Caribbean, Spain still controlled Cuba and Puerto Rico, while in the western Pacific, she had the Philippines and Guam. Yet all four would be lost definitively in the Spanish-American War of 1898 with the United States.

It was over. Save for a few forlorn patches of land on the African continent, Spain no longer had any overseas possessions. A major soul-searching ensued among Spanish intellectuals that resulted in a literary movement known as the Generation of Ninety Eight. There were some major Basque figures in their ranks—but that is another story.

Bibliography

Arciniega, Rosa. *Pedro Sarmiento de Gamboa: El Ulises de América.* Buenos Aires: Editorial Sudamericana, 1956.

Arteche, José de. *Cuatro relatos.* Pamplona: Editorial Gómez, 1959.

——. *Urdaneta, el dominador de los espacios del Océano Pacífico.* Madrid: Espasa Calpe, 1943.

Azcona Pastor, José Manuel. *Possible Paradises: Basque Emigration in Latin America.* Reno: University of Nevada Press, 2004.

Ballesteros Beretta, Antonio. *El cántabro Juan de la Cosa y el descubrimiento de América.* Santander: Diputación Regional de Cantabria, 1987.

Bard, Rachel. *Navarra: The Durable Kingdom.* Reno: University of Nevada Press, 1982.

Baudot Monroy, María. "Orígenes familiares y carrera profesional de Julián de Arriaga, Secretario de Estado de Marina de Indias (1700–1776)." *Espacio, Tiempo y Forma, Serie IV, Historia Moderna* 17 (2004): 166

Bawlf, Samuel. *The Secret Voyage of Sir Francis Drake, 1577–1580.* Vancouver: Douglas and McIntyre, 2003.

Beaglehole, J. C. *The Exploration of the Pacific.* London: Adam and Charles Black, 1966.

Bergreen, Laurence. *Columbus: The Four Voyages.* New York: Viking, 2011.

Bilbao, Jon. *Vascos en Cuba (1492–1511).* Buenos Aires: Editorial Ekin, 1958.

Borja, Marciano R. de. *Basques in the Philippines.* Reno: University of Nevada Press, 2005.

Bourne, Edward Gaylord. *Spain in America, 1450–1580.* Vol. 3, *The American Nation, a History: From Original Sources by Asso-*

ciated Authors. Edited by Albert Bushnell Hart. New York: Harper, 1904.

Boxer, C. R. The Portuguese Seaborne Empire: 1415–1825. New York: Alfred A. Knopf, 1969.

Caro Baroja, Julio. Los judíos en la España moderna y contemporánea. 3 vols. Madrid: Ediciones ISTMO, 1961.

————. Los vascos y el mar. San Sebastián: Txertoa, 1981.

Casas, Bartolomé de las. Historia de las Indias. 3 vols. Mexico City: Fondo de Cultura Económica, 1951.

Chipman, Donald E. Nuno de Guzman and the Province of Panuco in New Spain 1518–1533. Glendale: Arthur H. Clark, 1967.

Ciriquiain-Gaiztarro, Mariano. Los vascos en la pesca de la ballena. Donostia-San Sebastián: Biblioteca Vascongada de los Amigos del País, 1961.

Clavería Arza, Carlos. Los vascos en el mar. Pamplona: Editorial Aramburu, 1966.

Clissold, Stephen. Conquistador: The Life of Don Pedro de Sarmiento. London: Derek Verschoyle, 1954.

Díaz de Castillo, Bernal. Historia verdadera de la conquista de la Nueva España. 2 vols. Madrid: Historia 16, 1984.

Diaz-Trechuelo Spínola, María Lourdes. La Real Compañía de Filipinas. Sevilla: Escuela de Estudios Hispano-Americanos de Sevilla, Consejo Superior de Investigaciones Científicas, 1965.

Disney, A. R. A History of Portugal and the Portuguese Empire: From the Beginnings to 1807. 2 vols. Cambridge: Cambridge University Press, 2011.

Dodge, Ernest S. Islands and Empires: Western Impact on the Pacific and East Asia. Minneapolis: University of Minnesota Press, 1976.

Douglass, William A., and Jon Bilbao. Amerikanuak: Basques in the New World. Reno: University of Nevada Press, 1975.

Estíbaliz Ruiz de Azúa y Martínez de Ezquerecocha, María. Vascongados y América. Madrid: Editorial MAPFRE, 1992.

Fernández de Navarrete, Eustaquio. Historia de Juan Sebastián del Cano. Bilbao: Amigos del Libro Vasco, 1985.

Gallez, Paul. *Cristóbal de Haro: Banqueros y pimenteros en busca del estrecho magallánico*. Bahía Blanca: Instituto Patagónico, 1991.

Garate, Donald T. *Juan Bautista de Anza*. Reno: University of Nevada Press, 2003.

Garikano, Asun. *Kaliforniakoak (1533–1848): Euskaldunen lanak Kaliforniaren esplorazio eta kolonizazio garaian*. Iruñea-Pamplona: Pamiela, 2013.

Génova Sotíl, Juan. "Ortiz de Retes, por aguas australes." In *Descubrimientos españoles en el Mar del Sur*, 3 vols., writen by Amancio Landín Carrasco et al. Madrid: Editorial Naval, 1992.

Gil, Juan. "El entorno vasco de Andrés de Urdaneta." In *Andrés de Urdaneta: Un hombre moderno*, edited by Susana Truchuelo Garcí. Lasarte-Oria: Ordiziako Udala, 2009.

Guillén Salvetti, Fernando, and Amancio Landín Carrasco. "Miscelánea." In *Descubrimientos españoles en el Mar del Sur*, 3 vols., writen by Amancio Landín Carrasco et al. Madrid: Editorial Naval, 1992.

Guillén Salvetti, Fernando, and Carlos Vila Miranda. "La desdichada expedición de García Jofre de Loaísa." In *Descubrimientos españoles en el Mar del Sur*, 3 vols., writen by Amancio Landín Carrasco et al. Madrid: Editorial Naval, 1992.

Herrera y Tordesillas, Antonio de. *Historia general de los hechos de los castellanos en las islas y tierras firmes de el Mar Océano*. 10 vols. Asunción del Paraguay: Guarania, 1944–47.

Hittell, Theodore H. *History of California*. 4 vols. San Francisco: N. J. Stone, 1898.

Holmes, Maurice G. *From New Spain by Sea to the Californias 1519–1668*. Glendale: Arthur H. Clark, 1963.

Ispizúa, Segundo de. *Historia de los vascos en América*. 6 vols. Bilbao: Impr. J. A. de Lerchundi, 1914–19.

Kellenbenz, Hermann. *Los Fugger en España y Portugal hasta 1560*. Salamanca: Junta de Castilla y Léon, Consejería de Educación y Cultura, 2000.

Kelly, Celsus. *Calendar of Documents: Spanish Voyages in the South Pacific from Alvaro de Mendaña to Alejandro Malaspina 1567–1794 and the Franciscan Missionary Plans for the Peoples of the*

Austral Lands 1617–1634. Madrid: Franciscan Historical Studies [Australia] in association with Archive Ibero-Americano, 1965.

———. *La Austrialia del Espíritu Santo: The Journal of Fray Martín De Munilla O.F.M. and Other Documents Relating to the Voyage of Pedro Fernández de Quirós to the South Seas (1605–1606) and the Franciscan Missionary Plan (1617–1627)*. 2 vols. Cambridge: Cambridge University Press and Hakluyt Society, 1966.

Kurlansky, Mark. *The Basque History of the World*. London: Jonathan Cape, 1999.

———. *Cod: A Biography of a Fish That Changed the World*. New York: Penguin Books, 1998.

Laburu, Miguel. "Jalones en la historia de la arquitectura naval vasca." In *Itxasoa: El mar de Euskalerria*, vol. 2, *La naturaleza, el hombre y su historia*, edited by Enrique Ayerbe. Donostia/ San Sebastián: Eusko Kultur Eragintza Etor, 1988.

Lafarga Lozano, Adolfo. *Los vascos en el descubrimiento y colonización de América*. Bilbao: Editorial La Gran Enciclopedia Vasca, 1973.

Landín Carrasco, Amancio, and Luis Sánchez Masiá. "Archipiélagos de Marquesas y Santa Cruz." In *Descubrimientos españoles en el Mar del Sur*, 3 vols., writen by Amancio Landín Carrasco. Madrid: Editorial Naval, 1992.

———. "El descubrimiento de las Islas Solomón." In *Descubrimientos españoles en el Mar del Sur*, 3 vols., writen by Amancio Landín Carrasco et al. Madrid: Editorial Naval, 1992.

———. "Urdaneta y la vuelta de poniente." In *Descubrimientos españoles en el Mar del Sur*, 3 vols., writen by Amancio Landín Carrasco et al. Madrid: Editorial Naval, 1992.

———. "El viaje Redondo de Alonso de Arellano." In *Descubrimientos españoles en el Mar del Sur*, 3 vols., writen by Amancio Landín Carrasco et al. Madrid: Editorial Naval, 1992.

———. "Los viajes promovidos por el virrey Amat." In *Descubrimientos españoles en el Mar del Sur*, 3 vols., writen by Amancio Landín Carrasco et al. Madrid: Editorial Naval, 1992.

Langdon, Robert. *The Lost Caravel.* Sydney: Pacific Publications, 1975.

———. *The Lost Caravel Re-explored.* Canberra: Brolga Press, 1978.

Lucena, Manuel. *Juan Sebastián Elcano.* Barcelona: Ariel, 2003.

Maestro Castaneda, Juan Carlos. "Orígenes y formación marinera de un gran hombre de estado: Julián de Arriaga (1700–1749)." In *Euskal Herria y el Nuevo Mundo: La contribución de los vascos a la formación de las Américas,* edited by Ronald Escobedo Mansilla, Ana de Zaballa Beascoechea, and Óscar Álvarez Gila. Vitoria-Gasteiz: Servicio Editorial, Universidad del País Vasco, 1996.

Mathes, W. Michael. *Vizcaíno and Spanish Expansion in the Pacific Ocean, 1580–1630.* San Francisco: California Historical Society, 1968.

Maude, H. E. *Slavers in Paradise: The Peruvian Slave Trade in Polynesia, 1862–1864.* Palo Alto and Canberra: Stanford University Press and Australian National University Press, 1981.

Mitchell, Mairin. *Elcano: The First Circumnavigator of the World.* London: Herder Publications, 1958.

———. *Friar Andrés de Urdaneta, O. S. A.* London: Macdonald and Evans, 1964.

Moriarty, James R. "The Discovery and Earliest Exploration of Baja California." *San Diego Historical Quarterly* 11, no. 1 (January 1965).

Morison, Samuel Eliot. *The European Discovery of America.* Vol. 2, *The Southern Voyages, A.D. 1492–1616.* New York: Oxford University Press, 1974.

Mosk, Sanford A. "The Cardona Company and the Pearl Fisheries of Lower California." *Pacific Historical Review* 3, no. 1 (March 1934): 50–51.

Nader, Helen. *The Mendoza Family in the Spanish Renaissance, 1350–1550.* New Brunswick, N.J.: Rutgers University Press, 1979.

Newitt, Malyn. *A History of Portuguese Overseas Expansion, 1400–1668.* London: Routledge, 2005.

Nuttall, Zelia, ed. *New Light on Drake: A Collection of Documents Relating to his Voyage of Circumnavigation 1577–1580.* Translated by Zelia Nuttall. London: Hakluyt Society, 1914.

O'Donnell, Hugo. *España en el descubrimiento, conquista, y defensa del Mar del Sur.* Madrid: Mapre, Editorial, 1992.

Parr, Charles McKew. *Ferdinand Magellan, Circumnavigator.* New York: Thomas A. Crowell, 1964.

Pastells, P. Pablo. *El descubrimiento del Estrecho de Magallanes: En conmemoración del IV centenario.* 2 vols. Madrid: Sucesores de Rivadeneyra, 1920.

Payne, Stanley. *A History of Spain and Portugal.* 2 vols. Madison: University of Wisconsin Press, 1973.

Piñeiro, Manuel Esteban. "Las academias técnicas en la España del siglo xvi." *Quaderns d'Historia de l'Enginyeria* 5 (2003–4): 10–18.

Pourade, Richard F. *The Explorers, 1492–1774.* San Diego: Union-Tribune Publishing, Copley Press, 1962.

Prescott, William H. *History of the Reign of Ferdinand and Isabella the Catholic.* 3 vols. Philadelphia: J. B. Lippincott and Company, 1873.

Sarmiento de Gamboa, Pedro. "Touching the Captains and Ships, Masters and Pilots, that his Majesty appointed for the fleet sent for the enterprise of the Strait of the Mother of God, previously called of Fernando de Magallanes, and a list of the settlers in the Strait." In *Narratives of the Voyages of Pedro Sarmiento de Gamboa to the Straits of Magellan,* edited and translated by Clements R. Markham. London: The Haklyut Society, 1895.

Schwarzenfeld, Gertrude von. *Charles V: Father of Europe.* Chicago: Henry Regnery, 1957.

Sola, Victor María de. *Juan Sebastián de Elcano: Ensayo biográfico.* Bilbao: La Editorial Vizcaína, 1962.

Spate, O. H. K. *The Spanish Lake.* Canberra: Australian National University Press, 1979.

Stevens, Henry N., ed. *New Light on the Discovery of Australia as Revealed by the Journal of Captain Don Diego de Prado y Tovar.* London: Hakluyt Society, 1930.

Telletxea Idigoras, José Ignacio. "Vascos y mar en el siglo XVI." In *Itsasoa: El mar de Euskalerria, la naturaleza, el hombre y su historia*, vol. 4. Edited by Enrique Ayerbe. Donostia-San Sebastián: Eusko Kultur Eragintza Etor, 1988.

———. "Historias de la mar." In *Itsasoa: El mar de Euskalerria*, vol. 2, *La naturaleza, el hombre y su historia*, edited by Enrique Ayerbe. Donostia/San Sebastián: Eusko Kultur Eragintza Etor, 1988.

Thomas, Hugh. *The Golden Empire: Spain, Charles V, and the Creation of America*. New York: Random House, 2011.

———. *Rivers of Gold: The Rise of the Spanish Empire, from Columbus to Magellan*. New York: Random House, 2003.

Thurman, Michael E. *The Naval Department of San Blas: New Spain's Bastion for Alta California and Nootka, 1767 to 1798*. Glendale: Arthur H. Clark, 1967.

Urrutia, Eduardo de. "Julián de Arriaga." *Euskalerriaren alde: Revista de cultura vasca* 4, nos. 76–77 (1914): 102.

Walsh, William Thomas. *Isabella of Spain: The Last Crusader*. New York: Robert M. McBride, 1930.

Zweig, Stefan. *Magellan: Pioneer of the Pacific*. London: Cassell, 1938.

Index

Made in the USA
Charleston, SC
18 July 2015